JUSTIN MARTYR

FIRST APOLOGY, SECOND APOLOGY & DIALOGUE WITH TRYPHO IN ONE VOLUME

Published by
GRAPEVINE BOOKS

www.grapevinebooks.com
email: contact@grapevinebooks.com

Ordering Information:
Quantity sales: Special discounts are available on quantity purchases by corporations, associations, and others.
For details, reach out to the publisher.

First published by Grapevine Books, 2025

Contents

The First Apology Of St. Justin Martyr 5

The Second Apology Of St. Justin Martyr 41

Dialogue With Trypho 49

The First Apology of St. Justin Martyr

CHAPTER 1. ADDRESS

To the Emperor Titus Ælius Adrianus Antoninus Pius Augustus Cæsar, and to his son Verissimus the Philosopher, and to Lucius the Philosopher, the natural son of Cæsar, and the adopted son of Pius, a lover of learning, and to the sacred Senate, with the whole People of the Romans, I, Justin, the son of Priscus and grandson of Bacchius, natives of Flavia Neapolis in Palestine, present this address and petition on behalf of those of all nations who are unjustly hated and wantonly abused, myself being one of them.

CHAPTER 2. JUSTICE DEMANDED

Reason directs those who are truly pious and philosophical to honour and love only what is true, declining to follow traditional opinions, if these be worthless. For not only does sound reason direct us to refuse the guidance of those who did or taught anything wrong, but it is incumbent on the lover of truth, by all means, and if death be threatened, even before his own life, to choose to do and say what is right. Do you, then, since you are called pious and philosophers, guardians of justice and lovers of learning, give good heed, and hearken to my address; and if you are indeed such, it will be manifested. For we have come, not to flatter you by this writing, nor please you by our address, but to beg that you pass judgment, after an accurate and searching investigation, not flattered by prejudice or by a desire of pleasing superstitious men, nor induced by irrational impulse or evil rumours which have long been prevalent, to give a decision which will prove to be against yourselves. For as for us, we reckon that no evil can be done us, unless we be convicted as evil-doers or be proved to be wicked men; and you, you can kill, but not hurt us.

CHAPTER 3. CLAIM OF JUDICIAL INVESTIGATION

But lest any one think that this is an unreasonable and reckless utterance, we demand that the charges against the Christians be investigated, and that, if these be substantiated, they be punished as they deserve; [or rather, indeed, we ourselves will punish them.] But if no one can convict us of anything, true reason forbids you, for the sake of a wicked rumour, to wrong blameless men, and indeed rather yourselves, who think fit to direct affairs, not by judgment, but by passion. And every sober-minded person will declare this to be the only fair and equitable adjustment, namely, that the subjects render an unexceptional account of their own life and doctrine; and that, on the other hand, the rulers should give their decision in obedience, not to violence and tyranny, but to piety and philosophy. For thus would both rulers and ruled reap benefit. For even one of the ancients somewhere said, Unless both rulers and ruled philosophize, it is impossible to make states blessed. It is our task, therefore, to afford to all an opportunity of inspecting our life and teachings, lest, on account of those who are accustomed to be ignorant of our affairs, we should incur the penalty due to them for mental blindness; and it is your business, when you hear us, to be found, as reason demands, good judges. For if, when you have learned the truth, you do not what is just, you will be before God without excuse.

CHAPTER 4. CHRISTIANS UNJUSTLY CONDEMNED FOR THEIR MERE NAME

By the mere application of a name, nothing is decided, either good or evil, apart from the actions implied in the name; and indeed, so far at least as one may judge from the name we are accused of, we are most excellent people. But as we do not think it just to beg to be acquitted on account of the name, if we be convicted as evil-doers, so, on the other hand, if we be found to have committed no offense, either in the matter of thus naming ourselves, or of our conduct as citizens, it is your part very earnestly to guard against incurring just punishment, by unjustly punishing those who are not convicted. For from a name neither praise nor punishment could reasonably spring, unless something excellent or base in action be proved. And those among yourselves who are accused you do not punish before they are convicted; but in our case you receive the name as proof against us, and this although, so far as the name goes, you ought rather to punish our accusers. For we are accused of being Christians, and to hate what is excellent (Chrestian) is unjust. Again, if any of the accused deny the name, and say that he is not a Christian, you acquit him, as having no evidence against him as a wrong-doer; but if any one acknowledge that he is a Christian, you punish him on account of this acknowledgment. Justice requires that you inquire into the life both of him who confesses and of him who denies, that by his deeds it may be apparent what kind of man each is. For as some who have been taught by the Master, Christ, not to deny Him, give encouragement to others when they are put to the question, so in all probability do those who lead wicked lives give occasion to those who, without consideration, take upon them to accuse all the Christians of impiety and wickedness. And this also is not right. For of philosophy, too, some assume the name and the garb who do nothing worthy of their profession; and you are well aware, that those of the ancients whose opinions and teachings were quite diverse, are yet all called by the one name of philosophers. And of these some taught atheism; and the poets who have flourished among you raise a laugh out of the uncleanness of Jupiter with his own children. And those who now adopt such instruction are not restrained by you; but, on the contrary, you bestow prizes and honours upon those who euphoniously insult the gods.

CHAPTER 5. CHRISTIANS CHARGED WITH ATHEISM

Why, then, should this be? In our case, who pledge ourselves to do no wickedness, nor to hold these atheistic opinions, you do not examine the charges made against us; but, yielding to unreasoning passion, and to the instigation of evil demons, you punish us without consideration or judgment. For the truth shall be spoken; since of old these evil demons, effecting apparitions of themselves, both defiled women and corrupted boys, and showed such fearful sights to men, that those who did not use their reason in judging of the actions that were done, were struck with terror; and being carried away by fear, and not knowing that these were demons, they called them gods, and gave to each the name which each of the demons chose for himself. And when Socrates endeavoured, by true reason and examination, to bring these things to light, and deliver men from the demons, then the demons themselves, by means of men who rejoiced in iniquity, compassed his death, as an atheist and a profane person, on the charge that he was introducing new divinities; and in our case they display a similar activity. For not only among the Greeks did reason (Logos) prevail to condemn these things through Socrates, but also among the Barbarians were they condemned by Reason (or the Word, the Logos) Himself, who took shape, and became man, and was called Jesus Christ; and in obedience to Him, we not only deny that they who did such things as these are gods, but assert that they are wicked and impious demons, whose actions will not bear comparison with those even of men desirous of virtue.

CHAPTER 6. CHARGE OF ATHEISM REFUTED

Hence are we called atheists. And we confess that we are atheists, so far as gods of this sort are concerned, but not with respect to the most true God, the Father of righteousness and temperance and the other virtues, who is free from all impurity. But both Him, and the Son (who came forth from Him and taught us these things, and the host of the other good angels who follow and are made like to Him), and the prophetic Spirit, we worship and adore, knowing them in reason and truth, and declaring without grudging to every one who wishes to learn, as we have been taught.

CHAPTER 7. EACH CHRISTIAN MUST BE TRIED BY HIS OWN LIFE

But some one will say, Some have ere now been arrested and convicted as evil-doers. For you condemn many, many a time, after inquiring into the life of each of the accused severally, but not on account of those of whom we have been speaking. And this we acknowledge, that as among the Greeks those who teach such theories as please themselves are all called by the one name Philosopher, though their doctrines be diverse, so also among the Barbarians this name on which accusations are accumulated is the common property of those who are and those who seem wise. For all are called Christians. Wherefore we demand that the deeds of all those who are accused to you be judged, in order that each one who is convicted may be punished as an evil-doer, and not as a Christian; and if it is clear that any one is blameless, that he may be acquitted, since by the mere fact of his being a Christian he does no wrong. For we will not require that you punish our accusers; they being sufficiently punished by their present wickedness and ignorance of what is right.

CHAPTER 8. CHRISTIANS CONFESS THEIR FAITH IN GOD

And reckon that it is for your sakes we have been saying these things; for it is in our power, when we are examined, to deny that we are Christians; but we would not live by telling a lie. For, impelled by the desire of the eternal and pure life, we seek the abode that is with God, the Father and Creator of all, and hasten to confess our faith, persuaded and convinced as we are that they who have proved to God by their works that they followed Him, and loved to abide with Him where there is no sin to cause disturbance, can obtain these things. This, then, to speak shortly, is what we expect and have learned from Christ, and teach. And Plato, in like manner, used to say that Rhadamanthus and Minos would punish the wicked who came before them; and we say that the same thing will be done, but at the hand of Christ, and upon the wicked in the same bodies united again to their spirits which are now to undergo everlasting punishment; and not only, as Plato said, for a period of a thousand years. And if any one say that this is incredible or impossible, this error of ours is one which concerns ourselves only, and no other person, so long as you cannot convict us of doing any harm.

CHAPTER 9. FOLLY OF IDOL WORSHIP

And neither do we honour with many sacrifices and garlands of flowers such deities as men have formed and set in shrines and called gods; since we see that these are soulless and dead, and have not the form of God (for we do not consider that God has such a form as some say that they imitate to His honour), but have the names and forms of those wicked demons which have appeared. For why need we tell you who already know, into what forms the craftsmen, Isaiah **44**:**9-20**; Jeremiah **10**:**3**. carving and cutting, casting and hammering, fashion the materials? And often out of vessels of dishonour, by merely changing the form, and making an image of the requisite shape, they make what they call a god; which we consider not only senseless, but to be even insulting to God, who, having ineffable glory and form, thus gets His name attached to things that are corruptible, and require constant service. And that the artificers of these are both intemperate, and, not to enter into particulars, are practised in every vice, you very well know; even their own girls who work along with them they corrupt. What infatuation! That dissolute men should be said to fashion and make gods for your worship, and that you should appoint such men the guardians of the temples where they are enshrined; not recognising that it is unlawful even to think or say that men are the guardians of gods.

CHAPTER 10. HOW GOD IS TO BE SERVED

But we have received by tradition that God does not need the material offerings which men can give, seeing, indeed, that He Himself is the provider of all things. And we have been taught, and are convinced, and do believe, that He accepts those only who imitate the excellences which reside in Him, temperance, and justice, and philanthropy, and as many virtues as are peculiar to a God who is called by no proper name. And we have been taught that He in the beginning did of His goodness, for man's sake, create all things out of unformed matter; and if men by their works show themselves worthy of this His design, they are deemed worthy, and so we have received — of reigning in company with Him, being delivered from corruption and suffering. For as in the beginning He created us when we were not, so do we consider that, in like manner, those who choose what is pleasing to Him are, on account of their choice, deemed worthy of incorruption and of fellowship with Him. For the coming into being at first was not in our own power; and in order that we may follow those things which please Him, choosing them by means of the rational faculties He has Himself endowed us with, He both persuades us and leads us to faith. And we think it for the advantage of all men that they are not restrained from learning these things, but are even urged thereto. For the restraint which human laws could not effect, the Word, inasmuch as He is divine, would have effected, had not the wicked demons, taking as their ally the lust of wickedness which is in every man, and which draws variously to all manner of vice, scattered many false and profane accusations, none of which attach to us.

CHAPTER 11. WHAT KINGDOM CHRISTIANS LOOK FOR

And when you hear that we look for a kingdom, you suppose, without making any inquiry, that we speak of a human kingdom; whereas we speak of that which is with God, as appears also from the confession of their faith made by those who are charged with being Christians, though they know that death is the punishment awarded to him who so confesses. For if we looked for a human kingdom, we should also deny our Christ, that we might not be slain; and we should strive to escape detection, that we might obtain what we expect. But since our thoughts are not fixed on the present, we are not concerned when men cut us off; since also death is a debt which must at all events be paid.

CHAPTER 12. CHRISTIANS LIVE AS UNDER GOD'S EYE

And more than all other men are we your helpers and allies in promoting peace, seeing that we hold this view, that it is alike impossible for the wicked, the covetous, the conspirator, and for the virtuous, to escape the notice of God, and that each man goes to everlasting punishment or salvation according to the value of his actions. For if all men knew this, no one would choose wickedness even for a little, knowing that he goes to the everlasting punishment of fire; but would by all means restrain himself, and adorn himself with virtue, that he might obtain the good gifts of God, and escape the punishments. For those who, on account of the laws and punishments you impose, endeavour to escape detection when they offend (and they offend, too, under the impression that it is quite possible to escape your detection, since you are but men), those persons, if they learned and were convinced that nothing, whether actually done or only intended, can escape the knowledge of God, would by all means live decently on account of the penalties threatened, as even you yourselves will admit. But you seem to fear lest all men become righteous, and you no longer have any to punish. Such would be the concern of public executioners, but not of good princes. But, as we before said, we are persuaded that these things are prompted by evil spirits, who demand sacrifices and service even from those who live unreasonably; but as for you, we presume that you who aim at [a reputation for] piety and philosophy will do nothing unreasonable. But if you also, like the foolish, prefer custom to truth, do what you have power to do. But just so much power have rulers who esteem opinion more than truth, as robbers have in a desert. And that you will not succeed is declared by the Word, than whom, after God who begot Him, we know there is no ruler more kingly and just. For as all shrink from succeeding to the poverty or sufferings or obscurity of their fathers, so whatever the Word forbids us to choose, the sensible man will not choose. That all these things should come to pass, I say, our Teacher foretold, He who is both Son and Apostle of God the Father of all and the Ruler, Jesus Christ; from whom also we have the name of Christians. Whence we become more assured of all the things He taught us, since whatever He beforehand foretold should come to pass, is seen in fact coming to pass; and this is the work of God, to tell of a thing before it happens, and as it was foretold so to show it happening. It were possible to pause here and add no more, reckoning that we demand what is just and true; but because we are well aware that it is not easy suddenly to change a mind possessed by ignorance, we intend to add a few things, for the sake of persuading those who love the truth, knowing that it is not impossible to put ignorance to flight by presenting the truth.

CHAPTER 13. CHRISTIANS SERVE GOD RATIONALLY

What sober-minded man, then, will not acknowledge that we are not atheists, worshipping as we do the Maker of this universe, and declaring, as we have been taught, that He has no need of streams of blood and libations and incense; whom we praise to the utmost of our power by the exercise of prayer and thanksgiving for all things wherewith we are supplied, as we have been taught that the only honour that is worthy of Him is not to consume by fire what He has brought into being for our sustenance, but to use it for ourselves and those who need, and with gratitude to Him to offer thanks by invocations and hymns for our creation, and for all the means of health, and for the various qualities of the different kinds of things, and for the changes of the seasons; and to present before Him petitions for our existing again in incorruption through faith in Him. Our teacher of these things is Jesus Christ, who also was born for this purpose, and was crucified under Pontius Pilate, procurator of Judæa, in the times of Tiberius Cæsar; and that we reasonably worship Him, having learned that He is the Son of the true God Himself, and holding Him in the second place, and the prophetic Spirit in the third, we will prove. For they proclaim our madness to consist in this, that we give to a crucified man a place second to the unchangeable and eternal God, the Creator of all; for they do not discern the mystery that is herein, to which, as we make it plain to you, we pray you to give heed.

CHAPTER 14. THE DEMONS MISREPRESENT CHRISTIAN DOCTRINE

For we forewarn you to be on your guard, lest those demons whom we have been accusing should deceive you, and quite divert you from reading and understanding what we say. For they strive to hold you their slaves and servants; and sometimes by appearances in dreams, and sometimes by magical impositions, they subdue all who make no strong opposing effort for their own salvation. And thus do we also, since our persuasion by the Word, stand aloof from them (i.e., the demons), and follow the only unbegotten God through His Son — we who formerly delighted in fornication, but now embrace chastity alone; we who formerly used magical arts, dedicate ourselves to the good and unbegotten God; we who valued above all things the acquisition of wealth and possessions, now bring what we have into a common stock, and communicate to every one in need; we who hated and destroyed one another, and on account of their different manners would not live with men of a different tribe, now, since the coming of Christ, live familiarly with them, and pray for our enemies, and endeavour to persuade those who hate us unjustly to live conformably to the good precepts of Christ, to the end that they may become partakers with us of the same joyful hope of a reward from God the ruler of all. But lest we should seem to be reasoning sophistically, we consider it right, before giving you the promised explanation, to cite a few precepts given by Christ Himself. And be it yours, as powerful rulers, to inquire whether we have been taught and do teach these things truly. Brief and concise utterances fell from Him, for He was no sophist, but His word was the power of God.

CHAPTER 15. WHAT CHRIST HIMSELF TAUGHT

Concerning chastity, He uttered such sentiments as these: Whosoever looks upon a woman to lust after her, has committed adultery with her already in his heart before God. And, If your right eye offend you, cut it out; for it is better for you to enter into the kingdom of heaven with one eye, than, having two eyes, to be cast into everlasting fire. And, Whosoever shall marry her that is divorced from another husband, commits adultery. And, There are some who have been made eunuchs of men, and some who were born eunuchs, and some who have made themselves eunuchs for the kingdom of heaven's sake; but all cannot receive this saying. Matthew **19**:**12** So that all who, by human law, are twice married, are in the eye of our Master sinners, and those who look upon a woman to lust after her. For not only he who in act commits adultery is rejected by Him, but also he who desires to commit adultery: since not only our works, but also our thoughts, are open before God. And many, both men and women, who have been Christ's disciples from childhood, remain pure at the age of sixty or seventy years; and I boast that I could produce such from every race of men. For what shall I say, too, of the countless multitude of those who have reformed intemperate habits, and learned these things? For Christ called not the just nor the chaste to repentance, but the ungodly, and the licentious, and the unjust; His words being, I came not to call the righteous, but sinners to repentance. Matthew **9**:**13** For the heavenly Father desires rather the repentance than the punishment of the sinner. And of our love to all, He taught thus: If you love them that love you, what new thing are you doing? For even fornicators do this. But I say unto you, Pray for your enemies, and love them that hate you, and bless them that curse you, and pray for them that despitefully use you. Matthew **5**:**46**, **44**; Luke **6**:**28** And that we should communicate to the needy, and do nothing for glory, He said, Give to him that asks, and from him that would borrow turn not away; for if you lend to them of whom you hope to receive, what new thing are you doing? Even the publicans do this. Lay not up for yourselves treasure upon earth, where moth and rust does corrupt, and where robbers break through; but lay up for yourselves treasure in heaven, where neither moth nor rust does corrupt. For what is a man profited, if he shall gain the whole world, and lose his own soul? Or what shall a man give in exchange for it? Lay up treasure, therefore, in heaven, where neither moth nor rust does corrupt. And, Be kind and merciful, as your Father also is kind and merciful, and makes His sun to rise on sinners, and the righteous, and the wicked. Take no thought what you shall eat, or what you shall put on: are you not better than the birds and the beasts? And God feeds them. Take no thought, therefore, what you shall eat, or what you shall put on; for your heavenly Father knows that you have need of these things. But seek the kingdom of heaven, and all these things shall be added unto you. For where his treasure is, there also is the mind of a man. And, Do not these things to be seen of men; otherwise you have no reward from your Father which is in heaven. Matthew **6**:**1**

CHAPTER 16. CONCERNING PATIENCE AND SWEARING

And concerning our being patient of injuries, and ready to serve all, and free from anger, this is what He said: To him that smites you on the one cheek, offer also the other; and him that takes away your cloak or coat, forbid not. And whosoever shall be angry, is in danger of the fire. And every one that compels you to go with him a mile, follow him two. And let your good works shine before men, that they, seeing them, may glorify your Father which is in heaven. For we ought not to strive; neither has He desired us to be imitators of wicked men, but He has exhorted us to lead all men, by patience and gentleness, from shame and the love of evil. And this indeed is proved in the case of many who once were of your way of thinking, but have changed their violent and tyrannical disposition, being overcome either by the constancy which they have witnessed in their neighbours' lives, or by the extraordinary forbearance they have observed in their fellow-travellers when defrauded, or by the honesty of those with whom they have transacted business.

And with regard to our not swearing at all, and always speaking the truth, He enjoined as follows: Swear not at all; but let your yea be yea, and your nay, nay; for whatsoever is more than these comes of evil. Matthew **5**:**34**, **27** And that we ought to worship God alone, He thus persuaded us: The greatest commandment is, You shall worship the Lord your God, and Him only shall you serve, with all your heart, and with all your strength, the Lord God that made you. Mark **12**:**30** And when a certain man came to Him and said, Good Master, He answered and said, There is none good but God only, who made all things. Matthew **19**:**6**, **17** And let those who are not found living as He taught, be understood to be no Christians, even though they profess with the lip the precepts of Christ; for not those who make profession, but those who do the works, shall be saved, according to His word: Not every one who says to Me, Lord, Lord, shall enter into the kingdom of heaven, but he that does the will of My Father which is in heaven. For whosoever hears Me, and does My sayings, hears Him that sent Me. And many will say unto Me, Lord, Lord, have we not eaten and drunk in Your name, and done wonders? And then will I say unto them, Depart from Me, you workers of iniquity. Then shall there be wailing and gnashing of teeth, when the righteous shall shine as the sun, and the wicked are sent into everlasting fire. For many shall come in My name, clothed outwardly in sheep's clothing, but inwardly being ravening wolves. By their works you shall know them. And every tree that brings not forth good fruit, is hewn down and cast into the fire. And as to those who are not living pursuant to these His teachings, and are Christians only in name, we demand that all such be punished by you.

CHAPTER 17. CHRIST TAUGHT CIVIL OBEDIENCE

And everywhere we, more readily than all men, endeavour to pay to those appointed by you the taxes both ordinary and extraordinary, as we have been taught by Him; for at that time some came to Him and asked Him, if one ought to pay tribute to Cæsar; and He answered, Tell Me, whose image does the coin bear? And they said, Cæsar's. And again He answered them, Render therefore to Cæsar the things that are Cæsar's, and to God the things that are God's. Whence to God alone we render worship, but in other things we gladly serve you, acknowledging you as kings and rulers of men, and praying that with your kingly power you be found to possess also sound judgment. But if you pay no regard to our prayers and frank explanations, we shall suffer no loss, since we believe (or rather, indeed, are persuaded) that every man will suffer punishment in eternal fire according to the merit of his deed, and will render account according to the power he has received from God, as Christ intimated when He said, To whom God has given more, of him shall more be required. Luke **12:48**

CHAPTER 18. PROOF OF IMMORTALITY AND THE RESURRECTION

For reflect upon the end of each of the preceding kings, how they died the death common to all, which, if it issued in insensibility, would be a godsend to all the wicked. But since sensation remains to all who have ever lived, and eternal punishment is laid up (i.e., for the wicked), see that you neglect not to be convinced, and to hold as your belief, that these things are true. For let even necromancy, and the divinations you practise by immaculate children, and the evoking of departed human souls, and those who are called among the magi, Dream-senders and Assistant-spirits (Familiars), and all that is done by those who are skilled in such matters — let these persuade you that even after death souls are in a state of sensation; and those who are seized and cast about by the spirits of the dead, whom all call dæmoniacs or madmen; and what you repute as oracles, both of Amphilochus, Dodana, Pytho, and as many other such as exist; and the opinions of your authors, Empedocles and Pythagoras, Plato and Socrates, and the pit of Homer, and the descent of Ulysses to inspect these things, and all that has been uttered of a like kind. Such favour as you grant to these, grant also to us, who not less but more firmly than they believe in God; since we expect to receive again our own bodies, though they be dead and cast into the earth, for we maintain that with God nothing is impossible.

CHAPTER 19. THE RESURRECTION POSSIBLE

And to any thoughtful person would anything appear more incredible, than, if we were not in the body, and some one were to say that it was possible that from a small drop of human seed bones and sinews and flesh be formed into a shape such as we see? For let this now be said hypothetically: if you yourselves were not such as you now are, and born of such parents [and causes], and one were to show you human seed and a picture of a man, and were to say with confidence that from such a substance such a being could be produced, would you believe before you saw the actual production? No one will dare to deny [that such a statement would surpass belief]. In the same way, then, you are now incredulous because you have never seen a dead man rise again. But as at first you would not have believed it possible that such persons could be produced from the small drop, and yet now you see them thus produced, so also judge that it is not impossible that the bodies of men, after they have been dissolved, and like seeds resolved into earth, should in God's appointed time rise again and put on incorruption. For what power worthy of God those imagine who say, that each thing returns to that from which it was produced, and that beyond this not even God Himself can do anything, we are unable to conceive; but this we see clearly, that they would not have believed it possible that they could have become such and produced from such materials, as they now see both themselves and the whole world to be. And that it is better to believe even what is impossible to our own nature and to men, than to be unbelieving like the rest of the world, we have learned; for we know that our Master Jesus Christ said, that what is impossible with men is possible with God, Matthew **19**:**26** and, Fear not them that kill you, and after that can do no more; but fear Him who after death is able to cast both soul and body into hell. Matthew **10**:**28** And hell is a place where those are to be punished who have lived wickedly, and who do not believe that those things which God has taught us by Christ will come to pass.

CHAPTER 20. HEATHEN ANALOGIES TO CHRISTIAN DOCTRINE

And the Sibyl and Hystaspes said that there should be a dissolution by God of things corruptible. And the philosophers called Stoics teach that even God Himself shall be resolved into fire, and they say that the world is to be formed anew by this revolution; but we understand that God, the Creator of all things, is superior to the things that are to be changed. If, therefore, on some points we teach the same things as the poets and philosophers whom you honour, and on other points are fuller and more divine in our teaching, and if we alone afford proof of what we assert, why are we unjustly hated more than all others? For while we say that all things have been produced and arranged into a world by God, we shall seem to utter the doctrine of Plato; and while we say that there will be a burning up of all, we shall seem to utter the doctrine of the Stoics: and while we affirm that the souls of the wicked, being endowed with sensation even after death, are punished, and that those of the good being delivered from punishment spend a blessed existence, we shall seem to say the same things as the poets and philosophers; and while we maintain that men ought not to worship the works of their hands, we say the very things which have been said by the comic poet Menander, and other similar writers, for they have declared that the workman is greater than the work.

CHAPTER 21. ANALOGIES TO THE HISTORY OF CHRIST

And when we say also that the Word, who is the first-birth of God, was produced without sexual union, and that He, Jesus Christ, our Teacher, was crucified and died, and rose again, and ascended into heaven, we propound nothing different from what you believe regarding those whom you esteem sons of Jupiter. For you know how many sons your esteemed writers ascribed to Jupiter: Mercury, the interpreting word and teacher of all; Æsculapius, who, though he was a great physician, was struck by a thunderbolt, and so ascended to heaven; and Bacchus too, after he had been torn limb from limb; and Hercules, when he had committed himself to the flames to escape his toils; and the sons of Leda, and Dioscuri; and Perseus, son of Danae; and Bellerophon, who, though sprung from mortals, rose to heaven on the horse Pegasus. For what shall I say of Ariadne, and those who, like her, have been declared to be set among the stars? And what of the emperors who die among yourselves, whom you deem worthy of deification, and in whose behalf you produce some one who swears he has seen the burning Cæsar rise to heaven from the funeral pyre? And what kind of deeds are recorded of each of these reputed sons of Jupiter, it is needless to tell to those who already know. This only shall be said, that they are written for the advantage and encouragement of youthful scholars; for all reckon it an honourable thing to imitate the gods. But far be such a thought concerning the gods from every well-conditioned soul, as to believe that Jupiter himself, the governor and creator of all things, was both a parricide and the son of a parricide, and that being overcome by the love of base and shameful pleasures, he came in to Ganymede and those many women whom he had violated and that his sons did like actions. But, as we said above, wicked devils perpetrated these things. And we have learned that those only are deified who have lived near to God in holiness and virtue; and we believe that those who live wickedly and do not repent are punished in everlasting fire.

CHAPTER 22. ANALOGIES TO THE SONSHIP OF CHRIST

Moreover, the Son of God called Jesus, even if only a man by ordinary generation, yet, on account of His wisdom, is worthy to be called the Son of God; for all writers call God the Father of men and gods. And if we assert that the Word of God was born of God in a peculiar manner, different from ordinary generation, let this, as said above, be no extraordinary thing to you, who say that Mercury is the angelic word of God. But if any one objects that He was crucified, in this also He is on a par with those reputed sons of Jupiter of yours, who suffered as we have now enumerated. For their sufferings at death are recorded to have been not all alike, but diverse; so that not even by the peculiarity of His sufferings does He seem to be inferior to them; but, on the contrary, as we promised in the preceding part of this discourse, we will now prove Him superior — or rather have already proved Him to be so — for the superior is revealed by His actions. And if we even affirm that He was born of a virgin, accept this in common with what you accept of Perseus. And in that we say that He made whole the lame, the paralytic, and those born blind, we seem to say what is very similar to the deeds said to have been done by Æsculapius.

CHAPTER 23. THE ARGUMENT

And that this may now become evident to you — (firstly) that whatever we assert in conformity with what has been taught us by Christ, and by the prophets who preceded Him, are alone true, and are older than all the writers who have existed; that we claim to be acknowledged, not because we say the same things as these writers said, but because we say true things: and (secondly) that Jesus Christ is the only proper Son who has been begotten by God, being His Word and first-begotten, and power; and, becoming man according to His will, He taught us these things for the conversion and restoration of the human race: and (thirdly) that before He became a man among men, some, influenced by the demons before mentioned, related beforehand, through the instrumentality of the poets, those circumstances as having really happened, which, having fictitiously devised, they narrated, in the same manner as they have caused to be fabricated the scandalous reports against us of infamous and impious actions, of which there is neither witness nor proof— we shall bring forward the following proof.

CHAPTER 24. VARIETIES OF HEATHEN WORSHIP

In the first place [we furnish proof], because, though we say things similar to what the Greeks say, we only are hated on account of the name of Christ, and though we do no wrong, are put to death as sinners; other men in other places worshipping trees and rivers, and mice and cats and crocodiles, and many irrational animals. Nor are the same animals esteemed by all; but in one place one is worshipped, and another in another, so that all are profane in the judgment of one another, on account of their not worshipping the same objects. And this is the sole accusation you bring against us, that we do not reverence the same gods as you do, nor offer to the dead libations and the savour of fat, and crowns for their statues, and sacrifices. For you very well know that the same animals are with some esteemed gods, with others wild beasts, and with others sacrificial victims.

CHAPTER 25. FALSE GODS ABANDONED BY CHRISTIANS

And, secondly, because we — who, out of every race of men, used to worship Bacchus the son of Semele, and Apollo the son of Latona (who in their loves with men did such things as it is shameful even to mention), and Proserpine and Venus (who were maddened with love of Adonis, and whose mysteries also you celebrate), or Æsculapius, or some one or other of those who are called gods — have now, through Jesus Christ, learned to despise these, though we be threatened with death for it, and have dedicated ourselves to the unbegotten and impassible God; of whom we are persuaded that never was he goaded by lust of Antiope, or such other women, or of Ganymede, nor was rescued by that hundred-handed giant whose aid was obtained through Thetis, nor was anxious on this account that her son Achilles should destroy many of the Greeks because of his concubine Briseis. Those who believe these things we pity, and those who invented them we know to be devils.

CHAPTER 26. MAGICIANS NOT TRUSTED BY CHRISTIANS

And, thirdly, because after Christ's ascension into heaven the devils put forward certain men who said that they themselves were gods; and they were not only not persecuted by you, but even deemed worthy of honours. There was a Samaritan, Simon, a native of the village called Gitto, who in the reign of Claudius Cæsar, and in your royal city of Rome, did mighty acts of magic, by virtue of the art of the devils operating in him. He was considered a god, and as a god was honoured by you with a statue, which statue was erected on the river Tiber, between the two bridges, and bore this inscription, in the language of Rome: — Simoni Deo Sancto, To Simon the holy God. And almost all the Samaritans, and a few even of other nations, worship him, and acknowledge him as the first god; and a woman, Helena, who went about with him at that time, and had formerly been a prostitute, they say is the first idea generated by him. And a man, Menander, also a Samaritan, of the town Capparetæa, a disciple of Simon, and inspired by devils, we know to have deceived many while he was in Antioch by his magical art. He persuaded those who adhered to him that they should never die, and even now there are some living who hold this opinion of his. And there is Marcion, a man of Pontus, who is even at this day alive, and teaching his disciples to believe in some other god greater than the Creator. And he, by the aid of the devils, has caused many of every nation to speak blasphemies, and to deny that God is the maker of this universe, and to assert that some other being, greater than He, has done greater works. All who take their opinions from these men, are, as we before said, called Christians; just as also those who do not agree with the philosophers in their doctrines, have yet in common with them the name of philosophers given to them. And whether they perpetrate those fabulous and shameful deeds — the upsetting of the lamp, and promiscuous intercourse, and eating human flesh — we know not; but we do know that they are neither persecuted nor put to death by you, at least on account of their opinions. But I have a treatise against all the heresies that have existed already composed, which, if you wish to read it, I will give you.

CHAPTER 27. GUILT OF EXPOSING CHILDREN

But as for us, we have been taught that to expose newly-born children is the part of wicked men; and this we have been taught lest we should do any one an injury, and lest we should sin against God, first, because we see that almost all so exposed (not only the girls, but also the males) are brought up to prostitution. And as the ancients are said to have reared herds of oxen, or goats, or sheep, or grazing horses, so now we see you rear children only for this shameful use; and for this pollution a multitude of females and hermaphrodites, and those who commit unmentionable iniquities, are found in every nation. And you receive the hire of these, and duty and taxes from them, whom you ought to exterminate from your realm. And any one who uses such persons, besides the godless and infamous and impure intercourse, may possibly be having intercourse with his own child, or relative, or brother. And there are some who prostitute even their own children and wives, and some are openly mutilated for the purpose of sodomy; and they refer these mysteries to the mother of the gods, and along with each of those whom you esteem gods there is painted a serpent, a great symbol and mystery. Indeed, the things which you do openly and with applause, as if the divine light were overturned and extinguished, these you lay to our charge; which, in truth, does no harm to us who shrink from doing any such things, but only to those who do them and bear false witness against us.

CHAPTER 28. GOD'S CARE FOR MEN

For among us the prince of the wicked spirits is called the serpent, and Satan, and the devil, as you can learn by looking into our writings. And that he would be sent into the fire with his host, and the men who follow him, and would be punished for an endless duration, Christ foretold. For the reason why God has delayed to do this, is His regard for the human race. For He foreknows that some are to be saved by repentance, some even that are perhaps not yet born. In the beginning He made the human race with the power of thought and of choosing the truth and doing right, so that all men are without excuse before God; for they have been born rational and contemplative. And if any one disbelieves that God cares for these things, he will thereby either insinuate that God does not exist, or he will assert that though He exists He delights in vice, or exists like a stone, and that neither virtue nor vice are anything, but only in the opinion of men these things are reckoned good or evil. And this is the greatest profanity and wickedness.

CHAPTER 29. CONTINENCE OF CHRISTIANS

And again [we fear to expose children], lest some of them be not picked up, but die, and we become murderers. But whether we marry, it is only that we may bring up children; or whether we decline marriage, we live continently. And that you may understand that promiscuous intercourse is not one of our mysteries, one of our number a short time ago presented to Felix the governor in Alexandria a petition, craving that permission might be given to a surgeon to make him an eunuch. For the surgeons there said that they were forbidden to do this without the permission of the governor. And when Felix absolutely refused to sign such a permission, the youth remained single, and was satisfied with his own approving conscience, and the approval of those who thought as he did. And it is not out of place, we think, to mention here Antinous, who was alive but lately, and whom all were prompt, through fear, to worship as a god, though they knew both who he was and what was his origin.

CHAPTER 30. WAS CHRIST NOT A MAGICIAN?

But lest any one should meet us with the question, What should prevent that He whom we call Christ, being a man born of men, performed what we call His mighty works by magical art, and by this appeared to be the Son of God? We will now offer proof, not trusting mere assertions, but being of necessity persuaded by those who prophesied [of Him] before these things came to pass, for with our own eyes we behold things that have happened and are happening just as they were predicted; and this will, we think appear even to you the strongest and truest evidence.

CHAPTER 31. OF THE HEBREW PROPHETS

There were, then, among the Jews certain men who were prophets of God, through whom the prophetic Spirit published beforehand things that were to come to pass, ere ever they happened. And their prophecies, as they were spoken and when they were uttered, the kings who happened to be reigning among the Jews at the several times carefully preserved in their possession, when they had been arranged in books by the prophets themselves in their own Hebrew language. And when Ptolemy king of Egypt formed a library, and endeavoured to collect the writings of all men, he heard also of these prophets, and sent to Herod, who was at that time king of the Jews, requesting that the books of the prophets be sent to him. And Herod the king did indeed send them, written, as they were, in the foresaid Hebrew language. And when their contents were found to be unintelligible to the Egyptians, he again sent and requested that men be commissioned to translate them into the Greek language. And when this was done, the books remained with the Egyptians, where they are until now. They are also in the possession of all Jews throughout the world; but they, though they read, do not understand what is said, but count us foes and enemies; and, like yourselves, they kill and punish us whenever they have the power, as you can well believe. For in the Jewish war which lately raged, Barchochebas, the leader of the revolt of the Jews, gave orders that Christians alone should be led to cruel punishments, unless they would deny Jesus Christ and utter blasphemy. In these books, then, of the prophets we found Jesus our Christ foretold as coming, born of a virgin, growing up to man's estate, and healing every disease and every sickness, and raising the dead, and being hated, and unrecognised, and crucified, and dying, and rising again, and ascending into heaven, and being, and being called, the Son of God. We find it also predicted that certain persons should be sent by Him into every nation to publish these things, and that rather among the Gentiles [than among the Jews] men should believe in Him. And He was predicted before He appeared, first **5000** years before, and again **3000**, then **2000**, then **1000**, and yet again **800**; for in the succession of generations prophets after prophets arose.

CHAPTER 32. CHRIST PREDICTED BY MOSES

Moses then, who was the first of the prophets, spoke in these very words: The sceptre shall not depart from Judah, nor a lawgiver from between his feet, until He come for whom it is reserved; and He shall be the desire of the nations, binding His foal to the vine, washing His robe in the blood of the grape. Genesis **49**:**10** It is yours to make accurate inquiry, and ascertain up to whose time the Jews had a lawgiver and king of their own. Up to the time of Jesus Christ, who taught us, and interpreted the prophecies which were not yet understood, [they had a lawgiver] as was foretold by the holy and divine Spirit of prophecy through Moses, that a ruler would not fail the Jews until He should come for whom the kingdom was reserved (for Judah was the forefather of the Jews, from whom also they have their name of Jews); and after He (i.e., Christ) appeared, you began to rule the Jews, and gained possession of all their territory. And the prophecy, He shall be the expectation of the nations, signified that there would be some of all nations who should look for Him to come again. And this indeed you can see for yourselves, and be convinced of by fact. For of all races of men there are some who look for Him who was crucified in Judæa, and after whose crucifixion the land was straightway surrendered to you as spoil of war. And the prophecy, binding His foal to the vine, and washing His robe in the blood of the grape, was a significant symbol of the things that were to happen to Christ, and of what He was to do. For the foal of an ass stood bound to a vine at the entrance of a village, and He ordered His acquaintances to bring it to Him then; and when it was brought, He mounted and sat upon it, and entered Jerusalem, where was the vast temple of the Jews which was afterwards destroyed by you. And after this He was crucified, that the rest of the prophecy might be fulfilled. For this washing His robe in the blood of the grape was predictive of the passion He was to endure, cleansing by His blood those who believe in Him. For what is called by the Divine Spirit through the prophet His robe, are those men who believe in Him in whom abides the seed of God, the Word. And what is spoken of as the blood of the grape, signifies that He who should appear would have blood, though not of the seed of man, but of the power of God. And the first power after God the Father and Lord of all is the Word, who is also the Son; and of Him we will, in what follows, relate how He took flesh and became man. For as man did not make the blood of the vine, but God, so it was hereby intimated that the blood should not be of human seed, but of divine power, as we have said above. And Isaiah, another prophet, foretelling the same things in other words, spoke thus: A star shall rise out of Jacob, and a flower shall spring from the root of Jesse; and His arm shall the nations trust. Isaiah **11**:**1** And a star of light has arisen, and a flower has sprung from the root of Jesse — this Christ. For by the power of God He was conceived by a virgin of the seed of Jacob, who was the father of Judah, who, as we have shown, was the father of the Jews; and Jesse was His forefather according to the oracle, and He was the son of Jacob and Judah according to lineal descent.

CHAPTER 33. MANNER OF CHRIST'S BIRTH PREDICTED

And hear again how Isaiah in express words foretold that He should be born of a virgin; for he spoke thus: Behold, a virgin shall conceive, and bring forth a son, and they shall say for His name, 'God with us.' Isaiah **7**:**14** For things which were incredible and seemed impossible with men, these God predicted by the Spirit of prophecy as about to come to pass, in order that, when they came to pass, there might be no unbelief, but faith, because of their prediction. But lest some, not understanding the prophecy now cited, should charge us with the very things we have been laying to the charge of the poets who say that Jupiter went in to women through lust, let us try to explain the words. This, then, Behold, a virgin shall conceive, signifies that a virgin should conceive without intercourse. For if she had had intercourse with any one whatever, she was no longer a virgin; but the power of God having come upon the virgin, overshadowed her, and caused her while yet a virgin to conceive. And the angel of God who was sent to the same virgin at that time brought her good news, saying, Behold, you shall conceive of the Holy Ghost, and shall bear a Son, and He shall be called the Son of the Highest, and you shall call His name Jesus; for He shall save His people from their sins, Luke **1**:**32**; Matthew **1**:**21** — as they who have recorded all that concerns our Saviour Jesus Christ have taught, whom we believed, since by Isaiah also, whom we have now adduced, the Spirit of prophecy declared that He should be born as we intimated before. It is wrong, therefore, to understand the Spirit and the power of God as anything else than the Word, who is also the first-born of God, as the foresaid prophet Moses declared; and it was this which, when it came upon the virgin and overshadowed her, caused her to conceive, not by intercourse, but by power. And the name Jesus in the Hebrew language means Σωτήρ (Saviour) in the Greek tongue. Wherefore, too, the angel said to the virgin, You shall call His name Jesus, for He shall save His people from their sins. And that the prophets are inspired by no other than the Divine Word, even you, as I fancy, will grant.

CHAPTER 34. PLACE OF CHRIST'S BIRTH FORETOLD

And hear what part of earth He was to be born in, as another prophet, Micah, foretold. He spoke thus: And you, Bethlehem, the land of Judah, are not the least among the princes of Judah; for out of you shall come forth a Governor, who shall feed My people. Micah **5**:**2** Now there is a village in the land of the Jews, thirty-five stadia from Jerusalem, in which Jesus Christ was born, as you can ascertain also from the registers of the taxing made under Cyrenius, your first procurator in Judæa.

CHAPTER 35. OTHER FULFILLED PROPHECIES

And how Christ after He was born was to escape the notice of other men until He grew to man's estate, which also came to pass, hear what was foretold regarding this. There are the following predictions: — Unto us a child is born, and unto us a young man is given, and the government shall be upon His shoulders; Isaiah **9**:**6** which is significant of the power of the cross, for to it, when He was crucified, He applied His shoulders, as shall be more clearly made out in the ensuing discourse. And again the same prophet Isaiah, being inspired by the prophetic Spirit, said, I have spread out my hands to a disobedient and gainsaying people, to those who walk in a way that is not good. They now ask of me judgment, and dare to draw near to God. Isaiah **65**:**2**, Isaiah **58**:**2** And again in other words, through another prophet, He says, They pierced My hands and My feet, and for My vesture they cast lots. And indeed David, the king and prophet, who uttered these things, suffered none of them; but Jesus Christ stretched forth His hands, being crucified by the Jews speaking against Him, and denying that He was the Christ. And as the prophet spoke, they tormented Him, and set Him on the judgment-seat, and said, Judge us. And the expression, They pierced my hands and my feet, was used in reference to the nails of the cross which were fixed in His hands and feet. And after He was crucified they cast lots upon His vesture, and they that crucified Him parted it among them. And that these things did happen, you can ascertain from the Acts of Pontius Pilate. And we will cite the prophetic utterances of another prophet, Zephaniah, to the effect that He was foretold expressly as to sit upon the foal of an ass and to enter Jerusalem. The words are these: Rejoice greatly, O daughter of Zion; shout, O daughter of Jerusalem: behold, your King comes unto you; lowly, and riding upon an ass, and upon a colt the foal of an ass. Zechariah **9**:**9**

CHAPTER 36. DIFFERENT MODES OF PROPHECY

But when you hear the utterances of the prophets spoken as it were personally, you must not suppose that they are spoken by the inspired themselves, but by the Divine Word who moves them. For sometimes He declares things that are to come to pass, in the manner of one who foretells the future; sometimes He speaks as from the person of God the Lord and Father of all; sometimes as from the person of Christ; sometimes as from the person of the people answering the Lord or His Father, just as you can see even in your own writers, one man being the writer of the whole, but introducing the persons who converse. And this the Jews who possessed the books of the prophets did not understand, and therefore did not recognise Christ even when He came, but even hate us who say that He has come, and who prove that, as was predicted, He was crucified by them.

CHAPTER 37. UTTERANCES OF THE FATHER

And that this too may be clear to you, there were spoken from the person of the Father through Isaiah the Prophet, the following words: The ox knows his owner, and the ass his master's crib; but Israel does not know, and My people has not understood. Woe, sinful nation, a people full of sins, a wicked seed, children that are transgressors, you have forsaken the Lord. And again elsewhere, when the same prophet speaks in like manner from the person of the Father, What is the house that you will build for Me? Says the Lord. The heaven is My throne, and the earth is My footstool. Isaiah **66**:**1** And again, in another place, Your new moons and your sabbaths My soul hates; and the great day of the fast and of ceasing from labour I cannot away with; nor, if you come to be seen of Me, will I hear you: your hands are full of blood; and if you bring fine flour, incense, it is abomination unto Me: the fat of lambs and the blood of bulls I do not desire. For who has required this at your hands? But loose every bond of wickedness, tear asunder the tight knots of violent contracts, cover the houseless and naked, deal your bread to the hungry. Isaiah **1**:**14**, Isaiah **58**:**6** What kind of things are taught through the prophets from [the person of] God, you can now perceive.

CHAPTER 38. UTTERANCES OF THE SON

And when the Spirit of prophecy speaks from the person of Christ, the utterances are of this sort: I have spread out My hands to a disobedient and gainsaying people, to those who walk in a way that is not good. Isaiah **65**:**2** And again: I gave My back to the scourges, and My cheeks to the buffetings; I turned not away My face from the shame of spittings; and the Lord was My helper: therefore was I not confounded: but I set My face as a firm rock; and I knew that I should not be ashamed, for He is near that justifies Me. Isaiah **50**:**6** And again, when He says, They cast lots upon My vesture, and pierced My hands and My feet. And I lay down and slept, and rose again, because the Lord sustained Me. And again, when He says, They spoke with their lips, they wagged the head, saying, Let Him deliver Himself. And that all these things happened to Christ at the hands of the Jews, you can ascertain. For when He was crucified, they did shoot out the lip, and wagged their heads, saying, Let Him who raised the dead save Himself. Matthew **27**:**39**

CHAPTER 39. DIRECT PREDICTIONS BY THE SPIRIT

And when the Spirit of prophecy speaks as predicting things that are to come to pass, He speaks in this way: For out of Zion shall go forth the law, and the word of the Lord from Jerusalem. And He shall judge among the nations, and shall rebuke many people; and they shall beat their swords into ploughshares, and their spears into pruning-hooks: nation shall not lift up sword against nation, neither shall they learn war any more. Isaiah **2**:**3** And that it did so come to pass, we can convince you. For from Jerusalem there went out into the world, men, twelve in number, and these illiterate, of no ability in speaking: but by the power of God they proclaimed to every race of men that they were sent by Christ to teach to all the word of God; and we who formerly used to murder one another do not only now refrain from making war upon our enemies, but also, that we may not lie nor deceive our examiners, willingly die confessing Christ. For that saying, The tongue has sworn but the mind is unsworn, might be imitated by us in this matter. But if the soldiers enrolled by you, and who have taken the military oath, prefer their allegiance to their own life, and parents, and country, and all kindred, though you can offer them nothing incorruptible, it were verily ridiculous if we, who earnestly long for incorruption, should not endure all things, in order to obtain what we desire from Him who is able to grant it.

CHAPTER 40. CHRIST'S ADVENT FORETOLD

And hear how it was foretold concerning those who published His doctrine and proclaimed His appearance, the above-mentioned prophet and king speaking thus by the Spirit of prophecy Day unto day utters speech, and night unto night shows knowledge. There is no speech nor language where their voice is not heard. Their voice has gone out into all the earth, and their words to the ends of the world. In the sun has He set His tabernacle, and he as a bridegroom going out of his chamber shall rejoice as a giant to run his course. And we have thought it right and relevant to mention some other prophetic utterances of David besides these; from which you may learn how the Spirit of prophecy exhorts men to live, and how He foretold the conspiracy which was formed against Christ by Herod the king of the Jews, and the Jews themselves, and Pilate, who was your governor among them, with his soldiers; and how He should be believed on by men of every race; and how God calls Him His Son, and has declared that He will subdue all His enemies under Him; and how the devils, as much as they can, strive to escape the power of God the Father and Lord of all, and the power of Christ Himself; and how God calls all to repentance before the day of judgment comes. These things were uttered thus: Blessed is the man who has not walked in the counsel of the ungodly, nor stood in the way of sinners, nor sat in the seat of the scornful: but his delight is in the law of the Lord; and in His law will he meditate day and night. And he shall be like a tree planted by the rivers of waters, which shall give his fruit in his season; and his leaf shall not wither, and whatsoever he does shall prosper. The ungodly are not so, but are like the chaff which the wind drives away from the face of the earth. Therefore the ungodly shall not stand in the judgment, nor sinners in the council of the righteous. For the Lord knows the way of the righteous; but the way of the ungodly shall perish. Why do the heathen rage, and the people imagine new things? The kings of the earth set themselves, and the rulers take counsel together, against the Lord, and against His Anointed, saying, Let us break their bands asunder, and cast their yoke from us. He that dwells in the heavens shall laugh at them, and the Lord shall have them in derision. Then shall He speak to them in His wrath, and vex them in His sore displeasure. Yet have I been set by Him a King on Zion His holy hill, declaring the decree of the Lord. The Lord said to Me, You are My Son; this day have I begotten You. Ask of Me, and I shall give You the heathen for Your inheritance, and the uttermost parts of the earth as Your possession. You shall herd them with a rod of iron; as the vessels of a potter shall You dash them in pieces.

Be wise now, therefore, O you kings; be instructed, all you judges of the earth. Serve the Lord with fear, and rejoice with trembling. Embrace instruction, lest at any time the Lord be angry, and you perish from the right way, when His wrath has been suddenly kindled. Blessed are all they that put their trust in Him.

CHAPTER 41. THE CRUCIFIXION PREDICTED

And again, in another prophecy, the Spirit of prophecy, through the same David, intimated that Christ, after He had been crucified, should reign, and spoke as follows: Sing to the Lord, all the earth, and day by day declare His salvation. For great is the Lord, and greatly to be praised, to be feared above all the gods. For all the gods of the nations are idols of devils; but God made the heavens. Glory and praise are before His face, strength and glorying are in the habitation of His holiness. Give Glory to the Lord, the Father everlasting. Receive grace, and enter His presence, and worship in His holy courts. Let all the earth fear before His face; let it be established, and not shaken. Let them rejoice among the nations. The Lord has reigned from the tree.

CHAPTER 42. PROPHECY USING THE PAST TENSE

But when the Spirit of prophecy speaks of things that are about to come to pass as if they had already taken place, — as may be observed even in the passages already cited by me, — that this circumstance may afford no excuse to readers [for misinterpreting them], we will make even this also quite plain. The things which He absolutely knows will take place, He predicts as if already they had taken place. And that the utterances must be thus received, you will perceive, if you give your attention to them. The words cited above, David uttered **1500** years before Christ became a man and was crucified; and no one of those who lived before Him, nor yet of His contemporaries, afforded joy to the Gentiles by being crucified. But our Jesus Christ, being crucified and dead, rose again, and having ascended to heaven, reigned; and by those things which were published in His name among all nations by the apostles, there is joy afforded to those who expect the immortality promised by Him.

CHAPTER 43. RESPONSIBILITY ASSERTED

But lest some suppose, from what has been said by us, that we say that whatever happens, happens by a fatal necessity, because it is foretold as known beforehand, this too we explain. We have learned from the prophets, and we hold it to be true, that punishments, and chastisements, and good rewards, are rendered according to the merit of each man's actions. Since if it be not so, but all things happen by fate, neither is anything at all in our own power. For if it be fated that this man, e.g., be good, and this other evil, neither is the former meritorious nor the latter to be blamed. And again, unless the human race have the power of avoiding evil and choosing good by free choice, they are not accountable for their actions, of whatever kind they be. But that it is by free choice they both walk uprightly and stumble, we thus demonstrate. We see the same man making a transition to opposite things. Now, if it had been fated that he were to be either good or bad, he could never have been capable of both the opposites, nor of so many transitions. But not even would some be good and others bad, since we thus make fate the cause of evil, and exhibit her as acting in opposition to herself; or that which has been already stated would seem to be true, that neither virtue nor vice is anything, but that things are only reckoned good or evil by opinion; which, as the true word shows, is the greatest impiety and wickedness. But this we assert is inevitable fate, that they who choose the good have worthy rewards, and they who choose the opposite have their merited awards. For not like other things, as trees and quadrupeds, which cannot act by choice, did God make man: for neither would he be worthy of reward or praise did he not of himself choose the good, but were created for this end; nor, if he were evil, would he be worthy of punishment, not being evil of himself, but being able to be nothing else than what he was made.

CHAPTER 44. NOT NULLIFIED BY PROPHECY

And the holy Spirit of prophecy taught us this, telling us by Moses that God spoke thus to the man first created: Behold, before your face are good and evil: choose the good. And again, by the other prophet Isaiah, that the following utterance was made as if from God the Father and Lord of all: Wash you, make you clean; put away evils from your souls; learn to do well; judge the orphan, and plead for the widow: and come and let us reason together, says the Lord: And if your sins be as scarlet, I will make them white as wool; and if they be red like as crimson, I will make them white as snow. And if you be willing and obey Me, you shall eat the good of the land; but if you do not obey Me, the sword shall devour you: for the mouth of the Lord has spoken it. Isaiah **1**:**16**, etc. And that expression, The sword shall devour you, does not mean that the disobedient shall be slain by the sword, but the sword of God is fire, of which they who choose to do wickedly become the fuel. Wherefore He says, The sword shall devour you: for the mouth of the Lord has spoken it. And if He had spoken concerning a sword that cuts and at once dispatches, He would not have said, shall devour. And so, too, Plato, when he says, The blame is his who chooses, and God is blameless, took this from the prophet Moses and uttered it. For Moses is more ancient than all the Greek writers. And whatever both philosophers and poets have said concerning the immortality of the soul, or punishments after death, or contemplation of things heavenly, or doctrines of the like kind, they have received such suggestions from the prophets as have enabled them to understand and interpret these things. And hence there seem to be seeds of truth among all men; but they are charged with not accurately understanding [the truth] when they assert contradictories. So that what we say about future events being foretold, we do not say it as if they came about by a fatal necessity; but God foreknowing all that shall be done by all men, and it being His decree that the future actions of men shall all be recompensed according to their several value, He foretells by the Spirit of prophecy that He will bestow meet rewards according to the merit of the actions done, always urging the human race to effort and recollection, showing that He cares and provides for men. But by the agency of the devils death has been decreed against those who read the books of Hystaspes, or of the Sibyl, or of the prophets, that through fear they may prevent men who read them from receiving the knowledge of the good, and may retain them in slavery to themselves; which, however, they could not always effect. For not only do we fearlessly read them, but, as you see, bring them for your inspection, knowing that their contents will be pleasing to all. And if we persuade even a few, our gain will be very great; for, as good husbandmen, we shall receive the reward from the Master.

CHAPTER 45. CHRIST'S SESSION IN HEAVEN FORETOLD

And that God the Father of all would bring Christ to heaven after He had raised Him from the dead, and would keep Him there until He has subdued His enemies the devils, and until the number of those who are foreknown by Him as good and virtuous is complete, on whose account He has still delayed the consummation — hear what was said by the prophet David. These are his words: The Lord said to My Lord, Sit at My right hand, until I make Your enemies Your footstool. The Lord shall send to You the rod of power out of Jerusalem; and rule You in the midst of Your enemies. With You is the government in the day of Your power, in the beauties of Your saints: from the womb of morning have I begotten You. That which he says, He shall send to You the rod of power out of Jerusalem, is predictive of the mighty word, which His apostles, going forth from Jerusalem, preached everywhere; and though death is decreed against those who teach or at all confess the name of Christ, we everywhere both embrace and teach it. And if you also read these words in a hostile spirit, you can do no more, as I said before, than kill us; which indeed does no harm to us, but to you and all who unjustly hate us, and do not repent, brings eternal punishment by fire.

CHAPTER 46. THE WORD IN THE WORLD BEFORE CHRIST

But lest some should, without reason, and for the perversion of what we teach, maintain that we say that Christ was born one hundred and fifty years ago under Cyrenius, and subsequently, in the time of Pontius Pilate, taught what we say He taught; and should cry out against us as though all men who were born before Him were irresponsible — let us anticipate and solve the difficulty. We have been taught that Christ is the first-born of God, and we have declared above that He is the Word of whom every race of men were partakers; and those who lived reasonably are Christians, even though they have been thought atheists; as, among the Greeks, Socrates and Heraclitus, and men like them; and among the barbarians, Abraham, and Ananias, and Azarias, and Misael, and Elias, and many others whose actions and names we now decline to recount, because we know it would be tedious. So that even they who lived before Christ, and lived without reason, were wicked and hostile to Christ, and slew those who lived reasonably. But who, through the power of the Word, according to the will of God the Father and Lord of all, He was born of a virgin as a man, and was named Jesus, and was crucified, and died, and rose again, and ascended into heaven, an intelligent man will be able to comprehend from what has been already so largely said. And we, since the proof of this subject is less needful now, will pass for the present to the proof of those things which are urgent.

CHAPTER 47. DESOLATION OF JUDÆA FORETOLD

That the land of the Jews, then, was to be laid waste, hear what was said by the Spirit of prophecy. And the words were spoken as if from the person of the people wondering at what had happened. They are these: Sion is a wilderness, Jerusalem a desolation. The house of our sanctuary has become a curse, and the glory which our fathers blessed is burned up with fire, and all its glorious things are laid waste: and You refrain Yourself at these things, and have held Your peace, and have humbled us very sore. Isaiah **64**:**10-12** And you are convinced that Jerusalem has been laid waste, as was predicted. And concerning its desolation, and that no one should be permitted to inhabit it, there was the following prophecy by Isaiah: Their land is desolate, their enemies consume it before them, and none of them shall dwell therein. Isaiah **1**:**7** And that it is guarded by you lest any one dwell in it, and that death is decreed against a Jew apprehended entering it, you know very well.

CHAPTER 48. CHRIST'S WORK AND DEATH FORETOLD

And that it was predicted that our Christ should heal all diseases and raise the dead, hear what was said. There are these words: At His coming the lame shall leap as an hart, and the tongue of the stammerer shall be clear speaking: the blind shall see, and the lepers shall be cleansed; and the dead shall rise, and walk about. Isaiah **35**:**6** And that He did those things, you can learn from the Acts of Pontius Pilate. And how it was predicted by the Spirit of prophecy that He and those who hoped in Him should be slain, hear what was said by Isaiah. These are the words: Behold now the righteous perishes, and no man lays it to heart; and just men are taken away, and no man considers. From the presence of wickedness is the righteous man taken, and his burial shall be in peace: he is taken from our midst. Isaiah **57**:**1**

CHAPTER 49. HIS REJECTION BY THE JEWS FORETOLD

And again, how it was said by the same Isaiah, that the Gentile nations who were not looking for Him should worship Him, but the Jews who always expected Him should not recognise Him when He came. And the words are spoken as from the person of Christ; and they are these I was manifest to them that asked not for Me; I was found of them that sought Me not: I said, Behold Me, to a nation that called not on My name. I spread out My hands to a disobedient and gainsaying people, to those who walked in a way that is not good, but follow after their own sins; a people that provokes Me to anger to My face. Isaiah **65**:**1-3** For the Jews having the prophecies, and being always in expectation of the Christ to come, did not recognise Him; and not only so, but even treated Him shamefully. But the Gentiles, who had never heard anything about Christ, until the apostles set out from Jerusalem and preached concerning Him, and gave them the prophecies, were filled with joy and faith, and cast away their idols, and dedicated themselves to the Unbegotten God through Christ. And that it was foreknown that these infamous things should be uttered against those who confessed Christ, and that those who slandered Him, and said that it was well to preserve the ancient customs, should be miserable, hear what was briefly said by Isaiah; it is this: Woe unto them that call sweet bitter, and bitter sweet. Isaiah **5**:**20**

CHAPTER 50. HIS HUMILIATION PREDICTED

But that, having become man for our sakes, He endured to suffer and to be dishonoured, and that He shall come again with glory, hear the prophecies which relate to this; they are these: Because they delivered His soul unto death, and He was numbered with the transgressors, He has borne the sin of many, and shall make intercession for the transgressors. For, behold, My Servant shall deal prudently, and shall be exalted, and shall be greatly extolled. As many were astonished at You, so marred shall Your form be before men, and so hidden from them Your glory; so shall many nations wonder, and the kings shall shut their mouths at Him. For they to whom it was not told concerning Him, and they who have not heard, shall understand. O Lord, who has believed our report? And to whom is the arm of the Lord revealed? We have declared before Him as a child, as a root in a dry ground. He had no form, nor glory; and we saw Him, and there was no form nor comeliness: but His form was dishonoured and marred more than the sons of men. A man under the stroke, and knowing how to bear infirmity, because His face was turned away: He was despised, and of no reputation. It is He who bears our sins, and is afflicted for us; yet we did esteem Him smitten, stricken, and afflicted. But He was wounded for our transgressions, He was bruised for our iniquities, the chastisement of peace was upon Him, by His stripes we are healed. All we, like sheep, have gone astray; every man has wandered in his own way. And He delivered Him for our sins; and He opened not His mouth for all His affliction. He was brought as a sheep to the slaughter, and as a lamb before his shearer is dumb, so He opens not His mouth. In His humiliation, His judgment was taken away. Isaiah **52**:**13-15**, Isaiah **53**:**1-8** Accordingly, after He was crucified, even all His acquaintances forsook Him, having denied Him; and afterwards, when He had risen from the dead and appeared to them, and had taught them to read the prophecies in which all these things were foretold as coming to pass, and when they had seen Him ascending into heaven, and had believed, and had received power sent thence by Him upon them, and went to every race of men, they taught these things, and were called apostles.

CHAPTER 51. THE MAJESTY OF CHRIST

And that the Spirit of prophecy might signify to us that He who suffers these things has an ineffable origin, and rules His enemies, He spoke thus: His generation who shall declare? Because His life is cut off from the earth: for their transgressions He comes to death. And I will give the wicked for His burial, and the rich for His death; because He did no violence, neither was any deceit in His mouth. And the Lord is pleased to cleanse Him from the stripe. If He be given for sin, your soul shall see His seed prolonged in days. And the Lord is pleased to deliver His soul from grief, to show Him light, and to form Him with knowledge, to justify the righteous who richly serves many. And He shall bear our iniquities. Therefore He shall inherit many, and He shall divide the spoil of the strong; because His soul was delivered to death: and He was numbered with the transgressors; and He bore the sins of many, and He was delivered up for their transgressions. Isaiah **53**:**8-12** Hear, too, how He was to ascend into heaven according to prophecy. It was thus spoken: Lift up the gates of heaven; be opened, that the King of glory may come in. Who is this King of glory? The Lord, strong and mighty. And how also He should come again out of heaven with glory, hear what was spoken in reference to this by the prophet Jeremiah. His words are: Behold, as the Son of man He comes in the clouds of heaven, and His angels with Him. Daniel **7:13**

CHAPTER 52. CERTAIN FULFILMENT OF PROPHECY

Since, then, we prove that all things which have already happened had been predicted by the prophets before they came to pass, we must necessarily believe also that those things which are in like manner predicted, but are yet to come to pass, shall certainly happen. For as the things which have already taken place came to pass when foretold, and even though unknown, so shall the things that remain, even though they be unknown and disbelieved, yet come to pass. For the prophets have proclaimed two advents of His: the one, that which is already past, when He came as a dishonoured and suffering Man; but the second, when, according to prophecy, He shall come from heaven with glory, accompanied by His angelic host, when also He shall raise the bodies of all men who have lived, and shall clothe those of the worthy with immortality, and shall send those of the wicked, endued with eternal sensibility, into everlasting fire with the wicked devils. And that these things also have been foretold as yet to be, we will prove. By Ezekiel the prophet it was said: Joint shall be joined to joint, and bone to bone, and flesh shall grow again; and every knee shall bow to the Lord, and every tongue shall confess Him. Ezekiel **37**:**7-8**; Isaiah **45**:**24** And in what kind of sensation and punishment the wicked are to be, hear from what was said in like manner with reference to this; it is as follows: Their worm shall not rest, and their fire shall not be quenched; Isaiah **66**:**24** and then shall they repent, when it profits them not. And what the people of the Jews shall say and do, when they see Him coming in glory, has been thus predicted by Zechariah the prophet: I will command the four winds to gather the scattered children; I will command the north wind to bring them, and the south wind, that it keep not back. And then in Jerusalem there shall be great lamentation, not the lamentation of mouths or of lips, but the lamentation of the heart; and they shall rend not their garments, but their hearts. Tribe by tribe they shall mourn, and then they shall look on Him whom they have pierced; and they shall say, Why, O Lord, have You made us to err from Your way? The glory which our fathers blessed, has for us been turned into shame.

CHAPTER 53. SUMMARY OF THE PROPHECIES

Though we could bring forward many other prophecies, we forbear, judging these sufficient for the persuasion of those who have ears to hear and understand; and considering also that those persons are able to see that we do not make mere assertions without being able to produce proof, like those fables that are told of the so-called sons of Jupiter. For with what reason should we believe of a crucified man that He is the first-born of the unbegotten God, and Himself will pass judgment on the whole human race, unless we had found testimonies concerning Him published before He came and was born as man, and unless we saw that things had happened accordingly — the devastation of the land of the Jews, and men of every race persuaded by His teaching through the apostles, and rejecting their old habits, in which, being deceived, they had their conversation; yea, seeing ourselves too, and knowing that the Christians from among the Gentiles are both more numerous and more true than those from among the Jews and Samaritans? For all the other human races are called Gentiles by the Spirit of prophecy; but the Jewish and Samaritan races are called the tribe of Israel, and the house of Jacob. And the prophecy in which it was predicted that there should be more believers from the Gentiles than from the Jews and Samaritans, we will produce: it ran thus: Rejoice, O barren, you that do not bear; break forth and shout, you that do not travail, because many more are the children of the desolate than of her that has an husband. Isaiah **54**:**1** For all the Gentiles were desolate of the true God, serving the works of their hands; but the Jews and Samaritans, having the word of God delivered to them by the prophets, and always expecting the Christ, did not recognise Him when He came, except some few, of whom the Spirit of prophecy by Isaiah had predicted that they should be saved. He spoke as from their person: Unless the Lord had left us a seed, we should have been as Sodom and Gomorrha. Isaiah **1**:**9** For Sodom and Gomorrha are related by Moses to have been cities of ungodly men, which God burned with fire and brimstone, and overthrew, no one of their inhabitants being saved except a certain stranger, a Chaldæan by birth, whose name was Lot; with whom also his daughters were rescued. And those who care may yet see their whole country desolate and burned, and remaining barren. And to show how those from among the Gentiles were foretold as more true and more believing, we will cite what was said by Isaiah the prophet; for he spoke as follows Israel is uncircumcised in heart, but the Gentiles are uncircumcised in the flesh. So many things therefore, as these, when they are seen with the eye, are enough to produce conviction and belief in those who embrace the truth, and are not bigoted in their opinions, nor are governed by their passions.

CHAPTER 54. ORIGIN OF HEATHEN MYTHOLOGY

But those who hand down the myths which the poets have made, adduce no proof to the youths who learn them; and we proceed to demonstrate that they have been uttered by the influence of the wicked demons, to deceive and lead astray the human race. For having heard it proclaimed through the prophets that the Christ was to come, and that the ungodly among men were to be punished by fire, they put forward many to be called sons of Jupiter, under the impression that they would be able to produce in men the idea that the things which were said with regard to Christ were mere marvellous tales, like the things which were said by the poets. And these things were said both among the Greeks and among all nations where they [the demons] heard the prophets foretelling that Christ would specially be believed in; but that in hearing what was said by the prophets they did not accurately understand it, but imitated what was said of our Christ, like men who are in error, we will make plain. The prophet Moses, then, was, as we have already said, older than all writers; and by him, as we have also said before, it was thus predicted: There shall not fail a prince from Judah, nor a lawgiver from between his feet, until He come for whom it is reserved; and He shall be the desire of the Gentiles, binding His foal to the vine, washing His robe in the blood of the grape. Genesis **49**:**10** The devils, accordingly, when they heard these prophetic words, said that Bacchus was the son of Jupiter, and gave out that he was the discoverer of the vine, and they number wine [or, the ass] among his mysteries; and they taught that, having been torn in pieces, he ascended into heaven. And because in the prophecy of Moses it had not been expressly intimated whether He who was to come was the Son of God, and whether He would, riding on the foal, remain on earth or ascend into heaven, and because the name of foal could mean either the foal of an ass or the foal of a horse, they, not knowing whether He who was foretold would bring the foal of an ass or of a horse as the sign of His coming, nor whether He was the Son of God, as we said above, or of man, gave out that Bellerophon, a man born of man, himself ascended to heaven on his horse Pegasus. And when they heard it said by the other prophet Isaiah, that He should be born of a virgin, and by His own means ascend into heaven, they pretended that Perseus was spoken of. And when they knew what was said, as has been cited above, in the prophecies written aforetime, Strong as a giant to run his course, they said that Hercules was strong, and had journeyed over the whole earth. And when, again, they learned that it had been foretold that He should heal every sickness, and raise the dead, they produced Æsculapius.

CHAPTER 55. SYMBOLS OF THE CROSS

But in no instance, not even in any of those called sons of Jupiter, did they imitate the being crucified; for it was not understood by them, all the things said of it having been put symbolically. And this, as the prophet foretold, is the greatest symbol of His power and role; as is also proved by the things which fall under our observation. For consider all the things in the world, whether without this form they could be administered or have any community. For the sea is not traversed except that trophy which is called a sail abide safe in the ship; and the earth is not ploughed without it: diggers and mechanics do not their work, except with tools which have this shape. And the human form differs from that of the irrational animals in nothing else than in its being erect and having the hands extended, and having on the face extending from the forehead what is called the nose, through which there is respiration for the living creature; and this shows no other form than that of the cross. And so it was said by the prophet, The breath before our face is the Lord Christ. And the power of this form is shown by your own symbols on what are called vexilla [banners] and trophies, with which all your state possessions are made, using these as the insignia of your power and government, even though you do so unwittingly. And with this form you consecrate the images of your emperors when they die, and you name them gods by inscriptions. Since, therefore, we have urged you both by reason and by an evident form, and to the utmost of our ability, we know that now we are blameless even though you disbelieve; for our part is done and finished.

CHAPTER 56. THE DEMONS STILL MISLEAD MEN

But the evil spirits were not satisfied with saying, before Christ's appearance, that those who were said to be sons of Jupiter were born of him; but after He had appeared, and been born among men, and when they learned how He had been foretold by the prophets, and knew that He should be believed on and looked for by every nation, they again, as was said above, put forward other men, the Samaritans Simon and

Menander, who did many mighty works by magic, and deceived many, and still keep them deceived. For even among yourselves, as we said before, Simon was in the royal city Rome in the reign of Claudius Cæsar, and so greatly astonished the sacred senate and people of the Romans, that he was considered a god, and honoured, like the others whom you honour as gods, with a statue. Wherefore we pray that the sacred senate and your people may, along with yourselves, be arbiters of this our memorial, in order that if any one be entangled by that man's doctrines, he may learn the truth, and so be able to escape error; and as for the statue, if you please, destroy it.

CHAPTER 57. AND CAUSE PERSECUTION

Nor can the devils persuade men that there will be no conflagration for the punishment of the wicked; as they were unable to effect that Christ should be hidden after He came. But this only can they effect, that they who live irrationally, and were brought up licentiously in wicked customs, and are prejudiced in their own opinions, should kill and hate us; whom we not only do not hate, but, as is proved, pity and endeavour to lead to repentance. For we do not fear death, since it is acknowledged we must surely die; and there is nothing new, but all things continue the same in this administration of things; and if satiety overtakes those who enjoy even one year of these things, they ought to give heed to our doctrines, that they may live eternally free both from suffering and from want. But if they believe that there is nothing after death, but declare that those who die pass into insensibility, then they become our benefactors when they set us free from sufferings and necessities of this life, and prove themselves to be wicked, and inhuman, and bigoted. For they kill us with no intention of delivering us, but cut us off that we may be deprived of life and pleasure.

CHAPTER 58. AND RAISE UP HERETICS

And, as we said before, the devils put forward Marcion of Pontus, who is even now teaching men to deny that God is the maker of all things in heaven and on earth, and that the Christ predicted by the prophets is His Son, and preaches another god besides the Creator of all, and likewise another son. And this man many have believed, as if he alone knew the truth, and laugh at us, though they have no proof of what they say, but are carried away irrationally as lambs by a wolf, and become the prey of atheistical doctrines, and of devils. For they who are called devils attempt nothing else than to seduce men from God who made them, and from Christ His first-begotten; and those who are unable to raise themselves above the earth they have riveted, and do now rivet, to things earthly, and to the works of their own hands; but those who devote themselves to the contemplation of things divine, they secretly beat back; and if they have not a wise sober-mindedness, and a pure and passionless life, they drive them into godlessness.

CHAPTER 59. PLATO'S OBLIGATION TO MOSES

And that you may learn that it was from our teachers — we mean the account given through the prophets— that Plato borrowed his statement that God, having altered matter which was shapeless, made the world, hear the very words spoken through Moses, who, as above shown, was the first prophet, and of greater antiquity than the Greek writers; and through whom the Spirit of prophecy, signifying how and from what materials God at first formed the world, spoke thus: In the beginning God created the heaven and the earth. And the earth was invisible and unfurnished, and darkness was upon the face of the deep; and the Spirit of God moved over the waters. And God said, Let there be light; and it was so. So that both Plato and they who agree with him, and we ourselves, have learned, and you also can be convinced, that by the word of God the whole world was made out of the substance spoken of before by Moses. And that which the poets call Erebus, we know was spoken of formerly by Moses. Deuteronomy **32**:**22**

CHAPTER 60. PLATO'S DOCTRINE OF THE CROSS

And the physiological discussion concerning the Son of God in the Timæus of Plato, where he says, He placed him crosswise in the universe, he borrowed in like manner from Moses; for in the writings of Moses it is related how at that time, when the Israelites went out of Egypt and were in the wilderness, they fell in with poisonous beasts, both vipers and asps, and every kind of serpent, which slew the people; and that Moses, by the inspiration and influence of God, took brass, and made it into the figure of a cross, and set it in the holy tabernacle, and said to the people, If you look to this figure, and believe, you shall be saved thereby. Numbers **21**:**8** And when this was done, it is recorded that the serpents died, and it is handed down that the people thus escaped death. Which things Plato reading, and not accurately understanding, and not apprehending that it was the figure of the cross, but taking it to be a placing crosswise, he said that the power next to the first God was placed crosswise in the universe. And as to his speaking of a third, he did this because he read, as we said above, that which was spoken by Moses, that the Spirit of God moved over the waters. For he gives the second place to the Logos which is with God, who he said was placed crosswise in the universe; and the third place to the Spirit who was said to be borne upon the water, saying, And the third around the third. And hear how the Spirit of prophecy signified through Moses that there should be a conflagration. He spoke thus: Everlasting fire shall descend, and shall devour to the pit beneath. Deuteronomy **32**:**22** It is not, then, that we hold the same opinions as others, but that all speak in imitation of ours. Among us these things can be heard and learned from persons who do not even know the forms of the letters, who are uneducated and barbarous in speech, though wise and believing in mind; some, indeed, even maimed and deprived of eyesight; so that you may understand that these things are not the effect of human wisdom, but are uttered by the power of God.

CHAPTER 61. CHRISTIAN BAPTISM

I will also relate the manner in which we dedicated ourselves to God when we had been made new through Christ; lest, if we omit this, we seem to be unfair in the explanation we are making. As many as are persuaded and believe that what we teach and say is true, and undertake to be able to live accordingly, are instructed to pray and to entreat God with fasting, for the remission of their sins that are past, we praying and fasting with them. Then they are brought by us where there is water, and are regenerated in the same manner in which we were ourselves regenerated. For, in the name of God, the Father and Lord of the universe, and of our Saviour Jesus Christ, and of the Holy Spirit, they then receive the washing with water. For Christ also said, Unless you be born again, you shall not enter into the kingdom of heaven. John **3**:**5** Now, that it is impossible for those who have once been born to enter into their mothers' wombs, is manifest to all. And how those who have sinned and repent shall escape their sins, is declared by Esaias the prophet, as I wrote above; he thus speaks: Wash you, make you clean; put away the evil of your doings from your souls; learn to do well; judge the fatherless, and plead for the widow: and come and let us reason together, says the Lord. And though your sins be as scarlet, I will make them white like wool; and though they be as crimson, I will make them white as snow. But if you refuse and rebel, the sword shall devour you: for the mouth of the Lord has spoken it. Isaiah **1**:**16-20**

And for this [rite] we have learned from the apostles this reason. Since at our birth we were born without our own knowledge or choice, by our parents coming together, and were brought up in bad habits and wicked training; in order that we may not remain the children of necessity and of ignorance, but may become the children of choice and knowledge, and may obtain in the water the remission of sins formerly committed, there is pronounced over him who chooses to be born again, and has repented of his sins, the name of God the Father and Lord of the universe; he who leads to the laver the person that is to be washed calling him by this name alone. For no one can utter the name of the ineffable God; and if any one dare to say that there is a name, he raves with a hopeless madness. And this washing is called illumination, because they who learn these things are illuminated in their understandings. And in the name of Jesus Christ, who was crucified under Pontius Pilate, and in the name of the Holy Ghost, who through the prophets foretold all things about Jesus, he who is illuminated is washed.

CHAPTER 62. ITS IMITATION BY DEMONS

And the devils, indeed, having heard this washing published by the prophet, instigated those who enter their temples, and are about to approach them with libations and burnt-offerings, also to sprinkle themselves; and they cause them also to wash themselves entirely, as they depart [from the sacrifice], before they enter into the shrines in which their images are set. And the command, too, given by the priests to those who enter and worship in the temples, that they take off their shoes, the devils, learning what happened to the above-mentioned prophet Moses, have given in imitation of these things. For at that juncture, when Moses was ordered to go down into Egypt and lead out the people of the Israelites who were there, and while he was tending the flocks of his maternal uncle in the land of Arabia, our Christ conversed with him under the appearance of fire from a bush, and said, Put off your shoes, and draw near and hear. And he, when he had put off his shoes and drawn near, heard that he was to go down into Egypt and lead out the people of the Israelites there; and he received mighty power from Christ, who spoke to him in the appearance of fire, and went down and led out the people, having done great and marvellous things; which, if you desire to know, you will learn them accurately from his writings.

CHAPTER 63. HOW GOD APPEARED TO MOSES

And all the Jews even now teach that the nameless God spoke to Moses; whence the Spirit of prophecy, accusing them by Isaiah the prophet mentioned above, said The ox knows his owner, and the ass his master's crib; but Israel does not know Me, and My people do not understand. Isaiah **1**:**3** And Jesus the Christ, because the Jews knew not what the Father was, and what the Son, in like manner accused them; and Himself said, No one knows the Father, but the Son; nor the Son, but the Father, and they to whom the Son reveals Him. Matthew **11**:**27** Now the Word of God is His Son, as we have before said. And He is called Angel and Apostle; for He declares whatever we ought to know, and is sent forth to declare whatever is revealed; as our Lord Himself says, He that hears Me, hears Him that sent Me. Luke **10**:**16** From the writings of Moses also this will be manifest; for thus it is written in them, And the Angel of God spoke to Moses, in a flame of fire out of the bush, and said, I am that I am, the God of Abraham, the God of Isaac, the God of Jacob, the God of your fathers; go down into Egypt, and bring forth My people. Exodus **3**:**6** And if you wish to learn what follows, you can do so from the same writings; for it is impossible to relate the whole here. But so much is written for the sake of proving that Jesus the Christ is the Son of God and His Apostle, being of old the Word, and appearing sometimes in the form of fire, and sometimes in the likeness of angels; but now, by the will of God, having become man for the human race, He endured all the sufferings which the devils instigated the senseless Jews to inflict upon Him; who, though they have it expressly affirmed in the writings of Moses, And the angel of God spoke to Moses in a flame of fire in a bush, and said, I am that I am, the God of Abraham, and the God of Isaac, and the God of Jacob, yet maintain that He who said this was the Father and Creator of the universe. Whence also the Spirit of prophecy rebukes them, and says, Israel does not know Me, my people have not understood Me. Isaiah **1**:**3** And again, Jesus, as we have already shown, while He was with them, said, No one knows the Father, but the Son; nor the Son but the Father, and those to whom the Son will reveal Him. Matthew **11**:**27** The Jews, accordingly, being throughout of opinion that it was the Father of the universe who spoke to Moses, though He who spoke to him was indeed the Son of God, who is called both Angel and Apostle, are justly charged, both by the Spirit of prophecy and by Christ Himself, with knowing neither the Father nor the Son. For they who affirm that the Son is the Father, are proved neither to have become acquainted with the Father, nor to know that the Father of the universe has a Son; who also, being the first-begotten Word of God, is even God. And of old He appeared in the shape of fire and in the likeness of an angel to Moses and to the other prophets; but now in the times of your reign, having, as we before said, become Man by a virgin, according to the counsel of the Father, for the salvation of those who believe in Him, He endured both to be set at nought and to suffer, that by dying and rising again He might conquer death. And that which was said out of the bush to Moses, I am that I am, the God of Abraham, and the God of Isaac, and the God of Jacob, and the God of your fathers, Exodus **3**:**6** this signified that they, even though dead, are yet in existence, and are men belonging to Christ Himself. For they were the first of all men to busy themselves in the search after God; Abraham being the father of Isaac, and Isaac of Jacob, as Moses wrote.

CHAPTER 64. FURTHER MISREPRESENTATIONS OF THE TRUTH

From what has been already said, you can understand how the devils, in imitation of what was said by Moses, asserted that Proserpine was the daughter of Jupiter, and instigated the people to set up an image of her under the name of Kore [Cora, i.e., the maiden or daughter] at the spring-heads. For, as we wrote above, Moses said, In the beginning God made the heaven and the earth. And the earth was without form and unfurnished: and the Spirit of God moved upon the face of the waters. In imitation, therefore, of what is here said of the Spirit of God moving on the waters, they said that Proserpine [or Cora] was the daughter of Jupiter. And in like manner also they craftily feigned that Minerva was the daughter of Jupiter, not by sexual union, but, knowing that God conceived and made the world by the Word, they say that Minerva is the first conception [ἔννοια]; which we consider to be very absurd, bringing forward the form of the conception in a female shape. And in like manner the actions of those others who are called sons of Jupiter sufficiently condemn them.

CHAPTER 65. ADMINISTRATION OF THE SACRAMENTS

But we, after we have thus washed him who has been convinced and has assented to our teaching, bring him to the place where those who are called brethren are assembled, in order that we may offer hearty prayers in common for ourselves and for the baptized [illuminated] person, and for all others in every place, that we may be counted worthy, now that we have learned the truth, by our works also to be found good citizens and keepers of the commandments, so that we may be saved with an everlasting salvation. Having ended the prayers, we salute one another with a kiss. There is then brought to the president of the brethren bread and a cup of wine mixed with water; and he taking them, gives praise and glory to the Father of the universe, through the name of the Son and of the Holy Ghost, and offers thanks at considerable length for our being counted worthy to receive these things at His hands. And when he has concluded the prayers and thanksgivings, all the people present express their assent by saying Amen. This word Amen answers in the Hebrew language to γένοιτο [so be it]. And when the president has given thanks, and all the people have expressed their assent, those who are called by us deacons give to each of those present to partake of the bread and wine mixed with water over which the thanksgiving was pronounced, and to those who are absent they carry away a portion.

CHAPTER 66. OF THE EUCHARIST

And this food is called among us Εὐχαριστία [the Eucharist], of which no one is allowed to partake but the man who believes that the things which we teach are true, and who has been washed with the washing that is for the remission of sins, and unto regeneration, and who is so living as Christ has enjoined. For not as common bread and common drink do we receive these; but in like manner as Jesus Christ our Saviour, having been made flesh by the Word of God, had both flesh and blood for our salvation, so likewise have we been taught that the food which is blessed by the prayer of His word, and from which our blood and flesh by transmutation are nourished, is the flesh and blood of that Jesus who was made flesh. For the apostles, in the memoirs composed by them, which are called Gospels, have thus delivered unto us what was enjoined upon them; that Jesus took bread, and when He had given thanks, said, This do in remembrance of Me, Luke **22**:**19** this is My body; and that, after the same manner, having taken the cup and given thanks, He said, This is My blood; and gave it to them alone. Which the wicked devils have imitated in the mysteries of Mithras, commanding the same thing to be done. For, that bread and a cup of water are placed with certain incantations in the mystic rites of one who is being initiated, you either know or can learn.

CHAPTER 67. WEEKLY WORSHIP OF THE CHRISTIANS

And we afterwards continually remind each other of these things. And the wealthy among us help the needy; and we always keep together; and for all things wherewith we are supplied, we bless the Maker of all through His Son Jesus Christ, and through the Holy Ghost. And on the day called Sunday, all who live in cities or in the country gather together to one place, and the memoirs of the apostles or the writings of the prophets are read, as long as time permits; then, when the reader has ceased, the president verbally instructs, and exhorts to the imitation of these good things. Then we all rise together and pray, and, as we before said, when our prayer is ended, bread and wine and water are brought, and the president in like manner offers prayers and thanksgivings, according to his ability, and the people assent, saying Amen; and there is a distribution to each, and a participation of that over which thanks have been given, and to those who are absent a portion is sent by the deacons. And they who are well to do, and willing, give what each thinks fit; and what is collected is deposited with the president, who succours the orphans and widows and those who, through sickness or any other cause, are in want, and those who are in bonds and the strangers sojourning among us, and in a word takes care of all who are in need. But Sunday is the day on which we all hold our common assembly, because it is the first day on which God, having wrought a change in the darkness and matter, made the world; and Jesus Christ our Saviour on the same day rose from the dead. For He was crucified on the day before that of Saturn (Saturday); and on the day after that of Saturn, which is the day of the Sun, having appeared to His apostles and disciples, He taught them these things, which we have submitted to you also for your consideration.

CHAPTER 68. CONCLUSION

And if these things seem to you to be reasonable and true, honour them; but if they seem nonsensical, despise them as nonsense, and do not decree death against those who have done no wrong, as you would against enemies. For we forewarn you, that you shall not escape the coming judgment of God, if you continue in your injustice; and we ourselves will invite you to do that which is pleasing to God. And though from the letter of the greatest and most illustrious Emperor Adrian, your father, we could demand that you order judgment to be given as we have desired, yet we have made this appeal and explanation, not on the ground of Adrian's decision, but because we know that what we ask is just. And we have subjoined the copy of Adrian's epistle, that you may know that we are speaking truly about this. And the following is the copy:—

APPENDIX

EPISTLE OF ADRIAN ON BEHALF OF THE CHRISTIANS

I have received the letter addressed to me by your predecessor Serenius Granianus, a most illustrious man; and this communication I am unwilling to pass over in silence, lest innocent persons be disturbed, and occasion be given to the informers for practising villany. Accordingly, if the inhabitants of your province will so far sustain this petition of theirs as to accuse the Christians in some court of law, I do not prohibit them from doing so. But I will not suffer them to make use of mere entreaties and outcries. For it is far more just, if any one desires to make an accusation, that you give judgment upon it. If, therefore, any one makes the accusation, and furnishes proof that the said men do anything contrary to the laws, you shall adjudge punishments in proportion to the offenses. And this, by Hercules, you shall give special heed to, that if any man shall, through mere calumny, bring an accusation against any of these persons, you shall award to him more severe punishments in proportion to his wickedness.

EPISTLE OF ANTONINUS TO THE COMMON ASSEMBLY OF ASIA

The Emperor Cæsar Titus Ælius Adrianus Antoninus Augustus Pius, Supreme Pontiff, in the fifteenth year of his tribuneship, Consul for the third time, Father of the fatherland, to the Common Assembly of Asia, greeting: I should have thought that the gods themselves would see to it that such offenders should not escape. For if they had the power, they themselves would much rather punish those who refuse to worship them; but it is you who bring trouble on these persons, and accuse as the opinion of atheists that which they hold, and lay to their charge certain other things which we are unable to prove. But it would be advantageous to them that they should be thought to die for that of which they are accused, and they conquer you by being lavish of their lives rather than yield that obedience which you require of them. And regarding the earthquakes which have already happened and are now occurring, it is not seemly that you remind us of them, losing heart whenever they occur, and thus set your conduct in contrast with that of these men; for they have much greater confidence towards God than you yourselves have. And you, indeed, seem at such times to ignore the gods, and you neglect the temples, and make no recognition of the worship of God. And hence you are jealous of those who do serve Him, and persecute them to the death. Concerning such persons, some others also of the governors of provinces wrote to my most divine father; to whom he replied that they should not at all disturb such persons, unless they were found to be attempting anything against the Roman government. And to myself many have sent intimations regarding such persons, to whom I also replied in pursuance of my father's judgment. But if any one has a matter to bring against any person of this class, merely as such a person, let the accused be acquitted of the charge, even though he should be found to be such an one; but let the accuser be amenable to justice.

EPISTLE OF MARCUS AURELIUS TO THE SENATE, IN WHICH HE TESTIFIES THAT THE CHRISTIANS WERE THE CAUSE OF HIS VICTORY

The Emperor Cæsar Marcus Aurelius Antoninus, Germanicus, Parthicus, Sarmaticus, to the People of Rome, and to the sacred Senate greeting: I explained to you my grand design, and what advantages I gained on the confines of Germany, with much labour and suffering, in consequence of the circumstance that I was surrounded by the enemy; I myself being shut up in Carnuntum by seventy-four cohorts, nine miles off. And the enemy being at hand, the scouts pointed out to us, and our general Pompeianus showed us that there was close on us a mass of a mixed multitude of **977,000** men, which indeed we saw; and I was shut up by this vast host, having with me only a battalion composed of the first, tenth, double and marine legions. Having then examined my own position, and my host, with respect to the vast mass of barbarians and of the enemy, I quickly betook myself to prayer to the gods of my country. But being disregarded by them, I summoned those who among us go by the name of Christians. And having made inquiry, I discovered a great number and vast host of them, and raged against them, which was by no means becoming; for afterwards I learned their power. Wherefore they began the battle, not by preparing weapons, nor arms, nor bugles; for such preparation is hateful to them, on account of the God they bear about in their conscience. Therefore it is probable that those whom we suppose to be atheists, have God as their ruling power entrenched in their conscience. For having cast themselves on the ground, they prayed not only for me, but also for the whole army as it stood, that they might be delivered from the present thirst and famine. For during five days we had got no water, because there was none; for we were in the heart of Germany, and in the enemy's territory. And simultaneously with their casting themselves on the ground, and praying to God (a God of whom I am ignorant), water poured from heaven, upon us most refreshingly cool, but upon the enemies of Rome a withering hail. And immediately we recognised the presence of God following on the prayer — a God unconquerable and indestructible. Founding upon this, then, let us pardon such as are Christians, lest they pray for and obtain such a weapon against ourselves. And I counsel that no such person be accused on the ground of his being a Christian. But if any one be found laying to the charge of a Christian that he is a Christian, I desire that it be made manifest that he who is accused as a Christian, and acknowledges that he is one, is accused of nothing else than only this, that he is a Christian; but that he who arraigns him be burned alive. And I further desire, that he who is entrusted with the government of the province shall not compel the Christian, who confesses and certifies such a matter, to retract; neither shall he commit him. And I desire that these things be confirmed by a decree of the Senate. And I command this my edict to be published in the Forum of Trajan, in order that it may be read. The prefect Vitrasius Pollio will see that it be transmitted to all the provinces round about, and that no one who wishes to make use of or to possess it be hindered from obtaining a copy from the document I now publish.

The Second Apology of St. Justin Martyr

CHAPTER 1. INTRODUCTION

Romans, the things which have recently happened in your city under Urbicus, and the things which are likewise being everywhere unreasonably done by the governors, have compelled me to frame this composition for your sakes, who are men of like passions, and brethren, though you know it not, and though you be unwilling to acknowledge it on account of your glorying in what you esteem dignities. For everywhere, whoever is corrected by father, or neighbour, or child, or friend, or brother, or husband, or wife, for a fault, for being hard to move, for loving pleasure and being hard to urge to what is right (except those who have been persuaded that the unjust and intemperate shall be punished in eternal fire, but that the virtuous and those who lived like Christ shall dwell with God in a state that is free from suffering — we mean, those who have become Christians), and the evil demons, who hate us, and who keep such men as these subject to themselves, and serving them in the capacity of judges, incite them, as rulers actuated by evil spirits, to put us to death. But that the cause of all that has taken place under Urbicus may become quite plain to you, I will relate what has been done.

CHAPTER 2. URBICUS CONDEMNS THE CHRISTIANS TO DEATH

A certain woman lived with an intemperate husband; she herself, too, having formerly been intemperate. But when she came to the knowledge of the teachings of Christ she became sober-minded, and endeavoured to persuade her husband likewise to be temperate, citing the teaching of Christ, and assuring him that there shall be punishment in eternal fire inflicted upon those who do not live temperately and conformably to right reason. But he, continuing in the same excesses, alienated his wife from him by his actions. For she, considering it wicked to live any longer as a wife with a husband who sought in every way means of indulging in pleasure contrary to the law of nature, and in violation of what is right, wished to be divorced from him. And when she was overpersuaded by her friends, who advised her still to continue with him, in the idea that some time or other her husband might give hope of amendment, she did violence to her own feeling and remained with him. But when her husband had gone into Alexandria, and was reported to be conducting himself worse than ever, she — that she might not, by continuing in matrimonial connection with him, and by sharing his table and his bed, become a partaker also in his wickednesses and impieties — gave him what you call a bill of divorce, and was separated from him. But this noble husband of hers — while he ought to have been rejoicing that those actions which formerly she unhesitatingly committed with the servants and hirelings, when she delighted in drunkenness and every vice, she had now given up, and desired that he too should give up the same — when she had gone from him without his desire, brought an accusation against her, affirming that she was a Christian. And she presented a paper to you, the Emperor, a very bold apostrophe, like that of Huss to the Emperor Sigismund, which crimsoned his forehead with a blush of shame.]}--> requesting that first she be permitted to arrange her affairs, and afterwards to make her defense against the accusation, when her affairs were set in order. And this you granted. And her quondam husband, since he was now no longer able to prosecute her, directed his assaults against a man, Ptolemæus, whom Urbicus punished, and who had been her teacher in the Christian doctrines. And this he did in the following way. He persuaded a centurion — who had cast Ptolemæus into prison, and who was friendly to himself — to take Ptolemæus and interrogate him on this sole point: whether he were a Christian? And Ptolemæus, being a lover of truth, and not of a deceitful or false disposition, when he confessed himself to be a Christian, was bound by the centurion, and for a long time punished in the prison And, at last, when the man came to Urbicus, he was asked this one question only: whether he was a Christian? And again, being conscious of his duty, and the nobility of it through the teaching of Christ, he confessed his discipleship in the divine virtue. For he who denies anything either denies it because he condemns the thing itself, or he shrinks from confession because he is conscious of his own unworthiness or alienation from it, neither of which cases is that of the true Christian. And when Urbicus ordered him to be led away to punishment, one Lucius, who was also himself a Christian, seeing the unreasonable judgment that had thus been given, said to Urbicus: What is the ground of this judgment? Why have you punished this man, not as an adulterer, nor fornicator, nor murderer, nor thief, nor robber, nor convicted of any crime at all, but who has only confessed that he is called by the name of Christian? This judgment of yours, O Urbicus, does not become the Emperor Pius, nor the philosopher, the son of Cæsar, nor the sacred senate. And he said nothing else in answer to Lucius than this: You also seem to me to be such an one. And when Lucius answered, Most certainly I am, he again ordered him also to be led away. And he professed his thanks, knowing that he was delivered from such wicked rulers, and was going to the Father and King of the heavens. And still a third having come forward, was condemned to be punished.

CHAPTER 3. JUSTIN ACCUSES CRESCENS OF IGNORANT PREJUDICE AGAINST THE CHRISTIANS

I too, therefore, expect to be plotted against and fixed to the stake, by some of those I have named, or perhaps by Crescens, that lover of bravado and boasting; for the man is not worthy of the name of philosopher who publicly bears witness against us in matters which he does not understand, saying that the Christians are atheists and impious, and doing so to win favour with the deluded mob, and to please them. For if he assails us without having read the teachings of Christ, he is thoroughly depraved, and far worse than the illiterate, who often refrain from discussing or bearing false witness about matters they do not understand. Or, if he has read them and does not understand the majesty that is in them, or, understanding it, acts thus that he may not be suspected of being such [a Christian], he is far more base and thoroughly depraved, being conquered by illiberal and unreasonable opinion and fear. For I would have you to know that I proposed to him certain questions on this subject, and interrogated him, and found most convincingly that he, in truth, knows nothing. And to prove that I speak the truth, I am ready, if these disputations have not been reported to you, to conduct them again in your presence. And this would be an act worthy of a prince. But if my questions and his answers have been made known to you, you are already aware that he is acquainted with none of our matters; or, if he is acquainted with them, but, through fear of those who might hear him, does not dare to speak out, like Socrates, he proves himself, as I said before, no philosopher, but an opinionative man; at least he does not regard that Socratic and most admirable saying: But a man must in no way be honoured before the truth. But it is impossible for a Cynic, who makes indifference his end, to know any good but indifference.

CHAPTER 4. WHY THE CHRISTIANS DO NOT KILL THEMSELVES

But lest some one say to us, Go then all of you and kill yourselves, and pass even now to God, and do not trouble us, I will tell you why we do not so, but why, when examined, we fearlessly confess. We have been taught that God did not make the world aimlessly, but for the sake of the human race; and we have before stated that He takes pleasure in those who imitate His properties, and is displeased with those that embrace what is worthless either in word or deed. If, then, we all kill ourselves we shall become the cause, as far as in us lies, why no one should be born, or instructed in the divine doctrines, or even why the human race should not exist; and we shall, if we so act, be ourselves acting in opposition to the will of God. But when we are examined, we make no denial, because we are not conscious of any evil, but count it impious not to speak the truth in all things, which also we know is pleasing to God, and because we are also now very desirous to deliver you from an unjust prejudice.

CHAPTER 5. HOW THE ANGELS TRANSGRESSED

But if this idea take possession of some one, that if we acknowledge God as our helper, we should not, as we say, be oppressed and persecuted by the wicked; this, too, I will solve. God, when He had made the whole world, and subjected things earthly to man, and arranged the heavenly elements for the increase of fruits and rotation of the seasons, and appointed this divine law — for these things also He evidently made for man — committed the care of men and of all things under heaven to angels whom He appointed over them. But the angels transgressed this appointment, and were captivated by love of women, and begot children who are those that are called demons; and besides, they afterwards subdued the human race to themselves, partly by magical writings, and partly by fears and the punishments they occasioned, and partly by teaching them to offer sacrifices, and incense, and libations, of which things they stood in need after they were enslaved by lustful passions; and among men they sowed murders, wars, adulteries, intemperate deeds, and all wickedness. Whence also the poets and mythologists, not knowing that it was the angels and those demons who had been begotten by them that did these things to men, and women, and cities, and nations, which they related, ascribed them to god himself, and to those who were accounted to be his very offspring, and to the offspring of those who were called his brothers, Neptune and Pluto, and to the children again of these their offspring. For whatever name each of the angels had given to himself and his children, by that name they called them.

CHAPTER 6. NAMES OF GOD AND OF CHRIST, THEIR MEANING AND POWER

But to the Father of all, who is unbegotten there is no name given. For by whatever name He be called, He has as His elder the person who gives Him the name. But these words Father, and God, and Creator, and Lord, and Master, are not names, but appellations derived from His good deeds and functions. And His Son, who alone is properly called Son, the Word who also was with Him and was begotten before the works, when at first He created and arranged all things by Him, is called Christ, in reference to His being anointed and God's ordering all things through Him; this name itself also containing an unknown significance; as also the appellation God is not a name, but an opinion implanted in the nature of men of a thing that can hardly be explained. But Jesus, His name as man and Saviour, has also significance. For He was made man also, as we before said, having been conceived according to the will of God the Father, for the sake of believing men, and for the destruction of the demons. And now you can learn this from what is under your own observation. For numberless demoniacs throughout the whole world, and in your city, many of our Christian men exorcising them in the name of Jesus Christ, who was crucified under Pontius Pilate, have healed and do heal, rendering helpless and driving the possessing devils out of the men, though they could not be cured by all the other exorcists, and those who used incantations and drugs.

CHAPTER 7. THE WORLD PRESERVED FOR THE SAKE OF CHRISTIANS. MAN'S RESPONSIBILITY

Wherefore God delays causing the confusion and destruction of the whole world, by which the wicked angels and demons and men shall cease to exist, because of the seed of the Christians, who know that they are the cause of preservation in nature. Since, if it were not so, it would not have been possible for you to do these things, and to be impelled by evil spirits; but the fire of judgment would descend and utterly dissolve all things, even as formerly the flood left no one but him only with his family who is by us called Noah, and by you Deucalion, from whom again such vast numbers have sprung, some of them evil and others good. For so we say that there will be the conflagration, but not as the Stoics, according to their doctrine of all things being changed into one another, which seems most degrading. But neither do we affirm that it is by fate that men do what they do, or suffer what they suffer, but that each man by free choice acts rightly or sins; and that it is by the influence of the wicked demons that earnest men, such as Socrates and the like, suffer persecution and are in bonds, while Sardanapalus, Epicurus, and the like, seem to be blessed in abundance and glory. The Stoics, not observing this, maintained that all things take place according to the necessity of fate. But since God in the beginning made the race of angels and men with free-will, they will justly suffer in eternal fire the punishment of whatever sins they have committed. And this is the nature of all that is made, to be capable of vice and virtue. For neither would any of them be praiseworthy unless there were power to turn to both [virtue and vice]. And this also is shown by those men everywhere who have made laws and philosophized according to right reason, by their prescribing to do some things and refrain from others. Even the Stoic philosophers, in their doctrine of morals, steadily honour the same things, so that it is evident that they are not very felicitous in what they say about principles and incorporeal things. For if they say that human actions come to pass by fate, they will maintain either that God is nothing else than the things which are ever turning, and altering, and dissolving into the same things, and will appear to have had a comprehension only of things that are destructible, and to have looked on God Himself as emerging both in part and in whole in every wickedness; or that neither vice nor virtue is anything; which is contrary to every sound idea, reason, and sense.

CHAPTER 8. ALL HAVE BEEN HATED IN WHOM THE WORD HAS DWELT

And those of the Stoic school — since, so far as their moral teaching went, they were admirable, as were also the poets in some particulars, on account of the seed of reason [the Logos] implanted in every race of men — were, we know, hated and put to death — Heraclitus for instance, and, among those of our own time, Musonius and others. For, as we intimated, the devils have always effected, that all those who anyhow live a reasonable and earnest life, and shun vice, be hated. And it is nothing wonderful; if the devils are proved to cause those to be much worse hated who live not according to a part only of the word diffused [among men] but by the knowledge and contemplation of the whole Word, which is Christ. And they, having been shut up in eternal fire, shall suffer their just punishment and penalty. For if they are even now overthrown by men through the name of Jesus Christ, this is an intimation of the punishment in eternal fire which is to be inflicted on themselves and those who serve them. For thus did both all the prophets foretell, and our own teacher Jesus teach.

CHAPTER 9. ETERNAL PUNISHMENT NOT A MERE THREAT

And that no one may say what is said by those who are deemed philosophers, that our assertions that the wicked are punished in eternal fire are big words and bugbears, and that we wish men to live virtuously through fear, and not because such a life is good and pleasant; I will briefly reply to this, that if this be not so, God does not exist; or, if He exists, He cares not for men, and neither virtue nor vice is anything, and, as we said before, lawgivers unjustly punish those who transgress good commandments. But since these are not unjust, and their Father teaches them by the word to do the same things as Himself, they who agree with them are not unjust. And if one object that the laws of men are diverse, and say that with some, one thing is considered good, another evil, while with others what seemed bad to the former is esteemed good, and what seemed good is esteemed bad, let him listen to what we say to this. We know that the wicked angels appointed laws conformable to their own wickedness, in which the men who are like them delight; and the right Reason, when He came, proved that not all opinions nor all doctrines are good, but that some are evil, while others are good. Wherefore, I will declare the same and similar things to such men as these, and, if need be, they shall be spoken of more at large. But at present I return to the subject.

CHAPTER 10. CHRIST COMPARED WITH SOCRATES

Our doctrines, then, appear to be greater than all human teaching; because Christ, who appeared for our sakes, became the whole rational being, both body, and reason, and soul. For whatever either lawgivers or philosophers uttered well, they elaborated by finding and contemplating some part of the Word. But since they did not know the whole of the Word, which is Christ, they often contradicted themselves. And those who by human birth were more ancient than Christ, when they attempted to consider and prove things by reason, were brought before the tribunals as impious persons and busybodies. And Socrates, who was more zealous in this direction than all of them, was accused of the very same crimes as ourselves. For they said that he was introducing new divinities, and did not consider those to be gods whom the state recognised. But he cast out from the state both Homer and the rest of the poets, and taught men to reject the wicked demons and those who did the things which the poets related; and he exhorted them to become acquainted with the God who was to them unknown, by means of the investigation of reason, saying, That it is neither easy to find the Father and Maker of all, nor, having found Him, is it safe to declare Him to all. But these things our Christ did through His own power. For no one trusted in Socrates so as to die for this doctrine, but in Christ, who was partially known even by Socrates (for He was and is the Word who is in every man, and who foretold the things that were to come to pass both through the prophets and in His own person when He was made of like passions, and taught these things), not only philosophers and scholars believed, but also artisans and people entirely uneducated, despising both glory, and fear, and death; since He is a power of the ineffable Father, not the mere instrument of human reason.

CHAPTER 11. HOW CHRISTIANS VIEW DEATH

But neither should we be put to death, nor would wicked men and devils be more powerful than we, were not death a debt due by every man that is born. Wherefore we give thanks when we pay this debt. And we judge it right and opportune to tell here, for the sake of Crescens and those who rave as he does, what is related by Xenophon. Hercules, says Xenophon, coming to a place where three ways met, found Virtue and Vice, who appeared to him in the form of women: Vice, in a luxurious dress, and with a seductive expression rendered blooming by such ornaments, and her eyes of a quickly melting tenderness, said to Hercules that if he would follow her, she would always enable him to pass his life in pleasure and adorned with the most graceful ornaments, such as were then upon her own person; and Virtue, who was of squalid look and dress, said, But if you obey me, you shall adorn yourself not with ornament nor beauty that passes away and perishes, but with everlasting and precious graces. And we are persuaded that every one who flees those things that seem to be good, and follows hard after what are reckoned difficult and strange, enters into blessedness. For Vice, when by imitation of what is incorruptible (for what is really incorruptible she neither has nor can produce) she has thrown around her own actions, as a disguise, the properties of virtue, and qualities which are really excellent, leads captive earthly-minded men, attaching to Virtue her own evil properties. But those who understood the excellences which belong to that which is real, are also uncorrupt in virtue. And this every sensible person ought to think both of Christians and of the athletes, and of those who did what the poets relate of the so-called gods, concluding as much from our contempt of death, even when it could be escaped.

CHAPTER 12. CHRISTIANS PROVED INNOCENT BY THEIR CONTEMPT OF DEATH

For I myself, too, when I was delighting in the doctrines of Plato, and heard the Christians slandered, and saw them fearless of death, and of all other-things which are counted fearful, perceived that it was impossible that they could be living in wickedness and pleasure. For what sensual or intemperate man, or who that counts it good to feast on human flesh, could welcome death that he might be deprived of his enjoyments, and would not rather continue always the present life, and attempt to escape the observation of the rulers; and much less would he denounce himself when the consequence would be death? This also the wicked demons have now caused to be done by evil men. For having put some to death on account of the accusations falsely brought against us, they also dragged to the torture our domestics, either children or weak women, and by dreadful torments forced them to admit those fabulous actions which they themselves openly perpetrate; about which we are the less concerned, because none of these actions are really ours, and we have the unbegotten and ineffable God as witness both of our thoughts and deeds. For why did we not even publicly profess that these were the things which we esteemed good, and prove that these are the divine philosophy, saying that the mysteries of Saturn are performed when we slay a man, and that when we drink our fill of blood, as it is said we do, we are doing what you do before that idol you honour, and on which you sprinkle the blood not only of irrational animals, but also of men, making a libation of the blood of the slain by the hand of the most illustrious and noble man among you? And imitating Jupiter and the other gods in sodomy and shameless intercourse with woman, might we not bring as our apology the writings of Epicurus and the poets? But because we persuade men to avoid such instruction, and all who practise them and imitate such examples, as now in this discourse we have striven to persuade you, we are assailed in every kind of way. But we are not concerned, since we know that God is a just observer of all. But would that even now some one would mount a lofty rostrum, and shout with a loud voice; Be ashamed, be ashamed, you who charge the guiltless with those deeds which yourselves openly could commit, and ascribe things which apply to yourselves and to your gods to those who have not even the slightest sympathy with them. Be converted; become wise.

CHAPTER 13. HOW THE WORD HAS BEEN IN ALL MEN

For I myself, when I discovered the wicked disguise which the evil spirits had thrown around the divine doctrines of the Christians, to turn aside others from joining them, laughed both at those who framed these falsehoods, and at the disguise itself and at popular opinion and I confess that I both boast and with all my strength strive to be found a Christian; not because the teachings of Plato are different from those of Christ, but because they are not in all respects similar, as neither are those of the others, Stoics, and poets, and historians. For each man spoke well in proportion to the share he had of the spermatic word, seeing what was related to it. But they who contradict themselves on the more important points appear not to have possessed the heavenly wisdom, and the knowledge which cannot be spoken against. Whatever things were rightly said among all men, are the property of us Christians. For next to God, we worship and love the Word who is from the unbegotten and ineffable God, since also He became man for our sakes, that becoming a partaker of our sufferings, He might also bring us healing. For all the writers were able to see realities darkly through the sowing of the implanted word that was in them. For the seed and imitation impacted according to capacity is one thing, and quite another is the thing itself, of which there is the participation and imitation according to the grace which is from Him.

CHAPTER 14. JUSTIN PRAYS THAT THIS APPEAL BE PUBLISHED

And we therefore pray you to publish this little book, appending what you think right, that our opinions may he known to others, and that these persons may have a fair chalice of being freed from erroneous notions and ignorance of good, who by their own fault have become subject to punishment; that so these things may be published to men, because it is in the nature of man to know good and evil; and by their condemning us, whom they do not understand, for actions which they say are wicked, and by delighting in the gods who did such things, and even now require similar actions from men, and by inflicting on us death or bonds or some other such punishment, as if we were guilty of these things, they condemn themselves, so that there is no need of other judges.

CHAPTER 15. CONCLUSION

And I despised the wicked and deceitful doctrine of Simon of my own nation. And if you give this book your authority, we will expose him before all, that, if possible, they may be converted. For this end alone did we compose this treatise. And our doctrines are not shameful, according to a sober judgment, but are indeed more lofty than all human philosophy: and if not so, they are at least unlike the doctrines of the Sotadists, and Philænidians, and Dancers, and Epicureans, and such other teachings of the poets, which all are allowed to acquaint themselves with both as acted and as written. And henceforth we shall be silent, having done as much as we could, and having added the prayer that all men everywhere may be counted worthy of the truth. And would that you also, in a manner becoming piety and philosophy, would for your own sakes judge justly!

DIALOGUE WITH TRYPHO

CHAPTER I -- INTRODUCTION

While I was going about one morning in the walks of the Xystus, a certain man, with others in his company, having met me, and said, "Hail, O philosopher!" And immediately after saying this, he turned round and walked along with me; his friends likewise followed him. And I in turn having addressed him, said, "What is there important?"

And he replied, "I was instructed," says he, "by Corinthus the Socratic in Argos, that I ought not to despise or treat with indifference those who array themselves in this dress, but to show them all kindness, and to associate with them, as perhaps some advantage would spring from the intercourse either to some such man or to myself. It is good, moreover, for both, if either the one or the other be benefited. On this account, therefore, whenver I see any one in such costume, I gladly approach him, and now, for the same reason, have I willingly accosted you; and these accompany me, in the expectation of hearing for themselves something profitable from you."

"But who are you, most excellent man?" So I replied to him in jest.

Then he told me frankly both his name and his family. "Trypho," says he, "I am called; and I am a Hebrew of the circumcision, and having escaped from the war lately carried on there, I am spending my days in Greece, and chiefly at Corinth."

And in what," said I, "would you be profited by philosophy so much as by your own lawgiver and the prophets?"

Why not?" he replied. "Do no the philosophers turn every discourse on God? And do not questions continually arise to them about His unity and providence? Is not this truly the duty of philophy, to investigate the Deity?" "Assuredly," said I, "so we too have believed. But the most have not taken thought of this, whether there be one or more gods, and whether they have a regard for each one of us or not, as if this knowledge contributed nothing to our happiness; nay, they moreover attempt to persuade us that God takes care of the universe with its genera and species, but not of me and you, and each individually, since otherwise we would surely not need to pray to Him night and day. But it is not difficult to understand the upshot of this; for fearlessness and license in speaking result to such as maintain these opinions, doing and saying whatever they choose, neither dreading punishment nor hoping for any benefit from God. For how could they? They affirm that the same things shall always happen; and, further, that I and you shall again live in like manner, having become neither better men nor worse. But there are some others, who, having supposed the soul to be immortal and immaterial, believe that though they have committed evil they will not suffer punishment (for that which is immaterial is insensible), and that the soul, in consequence of its immortality, needs nothing from God."

And he, smiling gently, said, "Tell us your opinion of these matters, and what idea you entertain respecting God, and what you philosophy is."

CHAPTER II -- JUSTIN DESCRIBES HIS STUDIES IN PHILOSOPHY.

"I will tell you," said I, "what seems to me; for philosophy is, in fact, the greatest possession, and most honourable before God, to whom it leads us and alone commends us; and these are truly holy men who have bestowed attention on philosophy. What philosophy is, however, and the reason why it has been sent down to men, have escaped the observation of most; for there would be neither Platonists, nor Stoics, nor Peripatetics, nor Theoretics, nor Pythagoreans, this knowledge being one. I wish to tell you why it has become many-headed. It has happened that those who first handled it [i.e., philosophy], and who were therefore esteemed illustrious men, were succeeded by those who made no investigations concerning truth, but only admired the perseverance and self-discipline of the former, as well as the novelty of the doctrines; and each thought that to be true which he learned from his teacher: then, moreover, those latter persons handed down to their successors such things, and others similar to them; and this system was called by the name of him who was styled the father of the doctrine. Being at first desirous of personally conversing with one of these men, I surrendered myself to a certain Stoic; and having spent a considerable time with him, when I had not acquired any further knowledge of God (for he did not know himself, and said such instruction was unnecessary), I left him and betook myself to another, who was called a Peripatetic, and as he fancied, shrewd. And this man, after having entertained me for the first few days, requested me to settle the fee, in order that our intercourse might not be unprofitable. Him, too, for this reason I abandoned, believing him to be no philosopher at all. But when my soul was eagerly desirous to hear the peculiar and choice philosophy, I came to a Pythagorean, very celebrated--a man who thought much of his own wisdom. And then, when I had an interview with him, willing to become his hearer and disciple, he said, 'What then? Are you acquainted with music, astronomy, and geometry? Do you expect to perceive any of those things which conduce to a happy life, if you have not been first informed on those points which wean the soul from sensible objects, and render it fitted for objects which appertain to the mind, so that it can contemplate that which is honourable in its essence and that which is good in its essence?' Having commended many of these branches of learning, and telling me that they were necessary, he dismissed me when I confessed to him my ignorance. Accordingly I took it rather impatiently, as was to be expected when I failed in my hope, the more so because I deemed the man had some knowledge; but reflecting again on the space of time during which I would have to linger over those branches of learning, I was not able to endure longer procrastination. In my helpless condition it occurred to me to have a meeting with the Platonists, for their fame was great. I thereupon spent as much of my time as possible with one who had lately settled in our city,--a sagacious man, holding a high position among the Platonists,--and I progressed, and made the greatest improvements daily. And the perception of immaterial things quite overpowered me, and the contemplation of ideas furnished my mind with wings, so that in a little while I supposed that I had become wise; and such was my stupidity, I expected forthwith to look upon God, for this is the end of Plato's philosophy.

CHAPTER III -- JUSTIN NARRATES THE MANNER OF HIS CONVERSION.

"And while I was thus disposed, when I wished at one period to be filled with great quietness, and to shun the path of men, I used to go into a certain field not far from the sea. And when I was near that spot one day, which having reached I purposed to be by myself, a certain old man, by no means contemptible in appearance, exhibiting meek and venerable manners, followed me at a little distance. And when I turned round to him, having halted, I fixed my eyes rather keenly on him.

"And he said, 'Do you know me?'

I replied in the negative.

"'Why, then,' said he to me, 'do you so look at me?

"'I am astonished,' I said, 'because you have chanced to be in my company in the same place; for I had not expected to see any man here.'

"And he says to me, 'I am concerned about some of my household. These are gone away from me; and therefore have I come to make personal search for them, if, perhaps, they shall make their appearance somewhere. But why are you here?' said he to me.

"'I delight,' said I, 'in such walks, where my attention is not distracted, for converse with myself is uninterrupted; and such places are most fit for philology.'

"'Are you, then, a philologian,' said he, but no lover of deeds or of truth? and do you not aim at being a practical man so much as being a sophist?'

"'What greater work,' said I, 'could one accomplish than this, to show the reason which governs all, and having laid hold of it, and being mounted upon it, to look down on the errors of others, and their pursuits? But without philosophy and right reason, prudence would not be present to any man. Wherefore it is necessary for every man to philosophize, and to esteem this the greatest and most honourable work; but other things only of second-rate or third-rate importance, though, indeed, if they be made to depend on philosophy, they are of moderate value, and worthy of acceptance; but deprived of it, and not accompanying it, they are vulgar and coarse to those who pursue them.'

"'Does philosophy, then, make happiness?' said he, interrupting.

"'Assuredly,' I said, 'and it alone.'

"'What, then, is philosophy?' he says; 'and what is happiness? Pray tell me, unless something hinders you from saying.'

"'Philosophy, then,' said I, 'is the knowledge of that which really exists, and a clear perception of the truth; and happiness is the reward of such knowledge and wisdom.'

"'But what do you call God?' said he.

"'That which always maintains the same nature, and in the same manner, and is the cause of all other things--that, indeed, is God.' So I answered him; and he listened to me with pleasure, and thus again interrogated me:--

"'Is not knowledge a term common to different matters? For in arts of all kinds, he who knows any one of them is called a skilful man in the art of generalship, or of ruling, or of healing equally. But in divine and human affairs it is not so. Is there a knowledge which affords understanding of human and divine things, and then a thorough acquaintance with the divinity and the righteousness of them?'

"'Assuredly,' I replied.

"'What, then? Is it in the same way we know man and' God, as we know music, and arithmetic, and astronomy, or any other similar branch?'

"'By no means,' I replied.

"'You have not answered me correctly, then,' he said; 'for some [branches of knowledge] come to us by learning, or by some employment, while of others we have knowledge by sight. Now, if one were to tell you that there exists in India an animal with a nature unlike all others, but of such and such a kind, multiform and various, you would not know it before you saw it; but neither would you be competent to give any account of it, unless you should hear from one who had seen it.'

"'Certainly not,' I said.

"'How then,' he said, 'should the philosophers judge correctly about God, or speak any truth, when they have no knowledge of Him, having neither seen Him at any time, nor heard Him?'

"'But, father,' said I, 'the Deity cannot be seen merely by the eyes, as other living beings can, but is discernible to the mind alone, as Plato says; and I believe him.'

CHAPTER IV -- THE SOUL OF ITSELF CANNOT SEE GOD.

"'Is there then,' says he, 'such and so great power in our mind? Or can a man not perceive by sense sooner? Will the mind of man see God at any time, if it is uninstructed by the Holy Spirit?'

"'Plato indeed says,' replied I, 'that the mind's eye is of such a nature, and has been given for this end, that we may see that very Being when the mind is pure itself, who is the cause of all discerned by the mind, having no colour, no form, no greatness--nothing, indeed, which the bodily eye looks upon; but It is something of this sort, he goes on to say, that is beyond all essence, unutterable and inexplicable, but alone honourable and good, coming suddenly into souls well-dispositioned, on account of their affinity to and desire of seeing Him.'

"'What affinity, then,' replied he, 'is there between us and God? Is the soul also divine and immortal, and a part of that very regal mind? And even as that sees God, so also is it attainable by us to conceive of the Deity in our mind, and thence to become happy?'

"'Assuredly,' I said.

"'And do all the souls of all living beings comprehend Him?' he asked; 'or are the souls of men of one kind and the souls of horses and of asses of another kind?'

"'No; but the souls which are in all are similar,' I answered.

"'Then,' says he, 'shall both horses and asses see, or have they seen at some time or other, God?'

"'No,' I said; 'for the majority of men will not, saving such as shall live justly, purified by righteousness, and by every other virtue.'

"'It is not, therefore,' said he, 'on account of his affinity, that a man sees God, nor because he has a mind, but because he is temperate and righteous?'

"'Yes,' said I; 'and because he has that whereby he perceives God.'

"'What then? Do goats or sheep injure anyone?'

"'No one in any respect,' I said.

"'Therefore these animals will see [God] according to your account,' says he.

"'No; for their body being of such a nature, is an obstacle to them.'

"He rejoined,' If these animals could assume speech, be well assured that they would with greater reason ridicule our body; but let us now dismiss this subject, and let it be conceded to you as you say. Tell me, however, this: Does the soul see [God] so long as it is in the body, or after it has been removed from it?'

"'So long as it is in the form of a man, it is possible for it,' I continue, 'to attain to this by means of the mind; but especially when it has been set free from the body, and being apart by itself, it gets possession of that which it was wont continually and wholly to love.'

"'Does it remember this, then [the sight of God], when it is again in the man?'

"'It does not appear to me so,' I said.

"'What, then, is the advantage to those who have seen [God]? or what has he who has seen more than he who has not seen, unless he remember this fact, that he has seen?'

"'I cannot tell,' I answered.

"'And what do those suffer who are judged to be unworthy of this spectacle?' said he.

"'They are imprisoned in the bodies of certain wild beasts, and this is their punishment.'

"'Do they know, then, that it is for this reason they are in such forms, and that they have committed some sin?'

"'I do not think so.'

"'Then these reap no advantage from their punishment, as it seems: moreover, I would say that they are not punished unless they are conscious of the punishment.'

"'No indeed.'

"'Therefore souls neither see God nor trans-migrate into other bodies; for they would know that so they are punished, and they would be afraid to commit even the most trivial sin afterwards. But that they can perceive that God exists, and that righteousness and piety are honourable, I also quite agree with you,' said he.

"'You are right,' I replied.

CHAPTER V -- THE SOUL IS NOT IN ITS OWN NATURE IMMORTAL.

"'These philosophers know nothing, then, about these things; for they cannot tell what a soul is.'

"'It does not appear so.'

"'Nor ought it to be called immortal; for if it is immortal, it is plainly unbegotten.'

"'It is both unbegotten and immortal, according to some who are styled Platonists.'

"'Do you say that the world is also unbegotten?'

"'Some say so. I do not, however, agree with them.'

"'You are right; for what reason has one for supposing that a body so solid, possessing resistance, composite, changeable, decaying, and renewed every day, has not arisen from some cause? But if the world is begotten, souls also are necessarily begotten; and perhaps at one time they were not in existence, for they were made on account of men and other living creatures, if you will say that they have been begotten wholly apart, and not along with their respective bodies.' "'This seems to be correct.'

"'They are not, then, immortal?'

"'No; since the world has appeared to us to be begotten.'

"'But I do not say, indeed, that all souls die; for that were truly a piece of good fortune to the evil. What then? The souls of the pious remain in a better place, while those of the unjust and wicked are in a worse, waiting for the time of judgment. Thus some which have appeared worthy of God never die; but others are punished so long as God wills them to exist and to be punished.'

"'Is what you say, then, of a like nature with that which Plato in Timoeus hints about the world, when he says that it is indeed subject to decay, inasmuch as it has been created, but that it will neither be dissolved nor meet with the fate of death on account of the will of God? Does it seem to you the very same can be said of the soul, and generally of all things? For those things which exist after God, or shall at any time exist, these have the nature of decay, and are such as may be blotted out and cease to exist; for God alone is unbegotten and incorruptible, and therefore He is God, but all other things after Him are created and corruptible. For this reason souls both die and are punished: since, if they were unbegotten, they would neither sin, nor be filled with folly, nor be cowardly, and again ferocious; nor would they willingly transform into swine, and serpents, and dogs and it would not indeed be just to compel them, if they be unbegotten. For that which is unbegotten is similar to, equal to, and the same with that which is unbegotten; and neither in power nor in honour should the one be preferred to the other, and hence there are not many things which are unbegotten: for if there were some difference between them, you would not discover the cause of the difference, though you searched for it; but after letting the mind ever wander to infinity, you would at length, wearied out, take your stand on one Unbegotten, and say that this is the Cause of all. Did such escape the observation of Plato and Pythagoras, those wise men,' I said, 'who have been as a wall and fortress of philosophy to us?'

CHAPTER VI -- THESE THINGS WERE UNKNOWN TO PLATO AND OTHER PHILOSOPHERS.

"'It makes no matter to me,' said he, 'whether Plato or Pythagoras, or, in short, any other man held such opinions. For the truth is so; and you would perceive it from this. The soul assuredly is or has life. If, then, it is life, it would cause something else, and not itself, to live, even as motion would move something else than itself. Now, that the soul lives, no one would deny. But if it lives, it lives not as being life, but as the partaker of life; but that which partakes of anything, is different from that of which it does partake. Now the soul partakes of life, since God wills it to live. Thus, then, it will not even partake [of life] when God does not will it to live. For to live is not its attribute, as it is God's; but as a man does not live always, and the soul is not for ever conjoined with the body, since, whenever this harmony must be broken up, the soul leaves the body, and the man exists no longer; even so, whenever the soul must cease to exist, the spirit of life is removed from it, and there is no more soul, but it goes back to the place from whence it was taken.'

CHAPTER VII -- THE KNOWLEDGE OF TRUTH TO BE SOUGHT FROM THE PROPHETS ALONE.

"'Should any one, then, employ a teacher?' I say, 'or whence may any one be helped, if not even in them there is truth?'

"'There existed, long before this time, certain men more ancient than all those who are esteemed philosophers, both righteous and beloved by God, who spoke by the Divine Spirit, and foretold events which would take place, and which are now taking place. They are called prophets. These alone both saw and announced the truth to men, neither reverencing nor fearing any man, not influenced by a desire for glory, but speaking those things alone which they saw and which they heard, being filled with the Holy Spirit. Their writings are still extant, and he who has read them is very much helped in his knowledge of the beginning and end of things, and of those matters which the philosopher ought to know, provided he has believed them. For they did not use demonstration in their treatises, seeing that they were witnesses to the truth above all demonstration, and worthy of belief; and those events which have happened, and those which are happening, compel you to assent to the utterances made by them, although, indeed, they were entitled to credit on account of the miracles which they performed, since they both glorified the Creator, the God and Father of all things, and proclaimed His Son, the Christ [sent] by Him: which, indeed, the false prophets, who are filled with the lying unclean spirit, neither have done nor do, but venture to work certain wonderful deeds for the purpose of astonishing men, and glorify the spirits and demons of error. But pray that, above all things, the gates of light may be opened to you; for these things cannot be perceived or understood by all, but only by the man to whom God and His Christ have imparted wisdom.'

CHAPTER VIII -- JUSTIN BY HIS COLLOQUY IS KINDLED WITH LOVE TO CHRIST.

"When he had spoken these and many other things, which there is no time for mentioning at present, he went away, bidding me attend to them; and I have not seen him since. But straightway a flame was kindled in my soul; and a love of the prophets, and of those men who are friends of Christ, possessed me; and whilst revolving his words in my mind, I found this philosophy alone to be safe and profitable. Thus, and for this reason, I am a philosopher. Moreover, I would wish that all, making a resolution similar to my own, do not keep themselves away from the words of the Saviour. For they possess a terrible power in themselves, and are sufficient to inspire those who turn aside from the path of rectitude with awe; while the sweetest rest is afforded those who make a diligent practice of them. If, then, you have any concern for yourself, and if you are eagerly looking for salvation, and if you believe in God, you may--since you are not indifferent to the matter -- become acquainted with the Christ of God, and, after being initiated, live a happy life."

When I had said this, my beloved friends those who were with Trypho laughed; but he, smiling, says, "I approve of your other remarks, and admire the eagerness with which you study divine things; but it were better for you still to abide in the philosophy of Plato, or of some other man, cultivating endurance, self-control, and moderation, rather than be deceived by false words, and follow the opinions of men of no reputation. For if you remain in that mode of philosophy, and live blamelessly, a hope of a better destiny were left to you; but when you have forsaken God, and reposed confidence in man, what safety still awaits you? If, then, you are willing to listen to me (for I have already considered you a friend), first be circumcised, then observe what ordinances have been enacted with respect to the Sabbath, and the feasts, and the new moons of God; and, in a word, do all things which have been written in the law: and then perhaps you shall obtain mercy from God. But Christ--if He has indeed been born, and exists anywhere--is unknown, and does not even know Himself, and has no power until Elias come to anoint Him, and make Him manifest to all. And you, having accepted a groundless report, invent a Christ for yourselves, and for his sake are inconsiderately perishing."

CHAPTER IX -- THE CHRISTIANS HAVE NOT BELIEVED GROUNDLESS STORIES.

"I excuse and forgive you, my friend," I said. "For you know not what you say, but have been persuaded by teachers who do not understand the Scriptures; and you speak, like a diviner whatever comes into your mind. But if you are willing to listen to an account of Him, how we have not been deceived, and shall not cease to confess Him,--although men's reproaches be heaped upon us, although the most terrible tyrant compel us to deny Him,--I shall prove to you as you stand here that we have not believed empty fables, or words without any foundation but words filled with the Spirit of God, and big with power, and flourishing with grace."

Then again those who were in his company laughed, and shouted in an unseemly manner. Then I rose up and was about to leave; but he, taking hold of my garment, said I should not accomplish that until I had performed what I promised. "Let not, then, your companions be so tumultuous, or behave so disgracefully," I said. "But if they wish, let them listen in silence; or, if some better occupation prevent them, let them go away; while we, having retired to some spot, and resting there, may finish the discourse." It seemed good to Trypho that we should do so; and accordingly, having agreed upon it, we retired to the middle space of the Xystus. Two of his friends, when they had ridiculed and made game of our zeal, went off. And when we were come to that place, where there are stone seats on both sides, those with Trypho, having seated themselves on the one side, conversed with each other, some one of them having thrown in a remark about the war waged in Judaea.

CHAPTER X -- TRYPHO BLAMES THE CHRISTIANS FOR THIS ALONE--THE NON-OBSERVANCE OF THE LAW.

And when they ceased, I again addressed them thus:--

"Is there any other matter, my friends, in which we are blamed, than this, that we live not after the law, and are not circumcised in the flesh as your forefathers were, and do not observe sabbaths as you do? Are our lives and customs also slandered among you? And I ask this: have you also believed concerning us, that we eat men; and that after the feast, having extinguished the lights, we engage in promiscuous concubinage? Or do you condemn us in this alone, that we adhere to such tenets, and believe in an opinion, untrue, as you think?"

"This is what we are amazed at," said Trypho, "but those things about which the multitude speak are not worthy of belief; for they are most repugnant to human nature. Moreover, I am aware that your precepts in the so-called Gospel are so wonderful and so great, that I suspect no one can keep them; for I have carefully read them. But this is what we are most at a loss about: that you, professing to be pious, and supposing yourselves better than others, are not in any particular separated from them, and do not alter your mode of living from the nations, in that you observe no festivals or sabbaths, and do not have the rite of circumcision; and further, resting your hopes on a man that was crucified, you yet expect to obtain some good thing from God, while you do not obey His commandments. Have you not read, that soul shall be cut off from his people who shall not have been circumcised on the eighth day? And this has been ordained for strangers and for slaves equally. But you, despising this covenant rashly, reject the consequent duties, and attempt to persuade yourselves that you know God, when, however, you perform none of those things which they do who fear God. If, therefore, you can defend yourself on these points, and make it manifest in what way you hope for anything whatsoever, even though you do not observe the law, this we would very gladly hear from you, and we shall make other similar investigations."

CHAPTER XI -- THE LAW ABROGATED; THE NEW TESTAMENT PROMISED AND GIVEN BY GOD.

"There will be no other God, O Trypho, nor was there from eternity any other existing" (I thus addressed him), "but He who made and disposed all this universe. Nor do we think that there is one God for us, another for you, but that He alone is God who led your fathers out from Egypt with a strong hand and a high arm. Nor have we trusted in any other (for there is no other), but in Him in whom you also have trusted, the God of Abraham, and of Isaac, and of Jacob. But we do not trust through Moses or through the law; for then we would do the same as yourselves. But now--(for I have read that there shall be a final law, and a covenant, the chiefest of all, which it is now incumbent on all men to observe, as many as are seeking after the inheritance of God. For the law promulgated on Horeb is now old, and belongs to yourselves alone; but this is for all universally. Now, law placed against law has abrogated that which is before it, and a covenant which comes after in like manner has put an end to the previous one; and an eternal and final law--namely, Christ--has been given to us, and the covenant is trustworthy, after which there shall be no law, no commandment, no ordinance. Have you not read this which Isaiah says: 'Hearken unto Me, hearken unto Me, my people; and, ye kings, give ear unto Me: for a law shall go forth from Me, and My judgment shah be for a light to the nations. My righteousness approaches swiftly, and My salvation shall go forth, and nations shall trust in Mine arm?' And by Jeremiah, concerning this same new covenant, He thus speaks: 'Behold, the days come, saith the Lord, that I will make a new covenant with the house of Israel and with the house of Judah; not according to the covenant which I made with their fathers, in the day that I took them by the hand, to bring them out of the land of Egypt'). If, therefore, God proclaimed a new covenant which was to be instituted, and this for a light of the nations, we see and are persuaded that men approach God, leaving their idols and other unrighteousness, through the name of Him who was crucified, Jesus Christ, and abide by their confession even unto death, and maintain piety. Moreover, by the works and by the attendant miracles, it is possible for all to understand that He is the new law, and the new covenant, and the expectation of those who out of every people wait for the good things of God. For the true spiritual Israel, and descendants of Judah, Jacob, Isaac, and Abraham (who in uncircumcision was approved of and blessed by God on account of his faith, and called the father of many nations), are we who have been led to God through this crucified Christ, as shall be demonstrated while we proceed.

CHAPTER XII -- THE JEWS VIOLATE THE ETERNAL LAW, AND INTERPRET ILL THAT OF MOSES.

I also adduced another passage in which Isaiah exclaims: "'Hear My words, and your soul shall live; and I will make an everlasting covenant with you, even the sure mercies of David. Behold, I have given Him for a witness to the people: nations which know not Thee shall call on Thee; peoples who know not Thee shall escape to Thee, because of thy God, the Holy One of Israel; for He has glorified Thee.' This same law you have despised, and His new holy covenant you have slighted; and now you neither receive it, nor repent of your evil deeds. 'For your ears are closed, your eyes are blinded, and the heart is hardened,' Jeremiah has cried; yet not even then do you listen. The Lawgiver is present, yet you do not see Him; to the poor the Gospel is preached, the blind see, yet you do not understand. You have now need of a second circumcision, though you glory greatly in the flesh. The new law requires you to keep perpetual sabbath, and you, because you are idle for one day, suppose you are pious, not discerning why this has been commanded you: and if you eat unleavened bread, you say the will of God has been fulfilled. The Lord our God does not take pleasure in such observances: if there is any perjured person or a thief among you, let him cease to be so; if any adulterer, let him repent; then he has kept the sweet and true sabbaths of God. If any one has impure hands, let him wash and be pure.

CHAPTER XIII -- ISAIAH TEACHES THAT SINS ARE FORGIVEN THROUGH CHRIST'S BLOOD.

"For Isaiah did not send you to a bath, there to wash away murder and other sins, which not even all the water of the sea were sufficient to purge; but, as might have been expected, this was that saving bath of the olden time which followed s those who repented, and who no longer were purified by the blood of goats and of sheep, or by the ashes of an heifer, or by the offerings of fine flour, but by faith through the blood of Christ, and through His death, who died for this very reason, as Isaiah himself said, when he spake thus: 'The Lord shall make bare His holy arm in the eyes of all the nations, and all the nations and the ends of the earth shall see the salvation of God. Depart ye, depart ye, depart ye, go ye out from thence, and touch no unclean thing; go ye out of the midst of her, be ye clean that bear the vessels of the Lord, for ye go not with haste. For the Lord shall go before you; and the Lord, the God of Israel, shall gather you together. Behold, my servant shall deal prudently; and He shall be exalted, and be greatly glorified. As many were astonished at Thee, so Thy form and Thy glory shall be marred more than men. So shall many nations be astonished at Him, and the kings shall shut their mouths; for that which had not been told them concerning Him shall they see, and that which they had not heard shall they consider. Lord, who hath believed our report? and to whom is the arm of the Lord revealed? We have announced Him as a child before Him, as a root in a dry ground. He hath no form or comeliness, and when we saw Him He had no form or beauty; but His form is dishonoured, and fails more than the sons of men. He is a man in affliction, and acquainted with bearing sickness, because His face has been turned away; He was despised, and we esteemed Him not. He bears our sins, and is distressed for us; and we esteemed Him to be in toil and in affliction, and in evil treatment But He was wounded for our transgressions, He was bruised for our iniquities; the chastisement of our peace was upon Him. With His stripes we are healed. All we, like sheep, have gone astray. Every man has turned to his own way; and the Lord laid on Him our iniquities, and by reason of His oppression He opens not His mouth. He was brought as a sheep to the slaughter; and as a lamb before her shearer is dumb, so He openeth not His mouth. In His humiliation His judgment was taken away. And who shall declare His generation? For His life is taken from the earth. Because of the transgressions of my people He came unto death. And I will give the wicked for His grave, and the rich for His death, because He committed no iniquity, and deceit was not found in His mouth. And the Lord wills to purify Him from affliction. If he has been given for sin, your soul shall see a long-lived seed. And the Lord wills to take His soul away from trouble, to show Him light, and to form Him in understanding, to justify the righteous One who serves many well. And He shall bear our sins; therefore He shall inherit many, and shall divide the spoil of the strong, because His soul was delivered to death; and He was numbered with the transgressors, and He bare the sins of many, and was delivered for their transgression. Sing, O barren, who bearest not; break forth and cry aloud, thou who dost not travail in pain: for more are the children of the desolate than the children of the married wife.

For the Lord said, Enlarge the place of thy tent and of thy curtains; fix them, spare not, lengthen thy cords, and strengthen thy stakes; stretch forth to thy right and thy left; and thy seed shall inherit the Gentiles, and thou shalt make the desolate cities to be inherited. Fear not because thou art ashamed, neither be thou confounded because thou hast been reproached; for thou shalt forget everlasting shame, and shalt not remember the reproach of thy widowhood, because the Lord has made a name for Himself, and He who has redeemed thee shall be called through the whole earth the God of Israel. The Lord has called thee as a woman forsaken and grieved in spirit, as a woman hated from her youth.'

CHAPTER XIV -- RIGHTEOUSNESS IS NOT PLACED IN JEWISH RITES, BUT IN THE CONVERSION OF THE HEART GIVEN IN BAPTISM BY CHRIST.

"By reason, therefore, of this laver of repentance and knowledge of God, which has been ordained on account of the transgression of God's people, as Isaiah cries, we have believed, and testify that that very baptism which he announced is alone able to purify those who have repented; and this is the water of life. But the cisterns which you have dug for yourselves are broken and profitless to you. For what is the use of that baptism which cleanses the flesh and body alone? Baptize the soul from wrath and from covetousness, from envy, and from hatred; and, lo! the body is pure. For this is the symbolic significance of unleavened bread, that you do not commit the old deeds of wicked leaven. But you have understood all things in a carnal sense, and you suppose it to be piety if you do such things, while your souls are filled with deceit, and, in short, with every wickedness. Accordingly, also, after the seven days of eating unleavened bread, God commanded them to mingle new leaven, that is, the performance of other works, and not the imitation of the old and evil works. And because this is what this new Lawgiver demands of you, I shall again refer to the words which have been quoted by me, and to others also which have been passed over. They are related by Isaiah to the following effect: 'Hearken to me, and your soul shall live; and I will make with you an everlasting covenant, even the sure mercies of David. Behold, I have given Him for a witness to the people, a leader and commander to the nations. Nations which know not Thee shall call on Thee; and peoples who know not Thee shall escape unto Thee, because of Thy God, the Holy One of Israel, for He has glorified Thee. Seek ye God; and when you find Him, call on Him, so long as He may be nigh you. Let the wicked forsake his ways, and the unrighteous man his thoughts; and let him return unto the Lord, and he will obtain mercy, because He will abundantly pardon your sins. For my thoughts are not as your thoughts, neither are my ways as your ways; but as far removed as the heavens are from the earth, so far is my way removed from your way, and your thoughts from my thoughts. For as the snow or the rain descends from heaven, and shall not return till it waters the earth, and makes it bring forth and bud, and gives seed to the sower and bread for food, so shall My word be that goeth forth out of My mouth: it shall not return until it shall have accomplished all that I desired, and I shall make My commandments prosperous. For ye shall go out with joy, and be taught with gladness. For the mountains and the hills shall leap while they expect you, and all the trees of the fields shall applaud with their branches: and instead of the thorn shall come up the cypress, and instead of the brier shall come up the myrtle.

And the Lord shall be for a name, and for an everlasting sign, and He shall not fail!' Of these and such like words written by the prophets, O Trypho," said I, "some have reference to the first advent of Christ, in which He is preached as inglorious, obscure, and of mortal appearance: but others had reference to His second advent, when He shall appear in glory and above the clouds; and your nation shall see and know Him whom they have pierced, as Hosea, one of the twelve prophets, and Daniel, foretold.

CHAPTER XV -- IN WHAT THE TRUE FASTING CONSISTS.

"Learn, therefore, to keep the true fast of God, as Isaiah says, that you may please God. Isaiah has cried thus: 'Shout vehemently, and do not spare: lift up thy voice as with a trumpet, and show My people their transgressions, and the house of Jacob their sins. They seek Me from day to day, and desire to know My ways, as a nation that did righteousness, and forsook not the judgment of God. They ask of Me now righteous judgment, and desire to draw near to God, saying, Wherefore have we fasted, and Thou seest not? and afflicted our souls, and Thou hast not known? Because in the days of your fasting you find your own pleasure, and oppress all those who are subject to you. Behold, ye fast for strifes and debates, and smite the humble with your fists. Why do ye fast for Me, as to-day, so that your voice is heard aloud? This is not the fast which I have chosen, the day in which a man shall afflict his soul. And not even if you bend your neck like a ring, or clothe yourself in sackcloth and ashes, shall you call this a fast, and a day acceptable to the Lord. This is not the fast which I have chosen, saith the Lord; but loose every unrighteous bond, dissolve the terms of wrongous covenants, let the oppressed go free, and avoid every iniquitous contract. Deal thy bread to the hungry, and lead the homeless poor under thy dwelling; if thou seest the naked, clothe him; and do not hide thyself from thine own flesh. Then shall thy light break forth as the morning, and thy garments shall rise up quickly: and thy righteousness shall go before thee, and the glory of God shall envelope thee. Then shalt thou cry, and the Lord shall hear thee: while thou art speaking, He will say, Behold, I am here. And if thou take away from thee the yoke, and the stretching out of the hand, and the word of murmuring; and shalt give heartily thy bread to the hungry, and shalt satisfy the afflicted soul; then shall thy light arise in the darkness, and thy darkness shall be as the noon-day: and thy God shall be with thee continually, and thou shalt be satisfied according as thy soul desireth, and thy bones shall become fat, and shall be as a watered garden, and as a fountain of water, or as a land where water fails not.' 'Circumcise, therefore, the foreskin of your heart,' as the words of God in all these passages demand."

CHAPTER XVI -- CIRCUMCISION GIVEN AS A SIGN, THAT THE JEWS MIGHT BE DRIVEN AWAY FOR THEIR EVIL DEEDS DONE TO CHRIST AND THE CHRISTIANS.

"And God himself proclaimed by Moses, speaking thus: 'And circumcise the hardness of your hearts, and no longer stiffen the neck. For the Lord your God is both Lord of lords, and a great, mighty, and terrible God, who regardeth not persons, and taketh not rewards.' And in Leviticus: 'Because they have transgressed against Me, and despised

Me, and because they have walked contrary to Me, I also walked contrary to them, and I shall cut them off in the land of their enemies. Then shall their uncircumcised heart be turned.' For the circumcision according to the flesh, which is from Abraham, was given for a sign; that you may be separated from other nations, and from us; and that you alone may suffer that which you now justly suffer; and that your land may be desolate, and your cities burned with fire; and that strangers may eat your fruit in your presence, and not one of you may go up to Jerusalem.' For you are not recognised among the rest of men by any other mark than your fleshly circumcision. For none of you, I suppose, will venture to say that God neither did nor does foresee the events, which are future, nor fore-ordained his deserts for each one. Accordingly, these things have happened to you in fairness and justice, for you have slain the Just One, and His prophets before Him; and now you reject those who hope in Him, and in Him who sent Him--God the Almighty and Maker of all things--cursing in your synagogues those that believe on Christ. For you have not the power to lay hands upon us, on account of those who now have the mastery. But as often as you could, you did so. Wherefore God, by Isaiah, calls to you, saying, 'Behold how the righteous man perished, and no one regards it. For the righteous man is taken away from before iniquity. His grave shall be in peace, he is taken away from the midst. Draw near hither, ye lawless children, seed of the adulterers, and children of the whore. Against whom have you sported yourselves, and against whom have you opened the mouth, and against whom have you loosened the tongue?'

CHAPTER XVII -- THE JEWS SENT PERSONS THROUGH THE WHOLE EARTH TO SPREAD CALUMNIES ON CHRISTIANS.

"For other nations have not inflicted on us and on Christ this wrong to such an extent as you have, who in very deed are the authors of the wicked prejudice against the Just One, and us who hold by Him. For after that you had crucified Him, the only blameless and righteous Man,-- through whose swipes those who approach the Father by Him are healed,--when you knew that He had risen from the dead and ascended to heaven, as the prophets foretold He would, you not only did not repent of the wickedness which you had committed, but at that time you selected and sent out from Jerusalem chosen men through all the land to tell that the godless heresy of the Christians had sprung up, and to publish those things which all they who knew us not speak against us. So that you are the cause not only of your own unrighteousness, but in fact of that of all other men. And Isaiah cries justly: 'By reason of you, My name is blasphemed among the Gentiles.' And: 'Woe unto their soul! because they have devised an evil device against themselves, saying, Let us bind the righteous, for he is distasteful to us. Therefore they shall eat the fruit of their doings. Woe unto the wicked evil shall be rendered to him according to the works of his hands.' And again, in other words: 'Woe unto them that draw their iniquity as with a long cord, and their transgressions as with the harness of a heifer's yoke: who say, Let his speed come near; and let the counsel of the Holy One of Israel come, that we may know it. Woe unto them that call evil good, and good evil; that put light for darkness, and darkness for light; that put bitter for sweet, and sweet for bitter!' Accordingly, you displayed great zeal in publishing throughout all the land bitter and dark and unjust things against the only blameless and righteous Light sent by God.

For He appeared distasteful to you when He cried among you, 'It is written, My house is the house of prayer; but ye have made it a den of thieves!' He overthrew also the tables of the money-changers in the temple, and exclaimed, 'Woe unto you, Scribes and Pharisees, hypocrites! because ye pay tithe of mint and rue, but do not observe the love of God and justice. Ye whited sepulchres! appearing beautiful outward, but are within full of dead men's bones.' And to the Scribes, 'Woe unto you, Scribes! for ye have the keys, and ye do not enter in yourselves, and them that are entering in ye hinder; ye blind guides!'

CHAPTER XVIII -- CHRISTIANS WOULD OBSERVE THE LAW, IF THEY DID NOT KNOW WHY IT WAS INSTITUTED.

"For since you have read, O Trypho, as you yourself admitted, the doctrines taught by our Saviour, I do not think that I have done foolishly in adding some short utterances of His to the prophetic statements. Wash therefore, and be now clean, and put away iniquity from your souls, as God bids you be washed in this layer, and be circumcised with the true circumcision. For we too would observe the fleshly circumcision, and the Sabbaths, and in short all the feasts, if we did not know for what reason they were enjoined you,--namely, on account of your transgressions and the hardness of your hearts. For if we patiently endure all things contrived against us by wicked men and demons, so that even amid cruelties unutterable, death and torments, we pray for mercy to those who inflict such things upon us, and do not wish to give the least retort to any one, even as the new Lawgiver commanded us: how is it, Trypho, that we would not observe those rites which do not harm us,--I speak of fleshly circumcision, and Sabbaths, and feasts?

CHAPTER XIX -- CIRCUMCISION UNKNOWN BEFORE ABRAHAM. THE LAW WAS GIVEN BY MOSES ON ACCOUNT OF THE HARDNESS OF THEIR HEARTS.

"It is this about which we are at a loss, and with reason, because, while you endure such things, you do not observe all the other customs which we are now discussing."

"This circumcision is not, however, necessary for all men, but for you alone, in order that, as I have already said, you may suffer these things which you now justly suffer. Nor do we receive that useless baptism of cisterns, for it has nothing to do with this baptism of life. Wherefore also God has announced that you have forsaken Him, the living fountain, and digged for your selves broken cisterns which can hold no water. Even you, who are the circumcised according to the flesh, have need of our circumcision; but we, having the latter, do not require the former. For if it were necessary, as you suppose, God would not have made Adam uncircumcised would not have had respect to the gifts of Abel when, being uncircumcised, he offered sacrifice and would not have been pleased with the uncircumcision of Enoch, who was not found, because God had translated him. Lot, being uncircumcised, was saved from Sodom, the angels themselves and the Lord sending him out. Noah was the beginning of our race; yet, uncircumcised, along with his children he went into the ark. Melchizedek, the priest of the Most High, was uncircumcised; to whom also Abraham the first who received circumcision after the flesh, gave tithes, and he blessed him: after whose order God declared, by the mouth of David, that He would establish the everlasting priest. Therefore to you alone this circumcision was necessary, in order that the people may be no people, and the nation no nation; as also Hosea, one of the twelve prophets, declares. Moreover, all those righteous men already mentioned, though they kept no Sabbaths, were pleasing to God; and after them Abraham with all his descendants until Moses, under whom your nation appeared unrighteous and ungrateful to God, making a calf in the wilderness: wherefore God, accommodating Himself to that nation, enjoined them also to offer sacrifices, as if to His name, in order that you might not serve idols. Which precept, however, you have not observed; nay, you sacrificed your children to demons. And you were commanded to keep Sabbaths, that you might retain the memorial of God. For His word makes this announcement, saying, 'That ye may know that I am God who redeemed you.'

CHAPTER XX -- WHY CHOICE OF MEATS WAS PRESCRIBED.

"Moreover, you were commanded to abstain from certain kinds of food, in order that you might keep God before your eyes while you ate and drank, seeing that you were prone and very ready to depart from His knowledge, as Moses also affirms: 'The people ate and drank, and rose up to play.' And again: 'Jacob ate, and was satisfied, and waxed fat; and he who was beloved kicked: he waxed fat, he grew thick, he was enlarged, and he forsook God who had made him.' For it was told you by Moses in the book of Genesis, that God granted to Noah, being a just man, to eat of every animal, but not of flesh with the blood, which is dead." And as he was ready to say, "as the green herbs," I anticipated him: "Why do you not receive this statement, 'as the green herbs,' in the sense in which it was given by God, to wit, that just as God has granted the herbs for sustenance to man, even so has He given the animals for the diet of flesh? But, you say, a distinction was laid down thereafter to Noah, because we do not eat certain herbs. As you interpret it, the thing is incredible. And first I shall not occupy myself with this, though able to say and to hold that every vegetable is food, and fit to be eaten. But although we discriminate between green herbs, not eating all, we refrain from eating some, not because they are common or unclean, but because they are bitter, or deadly, or thorny. But we lay hands on and take of all herbs which are sweet, very nourishing and good, whether they are marine or land plants. Thus also God by the mouth of Moses commanded you to abstain from unclean and improper and violent animals: when, moreover, though you were eating manna in the desert, and were seeing all those wondrous acts wrought for you by God, you made and worshipped the golden calf. Hence he cries continually, and justly, 'They are foolish children, in whom is no faith.'

CHAPTER XXI -- SABBATHS WERE INSTITUTED ON ACCOUNT OF THE PEOPLE'S SINS, AND NOT FOR A WORK OF RIGHTEOUSNESS.

"Moreover, that God enjoined you to keep the Sabbath, and impose on you other precepts for a sign, as I have already said, on account of your unrighteousness, and that of your fathers,--as He declares that for the sake of the nations, lest His name be profaned among them, therefore He permitted some of you to remain alive,--these words of His can prove to you: they are narrated by Ezekiel thus: I am the Lord your God; walk in My statutes, and keep My judgments, and take no part in the customs of Egypt; and hallow My Sabbaths; and they shall be a sign between Me and you, that ye may know that I am the Lord your God. Notwithstanding ye rebelled against Me, and your children walked not in My statutes, neither kept My judgments to do them: which if a man do, he shall live in them. But they polluted My Sabbaths. And I said that I would pour out My fury upon them in the wilderness, to accomplish My anger upon them; yet I did it not; that My name might not be altogether profaned in the sight of the heathen. I led them out before their eyes, and I lifted up Mine hand unto them in the wilderness, that I would scatter them among the heathen, and disperse them through the countries; because they had not executed My judgments, but had despised My statutes, and polluted My Sabbaths, and their eyes were after the devices of their fathers. Wherefore I gave them also statutes which were not good, and judgments whereby they shall not live. And I shall pollute them in their own gifts, that I may destroy all that openeth the womb, when I pass through them.'

CHAPTER XXII -- SO ALSO WERE SACRIFICES AND OBLATIONS.

"And that you may learn that it was for the sins of your own nation, and for their idolatries and not because there was any necessity for such sacrifices, that they were likewise enjoined, listen to the manner in which He speaks of these by Amos, one of the twelve, saying: 'Woe unto you that desire the day of the Lord! to what end is this day of the Lord for you? It is darkness and not light, as when a man flees from the face of a lion, and a bear meets him; and he goes into his house, and leans his hands against the wall, and the serpent bites him. Shall not the day of the Lord be darkness and not light, even very dark, and no brightness in it? I have hated, I have despised your feast-days, and I will not smell in your solemn assemblies: wherefore, though ye offer Me your burnt-offerings and sacrifices, I will not accept them; neither will I regard the peace-offerings of your presence. Take thou away from Me the multitude of thy songs and psalms; I will not hear thine instruments. But let judgment be rolled down as water, and righteousness as an impassable torrent. Have ye offered unto Me victims and sacrifices in the wilderness, O house of Israel? saith the Lord. And have ye taken up the tabernacle of Moloch, and the star of your god Raphan, the figures which ye made for yourselves? And I will carry you away beyond Damascus, saith the Lord, whose name is the Almighty God. Woe to them that are at ease in Zion, and trust in the mountain of Samaria: those who are named among the chiefs have plucked away the first-fruits of the nations: the house of Israel have entered for themselves. Pass all of you unto Calneh, and see; and from thence go ye unto Hamath the great, and go down thence to Gath of the strangers, the noblest of all these kingdoms, if their boundaries are greater than your boundaries. Ye who come to the evil day, who are approaching, and who hold to false Sabbaths; who lie on beds of ivory, and are at ease upon their couches; who eat the lambs out of the flock, and the sucking calves out of the midst of the herd; who applaud at the sound of the musical instruments; they reckon them as stable, and not as fleeting, who drink wine in bowls, and anoint themselves with the chief ointments, but they are not grieved for the affliction of Joseph. Wherefore now they shall be captives, among the first of the nobles who are carried away; and the house of evil-doers shall be removed, and the neighing of horses shall be taken away from Ephraim. And again by Jeremiah: 'Collect your flesh, and sacrifices, and eat: for concerning neither sacrifices nor libations did I command your fathers in the day in which I took them by the hand to lead them out of Egypt. And again by David, in the forty-ninth Psalm, He thus said: 'The God of gods, the Lord hath spoken, and called the earth, from the rising of the sun unto the going down thereof. Out of Zion is the perfection of His beauty. God, even our God, shall come openly, and shall not keep silence. Fire shall burn before Him, and it shall be very temptestuous round about Him. He shall call to the heavens above, and to the earth, that He may judge His people. Assemble to Him His saints; those that have made a covenant with Him by sacrifices. And the heavens shall declare His righteousness, for God is judge. Hear, O My people, and I will speak to thee; O Israel, and I will testify to thee, I am God, even thy God. I will not reprove thee for thy sacrifices; thy burnt-offerings are continually before me. I will take no bullocks out of thy house, nor he-goats out of thy folds: for all the beasts of the field are Mine, the herds and the oxen on the mountains. I know all the fowls of the heavens, and the beauty of the field is Mine. If I were hungry, I would not tell thee; for the world is Mine, and the fulness thereof. Will I eat the flesh of bulls, or drink the blood of goats? Offer unto God the sacrifice of praise, and pay thy vows unto the Most High, and call upon Me in the day of trouble, and I will deliver thee, and thou shalt glorify Me. But unto the wicked God saith, What hast thou to do to declare My statutes, and to take My covenant into thy mouth? But thou hast hated instruction, and cast My words behind thee. When thou sawest a thief, thou consentedst with him; and hast been partaker with the adulterer. Thy mouth has framed evil, and thy tongue has enfolded deceit. Thou sittest and speakest against thy brother; thou slanderest thine own mother's son. These things hast thou done, and I kept silence; thou thoughtest that I would be like thyself in wickedness. I will reprove thee, and set thy sins in order before thine eyes. Now consider this, ye that forget God, lest He tear you in pieces, and there be none to deliver. The sacrifice of praise shall glorify Me; and there is the way in which I shall show him My salvation. Accordingly He neither takes sacrifices from you nor commanded them at first to be offered because they are needful to Him, but because of your sins. For indeed the temple, which is called the temple in Jerusalem, He admitted to be His house or court, not as though He needed it, but in order that you, in this view of it, giving yourselves to Him, might not worship idols. And that this is so, Isaiah says: 'What house have ye built Me? saith the Lord. Heaven is My throne, and earth is My footstool.'

CHAPTER XXXIII -- THE OPINION OF THE JEWS REGARDING THE LAW DOES AN INJURY TO GOD.

"But if we do not admit this, we shall be liable to fall into foolish opinions, as if it were not the same God who existed in the times of Enoch and all the rest, who neither were circumcised after the flesh, nor observed Sabbaths, nor any other rites, seeing that Moses enjoined such observances; or that God has not wished each race of mankind continually to perform the same righteous actions: to admit which, seems to be ridiculous and absurd. Therefore we must confess that He, who is ever the same, has commanded these and such like institutions on account of sinful men, and we must declare Him to be benevolent, foreknowing, needing nothing, righteous and good. But if this be not so, tell me, sir, what you think of those matters which we are investigating." And when no one responded: "Wherefore, Trypho, I will proclaim to you, and to those who wish to become proselytes, the divine message which I heard from that man. Do you see that the elements are not idle, and keep no Sabbaths? Remain as you were born. For if there was no need of circumcision before Abraham, or Of the observance of Sabbaths, of feasts and sacrifices, before Moses; no more need is there of them now, after that, according to the will of God, Jesus Christ the Son of God has been born without sin, of a virgin sprung from the stock of Abraham. For when Abraham himself was in un-circumcision, he was justified and blessed by reason of the faith which he reposed in God, as the Scripture tells. Moreover, the Scriptures and the facts themselves compel us to admit that He received circumcision for a sign, and not for righteousness. So that it was justly recorded concerning the people, that the soul which shall not be circumcised on the eighth day shall be cut off from his family. And, furthermore, the inability of the female sex to receive fleshly circumcision, proves that this circumcision has been given for a sign, and not for a work of righteousness. For God has given likewise to women the ability to observe all things which are righteous and virtuous; but we see that the bodily form of the male has been made different from the bodily form of the female; yet we know that neither of them is righteous or unrighteous merely for this cause, but [is considered righteous] by reason of piety and righteousness.

CHAPTER XXIV -- THE CHRISTIANS' CIRCUMCISION FAR MORE EXCELLENT.

"Now, sirs," I said, "it is possible for us to show how the eighth day possessed a certain mysterious import, which the seventh day did not possess, and which was promulgated by God through these rites. But lest I appear now to diverge to other subjects, understand what I say: the blood of that circumcision is obsolete, and we trust in the bloOd of salvation; there is now another covenant, and another law has gone forth from Zion. Jesus Christ circumcises all who will--as was declared above--with knives of stone; that they may be a righteous nation, a people keeping faith, holding to the truth, and maintaining peace. Come then with me, all who fear God, who wish to see the good of Jerusalem. Come, let us go to the light of the Lord; for He has liberated His people, the house of Jacob. Come, all nations; let us gather ourselves together at Jerusalem, no longer plagued by war for the sins of her people. 'For I was manifest to them that sought Me not; I was found of them that asked not for Me;' He exclaims by Isaiah: 'I said, Behold Me, unto nations which were not called by My name. I have spread out My hands all the day unto a disobedient and gainsaying people, which walked in a way that was not good, but after their own sins. It is a people that rovoketh Me to my face.'

CHAPTER XXV -- THE JEWS BOAST IN VAIN THAT THEY ARE SONS OF ABRAHAM.

"Those who justify themselves, and say they are sons of Abraham, shall be desirous even in a small degree to receive the inheritance along with you; as the Holy Spirit, by the mouth of Isaiah, cries, speaking thus while he personates them: 'Return from heaven, and behold from the habitation of Thy holiness and glory. Where is Thy zeal and strength? Where is the multitude of Thy mercy? for Thou hast sustained us, O Lord. For Thou art our Father, because Abraham is ignorant of us, and Israel has not recognised us. But Thou, O Lord, our Father, deliver us: from the beginning Thy name is upon us. O Lord, why hast Thou made us to err from Thy way? and hardened our hearts, so that we do not fear Thee? Return for Thy servants' sake, the tribes of Thine inheritance, that we may inherit for a little Thy holy mountain. We were as from the beginning, when Thou didst not bear rule over us, and when Thy name was not called upon us. If Thou wilt open the heavens, trembling shall seize the mountains before Thee: and they shall be melted, as wax melts before the fire; and fire shah consume the adversaries, and Thy name shall be manifest among the adversaries; the nations shall be put into disorder before Thy face. When Thou shall do glorious things, trembling shall seize the mountains before Thee. From the beginning we have not heard, nor have our eyes seen a God besides Thee: and Thy works, the mercy which Thou shall show to those who repent. He shall meet those who do righteousness, and they shall remember Thy ways. Behold, Thou art wroth, and we were sinning. Therefore we have erred and become all unclean, and all our righteousness is as the rags of a woman set apart: and we have faded away like leaves by reason of our iniquities; thus the wind will take us away. And there is none that calleth upon Thy name, or remembers to take hold of Thee; for Thou hast turned away Thy face from us, and hast given us up on account of our sins. And now return, O Lord, for we are all Thy people. The city of Thy holiness has become desolate. Zion has become as a wilderness, Jerusalem a curse; the house, our holiness, and the glory which our fathers blessed, has been burned with fire; and all the glorious nations have fallen along with it. And in addition to these [misfortunes], O Lord, Thou hast refrained Thyself, and art silent, and hast humbled us very much.'"

And Trypho remarked, "What is this you say? that none of us shall inherit anything on the holy mountain of God?"

CHAPTER XXVI -- NO SALVATION TO THE JEWS EXCEPT THROUGH CHRIST.

And I replied, "I do not say so; but those who have persecuted and do persecute Christ, if they do not repent, shall not inherit anything on the holy mountain. But the Gentiles, who have believed on Him, and have repented of the sins which they have committed, they shall receive the inheritance along with the patriarchs and the prophets, and the just men who are descended from Jacob, even although they neither keep the Sabbath, nor are circumcised, nor observe the feasts. Assuredly they shall receive the holy inheritance of God. For God speaks by Isaiah thus: 'I, the Lord God, have called Thee in righteousness, and will hold Thine hand, and will strengthen Thee; and I have given Thee for a covenant of the people, for a light of the Gentiles, to open the eyes of the blind, to bring out them that are bound from the chains, and those who sit in darkness from the prison-house.' And again: 'Lift up a standard s for the people; for, lo, the Lord has made it heard unto the end of the earth. Say ye to the daughters of Zion, Behold, thy Saviour has come; having His reward, and His work before His face: and He shall call it a holy nation, redeemed by the Lord. And thou shalt be called a city sought out, and not forsaken. Who is this that cometh from Edom? in red garments from Bosor? This that is beautiful in apparel, going up with great strength? I speak righteousness, and the judgment of salvation. Why are Thy garments red, and Thine apparel as from the trodden wine-press? Thou art full of the trodden grape. I have trodden the wine-press all alone, and of the people there is no man with Me; and I have trampled them in fury, and crushed them to the ground, and spilled their blood on the earth. For the day of retribution has come upon them, and the year of redemption is present. And I looked, and there was none to help; and I considered, and none assisted: and My arm delivered; and My fury came on them, and I trampled them in My fury, and spilled their blood on the earth.'"

CHAPTER XXVII -- WHY GOD TAUGHT THE SAME THINGS BY THE PROPHETS AS BY MOSES.

And Trypho said, "Why do you select and quote whatever you wish from the prophetic writings, but do not refer to those which expressly command the Sabbath to be observed? For Isaiah thus speaks: 'If thou shalt turn away thy foot from the Sabbaths, so as not to do thy pleasure on the holy day, and shalt call the Sabbaths the holy delights of thy God; if thou shalt not lift thy foot to work, and shalt not speak a word from thine own mouth; then thou shalt trust in the Lord, and He shall cause thee to go up to the good things of the land; and He shall feed thee with the inheritance of Jacob thy father: for the mouth of the Lord hath spoken it.'"

And I replied, "I have passed them by, my friends, not because such prophecies were contrary to me, but because you have understood, and do understand, that although God commands you by all the prophets to do the same things which He also commanded by Moses, it was on account of the hardness of your hearts, and your ingratitude towards Him, that He continually proclaims them, in order that, even in this way, if you repented, you might please Him, and neither sacrifice your children to demons, nor be partakers with thieves, nor lovers of gifts, nor hunters after revenge, nor fail in doing judgment for orphans, nor be inattentive to the justice due to the widow nor have your hands full of blood. 'For the daughters of Zion have walked with a high neck, both sporting by winking with their eyes, and sweeping along their dresses. For they are all gone aside,' He exclaims, 'they are all become useless. There is none that understands, there is not so much as one. With their tongues they have practised deceit, their throat is an open sepulchre, the poison of asps is under their lips, destruction and misery are in their paths, and the way of peace they have not known.' So that, as in the beginning, these things were enjoined you because of your wickedness, in like manner because of your stedfastness in it, or rather your increased proneness to it, by means of the same precepts He calls you to a remembrance or knowledge of it. But you are a people hard-hearted and without understanding, both blind and lame, children in whom is no faith, as He Himself says, honouring Him only with your lips, far from Him in your hearts, teaching doctrines that are your own and not His. For, tell me, did God wish the priests to sin when they offer the sacrifices on the Sabbaths? or those to sin, who are circumcised and do circumcise on the Sabbaths; since He commands that on the eighth day--even though it happen to be a Sabbath--those who are born shall be always circumcised? or could not the infants be operated upon one day previous or one day subsequent to the Sabbath, if He knew that it is a sinful act upon the Sabbaths? Or why did He not teach those--who are called righteous and pleasing to Him, who lived before Moses and Abraham, who were not circumcised in their foreskin, and observed no Sabbaths--to keep these institutions?"

CHAPTER XXVIII -- TRUE RIGHTEOUSNESS IS OBTAINED BY CHRIST.

And Trypho replied, "We heard you adducing this consideration a little ago, and we have given it attention: for, to tell the truth, it is worthy of attention; and that answer which pleases most--namely, that so it seemed good to Him--does not satisfy me. For this is ever the shift to which those have recourse who are unable to answer the question."

Then I said, "Since I bring from the Scriptures and the facts themselves both the proofs and the inculcation of them, do not delay or hesitate to put faith in me, although I am an uncircumcised man; so short a time is left you in which to become proselytes. If Christ's coming shall have anticipated you, in vain you will repent, in vain you will weep; for He will not hear yon. 'Break up your fallow ground,' Jeremiah has cried to the people, 'and sow not among thorns. Circumcise yourselves to the Lord, and circumcise the foreskin of your heart.' Do not sow, therefore, among thorns, and in untilled ground, whence you can have no fruit. Know Christ; and behold the fallow ground, good, good and fat, is in your hearts. 'For, behold, the days come, saith the Lord, that I will visit all them that are circumcised in their foreskins; Egypt, and Judah, and Edom, and the sons of Moab. For all the nations are uncircumcised, and all the house of Israel are uncircumcised in their hearts.' Do you see how that God does not mean this circumcision which is given for a sign? For it is of no use to the Egyptians, or the sons of Moab, or the sons of Edom. But though a man be a Scythian or a Persian, if he has the knowledge of God and of His Christ, and keeps the everlasting righteous decrees, he is circumcised with the good and useful circumcision, and is a friend of God, and God rejoices in his gifts and offerings. But I will lay before you, my friends, the very words of God, when He said to the people by Malachi, one of the twelve prophets, 'I have no pleasure in you, saith the Lord; and I shall not accept your sacrifices at your hands: for from the rising of the sun unto its setting My name shall be glorified among the Gentiles; and in every place a sacrifice is offered unto My name, even a pure sacrifice: for My name is honoured among the Gentiles, saith the Lord; but ye profane it.' And by David He said, 'A people whom I have not known, served Me; at the hearing of the ear they obeyed Me.'

CHAPTER XXIX -- CHRIST IS USELESS TO THOSE WHO OBSERVE THE LAW.

"Let us glorify God, all nations gathered together; for He has also visited us. Let us glorify Him by the King of glory, by the Lord of hosts. For He has been gracious towards the Gentiles also; and our sacrifices He esteems more grateful than yours. What need, then, have I of circumcision, who have been witnessed to by God? What need have I of that other baptism, who have been baptized with the Holy Ghost? I think that while I mention this, I would persuade even those who are possessed of scanty intelligence. For these words have neither been prepared by me, nor embellished by the art of man; but David sung them, Isaiah preached them, Zechariah proclaimed them, and Moses wrote them. Are you acquainted with them, Trypho? They are contained in your Scriptures, or rather not yours, but ours. For we believe them; but you, though you read them, do not catch the spirit that is in them. Be not offended at, or reproach us with, the bodily uncircumcision with which God has created us; and think it not strange that we drink hot water on the Sabbaths, since God directs the government of the universe on this day equally as on all others; and the priests, as on other days, so on this, are ordered to offer sacrifices; and there are so many righteous men who have performed none of these legal ceremonies, and yet are witnessed to by God Himself.

CHAPTER XXX -- CHRISTIANS POSSESS THE TRUE RIGHTEOUSNESS.

"But impute it to your own wickedness, that God even can be accused by those who have no understanding, of not having always instructed all in the same righteous statutes. For such institutions seemed to be unreasonable and unworthy of God to many men, who had not received grace to know that your nation were called to conversion and repentance of spirit, while they were in a sinful condition and labouring under spiritual disease; and that the prophecy which was announced subsequent to the death of Moses is everlasting. And this is mentioned in the Psalm, my friends. And that we, who have been made wise by them, confess that the statutes of the Lord are sweeter than honey and the honey-comb, is manifest from the fact that, though threatened with death, we do not deny His name. Moreover, it is also manifest to all, that we who believe in Him pray to be kept by Him from strange, i.e., from wicked and deceitful, spirits; as the word of prophecy, personating one of those who believe in Him, figuratively declares. For we do continually beseech God by Jesus Christ to preserve us from the demons which are hostile to the worship of God, and whom we of old time served, in order that, after our conversion by Him to God, we may be blameless. For we call Him Helper and Redeemer, the power of whose name even the demons do fear; and at this day, when they are exorcised in the name of Jesus Christ, crucified under Pontius Pilate, governor of Judaea, they are overcome. And thus it is manifest to all, that His Father has given Him so great power, by virtue of which demons are subdued to His name, and to the dispensation of His suffering.

CHAPTER XXXI -- IF CHRIST'S POWER BE NOW SO GREAT, HOW MUCH GREATER AT THE SECOND ADVENT!

"But if so great a power is shown to have followed and to be still following the dispensation of His suffering, how great shall that be which shall follow His glorious advent! For He shall come on the clouds as the Son of man, so Daniel foretold, and His angels shall come with Him. These are the words: 'I beheld till the thrones were set; and the Ancient of days did sit, whose garment was white as snow, and the hair of His head like the pure wool. His throne was like a fiery flame, His wheels as burning fire. A fiery stream issued and came forth from before Him. Thousand thousands ministered unto Him, and ten thousand times ten thousand stood before Him. The books were opened, and the judgment was set. I beheld then the voice of the great words which the horn speaks: and the beast was beat down, and his body destroyed, and given to the burning flame. And the rest of the beasts were taken away from their dominion, and a period of life was given to the beasts until a season and time. I saw in the vision of the night, and, behold, one like the Son of man coming with the clouds of heaven; and He came to the Ancient of days, and stood before Him. And they who stood by brought Him near; and there were given Him power and kingly honour, and all nations of the earth by their families, and all glory, serve Him. And His dominion is an everlasting dominion, which shall not be taken away; and His kingdom shall not be destroyed. And my spirit was chilled within my frame, and the visions of my head troubled me. I came near unto one of them that stood by, and inquired the precise meaning of all these things. In answer he speaks to me, and showed me the judgment of the matters: These great beasts are four kingdoms, which shall perish from the earth, and shall not receive dominion for ever, even for ever and ever. Then I wished to know exactly about the fourth beast, which destroyed all [the others] and was very terrible, its teeth of iron, and its nails of brass; which devoured, made waste, and stamped the residue with its feet: also about the ten horns upon its head, and of the one which came up, by means of which three of the former fell. And that horn had eyes, and a mouth speaking great things; and its countenance excelled the rest. And I beheld that horn waging war against the saints, and prevailing against them, until the Ancient of days came; and He gave judgment for the saints of the Most High. And the time came, and the saints of the Most High possessed the kingdom. And it was told me concerning the fourth beast: There shall be a fourth kingdom upon earth, which shall prevail over all these kingdoms, and shall devour the whole earth, and shall destroy and make it thoroughly waste. And the ten horns are ten kings that shall arise; and one shall arise after them; and he shall surpass the first in evil deeds, and he shall subdue three kings, and he shall speak words against the Most High, and shall overthrow the rest of the saints of the Most High, and shall expect to change the seasons and the times. And it shall be delivered into his hands for a time, and times, and half a time. And the judgment sat, and they shall take away his dominion, to consume and to destroy it unto the end. And the kingdom, and the power, and the great places of the kingdoms under the heavens, were given to the holy people of the Most High, to reign in an everlasting kingdom: and all powers shall be subject to Him, and shall obey Him. Hitherto is the end of the matter. I, Daniel, was possessed with a very great astonishment, and my speech was changed in me; yet I kept the matter in my heart.'"

CHAPTER XXXII -- TRYPHO OBJECTING THAT CHRIST IS DESCRIBED AS GLORIOUS BY DANIEL, JUSTIN DISTINGUISHES TWO ADVENTS.

And when I had ceased, Trypho said, "These and such like Scriptures, sir, compel us to wait for Him who, as Son of man, receives from the Ancient of days the everlasting kingdom. But this so-called Christ of yours was dishonourable and inglorious, so much so that the last curse contained in the law of God fell on him, for he was crucified."

Then I replied to him, "If, sirs, it were not said by the Scriptures which I have already quoted, that His form was inglorious, and His generation not declared, and that for His death the rich would suffer death, and with His stripes we should be healed, and that He would be led away like a sheep; and if I had not explained that there would be two advents of His,--one in which He was pierced by you; a second, when you shall know Him whom you have pierced, and your tribes shall mourn, each tribe by itself, the women apart, and the men apart, --then I must have been speaking dubious and obscure things. But now, by means of the contents of those Scriptures esteemed holy and prophetic amongst you, I attempt to prove all [that I have adduced], in the hope that some one of you may be found to be of that remnant which has been left by the grace of the Lord of Sabaoth for the eternal salvation. In order, therefore, that the matter inquired into may be plainer to you, I will mention to you other words also spoken by the blessed David, from which you will perceive that the Lord is called the Christ by the Holy Spirit of prophecy; and that the Lord, the Father of all, has brought Him again from the earth, setting Him at His own right hand, until He makes His enemies His footstool; which indeed happens from the time that our Lord Jesus Christ ascended to heaven, after He rose again from the dead, the times now running on to their consummation; and he whom Daniel foretells would have dominion for a time, and times, and an half, is even already at the door, about to speak blasphemous and daring things against the Most High. But you, being ignorant of how long he will have dominion, hold another opinion. For you interpret the 'time' as being a hundred years. But if this is so, the man of sin must, at the shortest, reign three hundred and fifty years, in order that we may compute that which is said by the holy Daniel--'and times'--to be two times only. All this I have said to you in digression, in order that you at length may be persuaded of what has been declared against you by God, that you are foolish sons; and of this, 'Therefore, behold, I will proceed to take away this people, and shall take them away; and I will strip the wise of their wisdom, and will hide the understanding of their prudent men;' and may cease to deceive yourselves and those who hear you, and may learn of us, who have been taught wisdom by the grace of Christ. The words, then, which were spoken by David, are these: 'The Lord said unto My Lord, Sit Thou at My right hand, until I make Thine enemies Thy footstool. The Lord shall send the rod of Thy strength out of Sion: rule Thou also in the midst of Thine enemies. With Thee shall be, in the day, the chief of Thy power, in the beauties of Thy saints. From the womb, before the morning star, have I begotten Thee. The Lord hath sworn, and will not repent: Thou art a priest for ever after the order of Melchizedek. The Lord is at Thy right hand: He has crushed kings in the day of His wrath: He shall judge among the heathen, He shall fill [with] the dead bodies. He shall drink of the brook in the way; therefore shall He lift up the head.'

CHAPTER XXXIII -- PS, CX. IS NOT SPOKEN OF HEZEKIAH. HE PROVES THAT CHRIST WAS FIRST HUMBLE, THEN SHALL BE GLORIOUS.

"And," I continued, "I am not ignorant that you venture to expound this psalm as if it referred to king Hezekiah; but that you arc mistaken, I shall prove to you from these very words forthwith. 'The Lord hath sworn, and will not repent,' it is said; and, 'Thou art a priest for ever, after the order of Melchizedek,' with what follows and precedes. Not even you will venture to object that Hezekiah was either a priest, or is the everlasting priest of God; but that this is spoken of our Jesus, these expressions show. But your ears are shut up, and your hearts are made dull. For by this statement, 'The Lord hath sworn, and will not repent: Thou art a priest for ever, after the order of Melchizedek,' with an oath God has shown Him (on account of your unbelief) to be the High Priest after the order of Melchizedek; i.e., as Melchizedek was described by Moses as the priest of the Most High, and he was a priest of those who were in uncircumcision, and blessed the circumcised Abraham who brought him tithes, so God has shown that His everlasting Priest, called also by the Hold Spirit Lord, would be Priest of those in uncircumcision. Those too in circumcision who approach Him, that is, believing Him and seeking blessings from Him, He will both receive and bless. And that He shall be first humble as a man, and then exalted, these words at the end of the Psalm show: 'He shall drink of the brook in the way,' and then, 'Therefore shall He lift up the head.'

CHAPTER XXXIV -- NOR DOES PS. LXXII. APPLY TO SOLOMON, WHOSE FAULTS CHRISTIANS SHUDDER AT.

"Further, to persuade you that you have not understood anything of the Scriptures, I will remind you of another psalm, dictated to David by the Holy Spirit, which you say refers to Solomon, who was also your king. But it refers also to our Christ. But you deceive yourselves by the ambiguous forms of speech. For where it is said, 'The law of the Lord is perfect,' you do not understand it of the law which was to be after Moses, but of the law which was given by Moses, although God declared that He would establish a new law and a new covenant. And where it has been said, 'O God, give Thy judgment to the king,' since Solomon was king, you say that the Psalm refers to him, although the words of the Psalm expressly proclaim that reference is made to the everlasting King, i.e., to Christ. For Christ is King, and Priest, and God, and Lord, and angel, and man, and captain, and stone, and a Son born, and first made subject to suffering, then returning to heaven, and again coming with glory, and He is preached as having the everlasting kingdom: so I prove from all the Scriptures. But that you may perceive what I have said, I quote the words of the Psalm; they are these: 'O God, give Thy judgment to the king, and Thy righteousness unto the king's son, to judge Thy people with righteousness, and Thy poor with judgment. The mountains shall take up peace to the people, and the little hills righteousness. He shall judge the poor of the people, and shah save the children of the needy, and shall abase the slanderer. He shall co-endure with the sun, and before the moon unto all generations. He shall come down like rain upon the fleece, as drops falling on the earth. In His days shall righteousness flourish, and abundance of peace until the moon be taken away. And He shall have dominion from sea to sea, and from the rivers unto the ends of the earth. Ethiopians shall fall down before Him, and His enemies shall lick the dust. The kings of Tarshish and the isles shall offer gifts; the kings of Arabia and Seba shall offer gifts; and all the kings of the earth shall worship Him, and all the nations shall serve Him: for He has delivered the poor from the man of power, and the needy that hath no helper. He shall spare the poor and needy, and shall save the souls of the needy: He shall redeem their souls from usury and injustice, and His name shall be honourable before them. And He shall live, and to Him shall be given of the gold of Arabia, and they shall pray continually for Him: they shall bless Him all the day. And there shall be a foundation on the earth, it shall be exalted on the tops of the mountains: His fruit shall be on Lebanon, and they of the city shall flourish like grass of the earth. His name shah be blessed for ever. His name shall endure before the sun; and all tribes of the earth shall be blessed in Him, all nations shall call Him blessed. Blessed be the Lord, the God of Israel, who only doeth wondrous things; and blessed be His glorious name for ever, and for ever and ever; and the whole earth shall be filled with His glory. Amen, amen.' And at the close of this Psalm which I have quoted, it is written, 'The hymns of David the son of Jesse are ended.' Moreover, that Solomon was a renowned and great king, by whom the temple called that at Jerusalem was built, I know; but that none of those things mentioned in the Psalm happened to him, is evident. For neither did all kings worship him; nor did he reign to the ends of the earth; nor did his enemies, failing before him, lick the dust. Nay, also, I venture to repeat what is written in the book of Kings as committed by him, how through a woman's influence he worshipped the idols of Sidon, which those of the Gentiles who know God, the Maker of all things through Jesus the crucified, do not venture to do, but abide every torture and vengeance even to the extremity of death, rather than worship idols, or eat meat offered to idols."

CHAPTER XXXV -- HERETICS CONFIRM THE CATHOLICS IN THE FAITH.

And Trypho said, "I believe, however, that many of those who say that they confess Jesus, and are called Christians, eat meats offered to idols, and declare that they are by no means injured in consequence." And I replied, "The fact that there are such men confessing themselves to be Christians, and admitting the crucified Jesus to be both Lord and Christ, yet not teaching His doctrines, but those of the spirits of error, causes us who are disciples of the true and pure doctrine of Jesus Christ, to be more faithful and stedfast in the hope announced by Him. For what things He predicted would take place in His name, these we do see being actually accomplished in our sight. For he said, 'Many shall come in My name, clothed outwardly in sheep's clothing, but inwardly they are ravening wolves." And, 'There shall be schisms and heresies.' And, 'Beware of false prophets, who shall come to you clothed outwardly in sheep's clothing, but inwardly they are ravening wolves.' And, 'Many false Christs and false apostles shall arise, and shall deceive many of the faithful.' There are, therefore, and there were many, my friends, who, coming forward in the name of Jesus, taught both to speak and act impious and blasphemous things; and these are called by us after the name of the men from whom each doctrine and opinion had its origin. (For some in one way, others in another, teach to blaspheme the Maker of all things, and Christ, who was foretold by Him as coming, and the God of Abraham, and of Isaac, and of Jacob, with whom we have nothing in common, since we know them to be atheists, impious, unrighteous, and sinful, and confessors of Jesus in name only, instead of worshippers of Him. Yet they style themselves Christians, just as certain among the Gentiles inscribe the name of God upon the works of their own hands, and partake in nefarious and impious rites.) Some are called Marcians, and some Valentinians, and some Basilidians, and some Saturnilians, and others by other names; each called after the originator of the individual opinion, just as each one of those who consider themselves philosophers, as I said before, thinks he must bear the name of the philosophy which he follows, from the name of the father of the particular doctrine. So that, in consequence of these events, we know that Jesus foreknew what would happen after Him, as well as in consequence of many other events which He foretold would befall those who believed on and confessed Him, the Christ. For all that we suffer, even when killed by friends, He foretold would take place; so that it is manifest no word or act of His can be found fault with. Wherefore we pray for you and for all other men who hate us; in order that you, having repented along with us, may not blaspheme Him who, by His works, by the mighty deeds even now wrought through His name, by the words He taught, by the prophecies announced concerning Him, is the blameless, and in all things irreproachable, Christ Jesus; but, believing on Him, may be saved in His second glorious advent, and may not be condemned to fire by Him."

CHAPTER XXXVI -- HE PROVES THAT CHRIST IS CALLED LORD OF HOSTS.

Then he replied, "Let these things be so as you say--namely, that it was foretold Christ would suffer, and be called a stone; and after His first appearance, in which it had been announced He would suffer, would come in glory, and be Judge finally of all, and eternal King and Priest. Now show if this man be He of whom these prophecies were made."

And I said, "As you wish, Trypho, I shall come to these proofs which you seek in the fitting place; but now you will permit me first to recount the prophecies, which I wish to do in order to prove that Christ is called both God and Lord of hosts, and Jacob, in parable by the Holy Spirit; and your interpreters, as God says, are foolish, since they say that reference is made to Solomon and not to Christ, when he bore the ark of testimony into the temple which he built. The Psalm of David is this: 'The earth is the Lord's, and the fulness thereof; the world, and all that dwell therein. He hath rounded it upon the seas, and prepared it upon the floods. Who shall ascend into the hill of the Lord? or who shall stand in His holy place? He that is clean of hands and pure of heart: who has not received his soul in vain, and has not sworn guilefully to his neighbour: he shall receive blessing from the Lord, and mercy from God his Saviour. This is the generation of them that seek the Lord, that seek the face of the God of Jacob. Lift up your gates, ye rulers; and be ye lift up, ye everlasting doors; and the King of glory shall come in. Who is this King of glory? The Lord strong and mighty in battle. Lift up your gates, ye rulers; and be ye lift up, ye everlasting doors; and the King of glory shall come in. Who is this King of glory? The Lord of hosts, He is the King of glory.' Accordingly, it is shown that Solomon is not the Lord of hosts; but when our Christ rose from the dead and ascended to heaven, the rulers in heaven, under appointment of

God, are commanded to open the gates of heaven, that He who is King of glory may enter in, and having ascended, may sit on the right hand of the Father until He make the enemies His footstool, as has been made manifest by another Psalm. For when the rulers of heaven saw Him of uncomely and dishonoured appearance, and inglorious, not recognising Him, they inquired, 'Who is this King of glory?' And the Holy Spirit, either from the person of His Father, or from His own person, answers them, 'The Lord of hosts, He is this King of glory.' For every one will confess that not one of those who presided over the gates of the temple at Jerusalem would venture to say concerning Solomon, though he was so glorious a king, or concerning the ark of testimony, 'Who is this King of glory?'

CHAPTER XXXVII -- THE SAME IS PROVED FROM OTHER PSALMS.

"Moreover, in the diapsalm of the forty-sixth Psalm, reference is thus made to Christ: 'God went up with a shout, the Lord with the sound of a trumpet. Sing ye to our God, sing ye: sing to our King, sing ye; for God is King of all the earth: sing with understanding. God has ruled over the nations. God sits upon His holy throne. The rulers of the nations were assembled along with the God of Abraham, for the strong ones of God are greatly exalted on the earth.' And in the ninety-eighth Psalm, the Holy Spirit reproaches you, and predicts Him whom you do not wish to be king to be King and Lord, both of Samuel, and of Aaron, and of Moses, and, in short, of all the others. And the words of the Psalm are these: 'The Lord has reigned, let the nations be angry: [it is] He who sits upon the cherubim, let the earth be shaken. The Lord is great in Zion, and He is high above all the nations. Let them confess Thy great name, for it is fearful and holy, and the honour of the King loves judgment. Thou hast prepared equity; judgment and righteousness hast Thou performed in Jacob. Exalt the Lord our God, and worship the footstool of His feet; for He is holy. Moses and Aaron among His priests, and Samuel among those who call upon His name. They called (says the Scripture) on the Lord, and He heard them. In the pillar of the cloud He spake to them; for they kept His testimonies, and the commandment which he gave them. O Lord our God, Thou heardest them: O God, Thou wert propitious to them, and [yet] taking vengeance on all their inventions. Exalt the Lord our God, and worship at His holy hill; for the Lord our God is holy.'"

CHAPTER XXXVIII -- IT IS AN ANNOYANCE TO THE JEW THAT CHRIST IS SAID TO BE ADORED. JUSTIN CONFIRMS IT, HOWEVER, FROM PS. XLV.

And Trypho said, "Sir, it were good for us if we obeyed our teachers, who laid down a law that we should have no intercourse with any of you, and that we should not have even any communication with you on these questions. For you utter many blasphemies, in that you seek to persuade us that this crucified man was with Moses and Aaron, and spoke to them in the pillar of the cloud; then that he became man, was crucified, and ascended up to heaven, and comes again to earth, and ought to be worshipped."

Then I answered, "I know that, as the word of God says, this great wisdom of God, the Maker of all things, and the Almighty, is hid from you. Wherefore, in sympathy with you, I am striving to the utmost that you may understand these matters which to you are paradoxical; but if not, that I myself may be innocent in the day of judgment. For you shall hear other words which appear still more paradoxical; but be not confounded, nay, rather remain still more zealous hearers and investigators, despising the tradition of your teachers, since they are convicted by the Holy Spirit of inability to perceive the truths taught by God, and of preferring to teach their own doctrines. Accordingly, in the forty-fourth [forty-fifth] Psalm, these words are in like manner referred to Christ: 'My heart has brought forth a good matter; I tell my works to the King. My tongue is the pen of a ready writer. Fairer in beauty than the sons of men: grace is poured forth into Thy lips: therefore bath God blessed Thee for ever. Gird Thy sword upon Thy thigh, O mighty One. Press on in Thy fairness and in Thy beauty, and prosper and reign, because of truth, and of meekness, and of righteousness: and Thy right hand shall instruct Thee marvellously. Thine arrows are sharpened, O mighty One; the people shall fall under Thee; in the heart of the enemies of the King [the arrows are fixed]. Thy throne, O God, is for ever and ever: a sceptre of equity is the sceptre of Thy kingdom. Thou hast loved righteousness, and hast hated iniquity; therefore thy God hath anointed Thee with the oil of gladness above Thy fellows. [He hath anointed Thee] with myrrh, and oil, and cassia, from Thy garments; from the ivory palaces, whereby they made Thee glad. Kings' daughters are in Thy honour. The queen stood at Thy right hand, clad in garments embroidered with gold. Hearken, O daughter, and behold, and incline thine ear, and forget thy people and the house of thy father: and the King shall desire thy beauty; because He is thy Lord, they shall worship Him also. And the daughter of Tyre [shall be there] with gifts. The rich of the people shall entreat Thy face. All the glory of the King's daughter within, clad in embroidered garments of needlework. The virgins that follow her shall be brought to the King; her neighbours shall be brought unto Thee: they shall be brought with joy and gladness: they shall be led into the King's shrine. Instead of thy fathers, thy sons have been born: Thou shalt appoint them rulers over all the earth. I shall remember Thy name in every generation: therefore the people shall confess Thee for ever, and for ever and ever.'

CHAPTER XXXIX -- THE JEWS HATE THE CHRISTIANS WHO BELIEVE THIS. HOW GREAT THE DISTINCTION IS BETWEEN BOTH!

"Now it is not surprising," I continued, "that you hate us who hold these opinions, and convict you of a continual hardness of heart. For indeed Elijah, conversing with God concerning you, speaks thus: 'Lord, they have slain Thy prophets, and digged down Thine altars: and I am left alone, and they seek my life.' And He answers him: 'I have still seven thousand men who have not bowed the knee to Baal.' Therefore, just as God did not inflict His anger on account of those seven thousand men, even so He has now neither yet inflicted judgment, nor does inflict it, knowing that daily some [of you] are becoming disciples in the name of Christ, and quitting the path of error; who are also receiving gifts, each as he is worthy, illumined through the name of this Christ. For one receives the spirit of understanding, another of counsel, another of strength, another of healing, another of foreknowledge, another of teaching, and another of the fear of God."

To this Trypho said to me, "I wish you knew that you are beside yourself, talking these sentiments."

And I said to him, "Listen, O friend, for I am not mad or beside myself; but it was prophesied that, after the ascent of Christ to heaven, He would deliver us from error and give us gifts. The words are these: 'He ascended up on high; He led captivity captive; He gave gifts to men.' Accordingly, we who have received gifts from Christ, who has ascended up on high, prove from the words of prophecy that you, 'the wise in yourselves, and the men of understanding in your own eyes,' are foolish, and honour God and His Christ by lip only. But we, who are instructed in the whole truth, honour Them both in acts, and in knowledge, and in heart, even unto death. But you hesitate to confess that He is Christ, as the Scriptures and the events witnessed and done in His name prove, perhaps for this reason, lest you be persecuted by the rulers, who, under the influence of the wicked and deceitful spirit, the serpent, will not cease putting to death and persecuting those who confess the name of Christ until He come again, and destroy them all, and render to each his deserts."

And Trypho replied, "Now, then, render us the proof that this man who you say was crucified and ascended into heaven is the Christ of God. For you have sufficiently proved by means of the Scriptures previously quoted by you, that it is declared in the Scriptures that Christ must suffer, and come again with glory, and receive the eternal kingdom over all the nations, every kingdom being made subject to Him: now show us that this man is He."

And I replied, "It has been already proved, sirs, to those who have ears, even from the facts which have been conceded by you; but that you may not think me at a loss, and unable to give proof of what you ask, as I promised, I shall do so at a fitting place. At present, I resume the consideration of the subject which I was discussing.

CHAPTER XL -- HE RETURNS TO THE MOSAIC LAWS, AND PROVES THAT THEY WERE FIGURES OF THE THINGS WHICH PERTAIN TO CHRIST.

"The mystery, then, of the lamb which God enjoined to be sacrificed as the passover, was a type of Christ; with whose blood, in proportion to their faith in Him, they anoint their houses, i.e., themselves, who believe on Him. For that the creation which God created--to wit, Adam--was a house for the spirit which proceeded from God, you all can understand. And that this injunction was temporary, I prove thus. God does not permit the lamb of the passover to be sacrificed in any other place than where His name was named; knowing that the days will come, after the suffering of Christ, when even the place in Jerusalem shall be given over to your enemies, and all the offerings, in short, shall cease; and that lamb which was commanded to be wholly roasted was a symbol of the suffering of the cross which Christ would undergo. For the lamb, which is roasted, is roasted and dressed up in the form of the cross. For one spit is transfixed right through from the lower parts up to the head, and one across the back, to which are attached the legs of the lamb. And the two goats which were ordered to be offered during the fast, of which one was sent away as the scape [goat], and the other sacrificed, were similarly declarative of the two appearances of Christ: the first, in which the elders of your people, and the priests, having laid hands on Him and put Him to death, sent Him away as the scope [goat]; and His second appearance, because in the same place in Jerusalem you shall recognise Him whom you have dishonoured, and who was an offering for all sinners willing to repent, and keeping the fast which Isaiah speaks of, loosening the terms of the violent contracts, and keeping the other precepts, likewise enumerated by him, and which I have quoted, which those believing in Jesus do. And further, you are aware that the offering of the two goats, which were enjoined to be sacrificed at the fast, was not permitted to take place similarly anywhere else, but only in Jerusalem.

CHAPTER XLI -- THE OBLATION OF FINE FLOUR WAS A FIGURE OF THE EUCHARIST.

"And the offering of fine flour, sirs," I said, "which was prescribed to be presented on behalf of those purified from leprosy, was a type of the bread of the Eucharist, the celebration of which our Lord Jesus Christ prescribed, in remembrance of the suffering which He endured on behalf of those who are purified in soul from all iniquity, in order that we may at the same time thank God for having created the world, with all things therein, for the sake of man, and for delivering us from the evil in which we were, and for utterly overthrowing principalities and powers by Him who suffered according to His will. Hence God speaks by the mouth of Malachi, one of the twelve [prophets], as I said before, about the sacrifices at that time presented by you: 'I have no pleasure in you, saith the Lord; and I will not accept your sacrifices at your hands: for, from the rising of the sun unto the going down of the same, My name has been glorified among the Gentiles, and in every place incense is offered to My name, and a pure offering: for My name is great among the Gentiles, saith the Lord: but ye profane it.' He then speaks of those Gentiles, namely us, who in every place offer sacrifices to Him, i.e., the bread of the Eucharist, and also the cup of the Eucharist, affirming both that we glorify His name, and that you profane . The command of circumcision, again, bidding [them] always circumcise the children on the eighth day, was a type of the true circumcision, by which we are circumcised from deceit and iniquity through Him who rose from the dead on the first day after the Sabbath, [namely through] our Lord Jesus Christ. For the first day after the Sabbath, remaining the first of all the days, is called, however, the eighth, according to the number of all the days of the cycle, and [yet] remains the first.

CHAPTER XLII -- THE BELLS ON THE PRIEST'S ROBE WERE A FIGURE OF THE APOSTLES.

"Moreover, the prescription that twelve bells be attached to the [robe] of the high priest, which hung down to the feet, was a symbol of the twelve apostles, who depend on the power of Christ, the eternal Priest; and through their voice it is that all the earth has been filled with the glory and grace of God and of His Christ. Wherefore David also says: 'Their sound has gone forth into all the earth, and their words to the ends of the world.' And Isaiah speaks as if he were personating the apostles, when they say to Christ that they believe not in their own report, but in the power of Him who sent them. And so he says: 'Lord, who hath believed our report? and to whom is the arm of the Lord revealed? We have preached before Him as if [He were] a child, as if a root in a dry ground.' (And what follows in order of the prophecy already quoted.) But when the passage speaks as from the lips of many, 'We have preached before Him,' and adds, 'as if a child,' it signifies that the wicked shall become subject to Him, and shall obey His command, and that all shall become as one child. Such a thing as you may witness in the body: although the members are enumerated as many, all are called one, and are a body. For, indeed, a commonwealth and a church, though many individuals in number, are in fact as one, called and addressed by one appellation. And in short, sirs," said I, "by enumerating all the other appointments of Moses I can demonstrate that they were types, and symbols, and declarations of those things which would happen to Christ, of those who it was foreknown were to believe in Him, and of those things which would also be done by Christ Himself. But since what I have now enumerated appears to me to be sufficient, I revert again to the order of the discourse.

CHAPTER XLIII -- HE CONCLUDES THAT THE LAW HAD AN END IN CHRIST, WHO WAS BORN OF THE VIRGIN.

"As, then, circumcision began with Abraham, and the Sabbath and sacrifices and offerings and feasts with Moses, and it has been proved they were enjoined on account of the hardness of your people's heart, so it was necessary, in accordance with the Father's will, that they should have an end in Him who was born of a virgin, of the family of Abraham and tribe of Judah, and of David; in Christ the Son of God, who was proclaimed as about to come to all the world, to be the everlasting law and the everlasting covenant, even as the forementioned prophecies show. And we, who have approached God through Him, have received not carnal, but spiritual circumcision, which Enoch and those like him observed. And we have received it through baptism, since we were sinners, by God's mercy; and all men may equally obtain it. But since the mystery of His birth now demands our attention I shall speak of it. Isaiah then asserted in regard to the generation of Christ, that it could not be declared by man, in words already quoted: 'Who shall declare His generation? for His life is taken from the earth: for the transgressions of my people was He led to death.' The Spirit of prophecy thus affirmed that the generation of Him who was to die, that we sinful men might be healed by His stripes, was such as could not be declared. Furthermore, that the men who believe in Him may possess the knowledge of the manner in which He came into the world, the Spirit of prophecy by the same Isaiah foretold how it would happen thus: 'And the Lord spoke again to Ahaz, saying, Ask for thyself a sign from the Lord thy God, in the depth, or in the height. And Ahaz said, I will not ask, neither will I tempt the Lord. And Isaiah said, Hear then, O house of David; Is it a small thing for you to contend with men, and how do you contend with the Lord? Therefore the Lord Himself will give you a sign. Behold, the virgin shall conceive, and shall bear a son, and his name shall be called Immanuel. Butter and honey shall he eat, before he knows or prefers the evil, and chooses out the good; for before the child knows good or ill, he rejects evil by choosing out the good. For before the child knows how to call father or mother, he shall receive the power of Damascus and the spoil of Samaria in presence of the king of Assyria. And the land shall be forsaken, which thou shalt with difficulty endure in consequence of the presence of its two kings. But God shall bring on thee, and on thy people, and on the house of thy father, days which have not yet come upon thee since the day in which Ephraim took away from Judah the king of Assyria.' Now it is evident to all, that in the race of Abraham according to the flesh no one has been born of a virgin, or is said to have been born [of a virgin], save this our Christ. But since you and your teachers venture to affirm that in the prophecy of Isaiah it is not said, 'Behold, the virgin shall conceive,' but, 'Behold, the young woman shall conceive, and bear a son;' and [since] you explain the prophecy as if [it referred] to Hezekiah, who was your king, I shall endeavor to [discuss shortly this point in opposition to you, and to show that reference is made to Him who is acknowledged by us as Christ.

CHAPTER XLIV -- THE JEWS IN VAIN PROMISE THEMSELVES SALVATION, WHICH CANNOT BE OBTAINED EXCEPT THROUGH CHRIST.

"For thus, so far as you are concerned, I shall be found in all respects innocent, if I strive earnestly to persuade you by bringing forward demonstrations. But if you remain hard-hearted, or weak in [forming] a resolution, on account of death, which is the lot of the Christians, and are unwilling to assent to the truth, you shall appear as the authors of your own [evils]. And you deceive yourselves while you fancy that, because you are the seed of Abraham after the flesh, therefore you shall fully inherit the good things announced to be bestowed by God through Christ. For no one, not even of them, has anything to look for, but only those who in mind are assimilated to the faith of Abraham, and who have recognised all the mysteries: for I say, that some injunctions were laid on you in reference to the worship of God and practice of righteousness; but some injunctions and acts were likewise mentioned in reference to the mystery of Christ, on account of the hardness of your people's hearts. And that this is so, God makes known in Ezekiel, [when] He said concerning it: 'If Noah and Jacob and Daniel should beg either sons or daughters, the request would not be granted them.' And in Isaiah, of the very same matter He spake thus: 'The Lord God said, they shall both go forth and look on the members [of the bodies] of the men that have transgressed. For their worm shall not die, and their fire shall not be quenched, and they shall be a gazing-stock to all flesh.' So that it becomes you to eradicate this hope from your souls, and hasten to know in what way forgiveness of sins, and a hope of inheriting the promised good things, shall be yours. But there is no other [way] than this,--to become acquainted with this Christ, to be washed in the fountain spoken of by Isaiah for the remission of sins; and for the rest, to live sinless lives."

CHAPTER XLV -- THOSE WHO WERE RIGHTEOUS BEFORE AND UNDER THE LAW SHALL BE SAVED BY CHRIST.

And Trypho said, "If I seem to interrupt these matters, which you say must be investigated, yet the question which I mean to put is urgent. Suffer me first."

And I replied, "Ask whatever you please, as it occurs to you; and I shall endeavour, after questions and answers, to resume and complete the discourse."

Then he said, "Tell me, then, shall those who lived according to the law given by

Moses, live in the same manner with Jacob, Enoch, and Noah, in the resurrection of the dead, or not?"

I replied to him, "When I quoted, sir, the words spoken by Ezekiel, that 'even if Noah and Daniel and Jacob were to beg sons and daughters, the request would not be granted them,' but that each one, that is to say, shall be saved by his own righteousness, I said also, that those who regulated their lives by the law of Moses would in like manner be saved. For what in the law of Moses is naturally good, and pious, and righteous, and has been prescribed to be done by those who obey it; and what was appointed to be performed by reason of the hardness of the people's hearts; was similarly recorded, and done also by those who were under the law. Since those who did that which is universally, naturally, and eternally good are pleasing to God, they shall be saved through this Christ in the resurrection equally with those righteous men who were before them, namely Noah, and Enoch, and Jacob, and whoever else there be, along with those who have known this Christ, Son of God, who was before the morning star and the moon, and submitted to become incarnate, and be born of this virgin of the family of David, in order that, by this dispensation, the serpent that sinned from the beginning, and the angels like him, may be destroyed, and that death may be contemned, and for ever quit, at the second coming of the Christ Himself, those who believe in Him and live acceptably,--and be no more: when some are sent to be punished unceasingly into judgment and condemnation of fire; but others shall exist in freedom from suffering, from corruption, and from grief, and in immortality."

CHAPTER XLVI -- TRYPHO ASKS WHETHER A MAN WHO KEEPS THE LAW EVEN NOW WILL BE SAVED. JUSTIN PROVES THAT IT CONTRIBUTES NOTHING TO RIGHTEOUSNESS.

"But if some, even now, wish to live in the observance of the institutions given by Moses, and yet believe in this Jesus who was crucified, recognising Him to be the Christ of God, and that it is given to Him to be absolute Judge of all, and that His is the everlasting kingdom, can they also be saved?" he inquired of me.

And I replied, "Let us consider that also together, whether one may now observe all the Mosaic institutions."

And he answered, "No. For we know that, as you said, it is not possible either anywhere to sacrifice the lamb of the passover, or to offer the goats ordered for the fast; or, in short, [to present] all the other offerings."

And I said, "Tell then yourself, I pray, some things which can be observed; for you will be persuaded that, though a man does not keep or has not performed the eternal decrees, he may assuredly be saved."

Then he replied, "To keep the Sabbath, to be circumcised, to observe months, and to be washed if you touch anything prohibited by Moses, or after sexual intercourse."

And I said, "Do you think that Abraham, Isaac, Jacob, Noah, and Job, and all the rest before or after them equally righteous, also Sarah the wife of Abraham, Rebekah the wife of Isaac, Rachel the wife of Jacob, and Leah, and all the rest of them, until the mother of Moses the faithful servant, who observed none of these [statutes], will be saved?"

And Trypho answered, "Were not Abraham and his descendants circumcised?"

And I said, "I know that Abraham and his descendants were circumcised. The reason why circumcision was given to them I stated at length in what has gone before; and if what has been said does not convince you, let us again search into the matter. But you are aware that, up to Moses, no one in fact who was righteous observed any of these rites at all of which we are talking, or received one commandment to observe, except that of circumcision, which began from Abraham."

And he replied, "We know it, and admit that they are saved."

Then I returned answer, "You perceive that God by Moses laid all such ordinances upon you on account of the hardness of your people's hearts, in order that, by the large number of them, you might keep God continually, and in every action, before your eyes, and never begin to act unjustly or impiously. For He enjoined you to place around you [a fringe] of purple dye, in order that you might not forget God; and He commanded you to wear a phylactery, certain characters, which indeed we consider holy, being engraved on very thin parchment; and by these means stirring you up to retain a constant remembrance of God: at the same time, however, convincing you, that in your hearts you have not even a faint remembrance of God's worship. Yet not even so were you dissuaded from idolatry: for in the times of Elijah, when [God] recounted the number of those who had not bowed the knee to Baal, He said the number was seven thousand; and in Isaiah He rebukes you for having sacrificed your children to idols. But we, because we refuse to sacrifice to those to whom we were of old accustomed to sacrifice, undergo extreme penalties, and rejoice in death,--believing that God will raise us up by His Christ, and will make us incorruptible, and undisturbed, and immortal; and we know that the ordinances imposed by reason of the hardness of your people's hearts, contribute nothing to the performance of righteousness and of piety."

CHAPTER XLVII -- JUSTIN COMMUNICATES WITH CHRISTIANS WHO OBSERVE THE LAW. NOT A FEW CATHOLICS DO OTHERWISE.

And Trypho again inquired, "But if some one, knowing that this is so, after he recognises that this man is Christ, and has believed in and obeys Him, wishes, however, to observe these [institutions], will he be saved?"

I said, "In my opinion, Trypho, such an one will be saved, if he does not strive in every way to persuade other men,--I mean those Gentiles who have been circumcised from error by Christ, to observe the same things as himself, telling them that they will not be saved unless they do so. This you did yourself at the commencement of the discourse, when you declared that I would not be saved unless I observe these institutions."

Then he replied, "Why then have you said, 'In my opinion, such an one will be saved,' unless there are some who affirm that such will not be saved?"

"There are such people, Trypho," I answered; "and these do not venture to have any intercourse with or to extend hospitality to such persons; but I do not agree with them. But if some, through weak-mindedness, wish to observe such institutions as were given by Moses, from which they expect some virtue, but which we believe were appointed by reason of the hardness of the people's hearts, along with their hope in this Christ, and [wish to perform] the eternal and natural acts of righteousness and piety, yet choose to live with the Christians and the faithful, as I said before, not inducing them either to be circumcised like themselves, or to keep the Sabbath, or to observe any other such ceremonies, then I hold that we ought to join ourselves to such, and associate with them in all things as kinsmen and brethren. But if, Trypho," I continued, "some of your race, who say they believe in this Christ, compel those Gentiles who believe in this Christ to live in all respects according to the law given by Moses, or choose not to associate so intimately with them, I in like manner do not approve of them. But I believe that even those, who have been persuaded by them to observe the legal dispensation along with their confession of God in Christ, shall probably be saved. And I hold, further, that such as have confessed and known this man to be Christ, yet who have gone back from some cause to the legal dispensation, and have denied that this man is Christ, and have repented not before death, shall by no means be saved. Further, I hold that those of the seed of Abraham who live according to the law, and do not believe in this Christ before death, shall likewise not be saved, and especially those who have anathematized and do anathematize this very Christ in the synagogues, and everything by which they might obtain salvation and escape the vengeance of fire. For the goodness and the loving-kindness of God, and His boundless riches, hold righteous and sinless the man who, as Ezekiel tells, repents of sins; and reckons sinful, unrighteous, and impious the man who fails away from piety and righteousness to unrighteousness and ungodliness. Wherefore also our Lord Jesus Christ said, 'In whatsoever things I shall take you, in these I shall judge you.' "

CHAPTER XLVIII -- BEFORE THE DIVINITY OF CHRIST IS PROVED, HE [TRYPHO] DEMANDS THAT IT BE SETTLED THAT HE IS CHRIST.

And Trypho said, "We have heard what you think of these matters. Resume the discourse where you left off, and bring it to an end. For some of it appears to me to be paradoxical, and wholly incapable of proof. For when you say that this Christ existed as God before the ages, then that He submitted to be born and become man, yet that He is not man of man, this[assertion] appears to me to be not merely paradoxical, but also foolish."

And I replied to this, "I know that the statement does appear to be paradoxical, especially to those of your race, who are ever unwilling to understand or to perform the[requirements] of God, but[ready to perform] those of your teachers, as God Himself declares. Now assuredly, Trypho," I continued,"[the proof] that this man is the Christ of God does not fail, though I be unable to prove that He existed formerly as Son of the Maker of all things, being God, and was born a man by the Virgin. But since I have certainly proved that this man is the Christ of God, whoever He be, even if I do not prove that He pre-existed, and submitted to be born a man of like passions with us, having a body, according to the Father's will; in this last matter alone is it just to say that I have erred, and not to deny that He is the Christ, though it should appear that He was born man of men, and[nothing more] is proved[than this], that He has become Christ by election. For there are some, my friends," I said, "of our race, who admit that He is Christ, while holding Him to be man of men; with whom I do not agree, nor would I, even though most of those who have[now] the same opinions as myself should say so; since we were enjoined by Christ Himself to put no faith in human doctrines, but in those proclaimed by the blessed prophets and taught by Himself."

CHAPTER XLIX -- TO THOSE WHO OBJECT THAT ELIJAH HAS NOT YET COME, HE REPLIES THAT HE IS THE PRECURSOR OF THE FIRST ADVENT.

And Trypho said, "Those who affirm him to have been a man, and to have been anointed by election, and then to have become Christ, appear to me to speak more plausibly than you who hold those opinions which you express. For we all expect that Christ will be a man[born] of men, and that Elijah when he comes will anoint him. But if this man appear to be Christ, he must certainly be known as man[born] of men; but from the circumstance that Elijah has not yet come, I infer that this man is not He[the Christ]."

Then I inquired of him, "Does not Scripture, in the book of Zechariah, say that Elijah shall come before the great and terrible day of the Lord?"

And he answered, "Certainly."

"If therefore Scripture compels you to admit that two advents of Christ were predicted to take place,--one in which He would appear suffering, and dishonoured, and without comeliness; but the other in which He would come glorious. and Judge of all, as has been made manifest in many of the forecited passages,--shall we not suppose that the word of God has proclaimed that Elijah shall be the precursor of the great and terrible day, that is, of His second advent?"

"Certainly," he answered.

"And, accordingly, our Lord in His teaching," I continued, "proclaimed that this very thing would take place, saying that Elijah would also come. And we know that this shall take place when our Lord Jesus Christ shall come in glory from heaven; whose first manifestation the Spirit of God who was in Elijah preceded as herald in[the person of] John, a prophet among your nation; after whom no other prophet appeared among you. He cried, as he sat by the river Jordan: 'I baptize you with water to repentance; but He that is stronger than I shall come, whose shoes I am not worthy to bear: He shall baptize you with the Holy Ghost and with fire: whose fan is in His hand, and He will thoroughly purge His floor, and will gather the wheat into the barn; but the chaff He will burn up with unquenchable fire.' And this very prophet your king Herod had shut up in prison; and when his birthday was celebrated, and the niece of the same Herod by her dancing had pleased him, he told her to ask whatever she pleased. Then the mother of the maiden instigated her to ask the head of John, who was in prison; and having asked it,[Herod] sent and ordered the head of John to be brought in on a charger. Wherefore also our Christ said,[when He was] on earth, to those who were affirming that Elijah must come before Christ: 'Elijah shall come, and restore all things; but I say unto you, that Elijah has already come, and they knew him not, but have done to him whatsoever they chose.' And it is written, 'Then the disciples understood that He spake to them about John the Baptist.' "

And Trypho said, "This statement also seems to me paradoxical; namely, that the prophetic Spirit of God, who was in Elijah, was also in John."

To this I replied, "Do you not think that the same thing happened in the case of Joshua the son of Nave(Nun), who succeeded to the command of the people after Moses, when Moses was commanded to lay his hands on Joshua, and God said to him, I will take of the spirit which is in thee, and put it on him?' "

And he said, "Certainly."

"As therefore," I say, "while Moses was still among men, God took of the spirit which was in Moses and put it on Joshua, even so God was able to cause[the spirit] of Elijah to come upon John; in order that, as Christ at His first coming appeared inglorious, even so the first coming of the spirit, which remained always pure in Elijah s like that of Christ, might be perceived to be inglorious. For the Lord said He would wage war against Amalek with concealed hand; and you will not deny that Amalek fell. But if it is said that only in the glorious advent of Christ war will be waged with Amalek, how great will the fulfilment of Scripture be which says, 'God will wage war against Amalek with concealed hand!' You can perceive that the concealed power of God was in Christ the crucified, before whom demons, and all the principalities and powers of the earth, tremble."

CHAPTER L -- IT IS PROVED FROM ISAIAH THAT JOHN IS THE PRECURSOR OF CHRIST.

And Trypho said, "You seem to me to have come out of a great conflict with many persons about all the points we have been searching into, and therefore quite ready to return answers to all questions put to you. Answer me then, first, how you can show that there is another God besides the Maker of all things; and then you will show,[further], that He submitted to be born of the Virgin."

I replied, "Give me permission first of all to quote certain passages from the prophecy of Isaiah, which refer to the office of forerunner discharged by John the Baptist and prophet before this our Lord Jesus Christ."

"I grant it," said he.

Then I said, "Isaiah thus foretold John's forerunning: 'And Hezekiah said to Isaiah, Good is the word of the Lord which He spake: Let there be peace and righteousness in my days.' And, 'Encourage the people; ye priests, speak to the heart of Jerusalem, and encourage her, because her humiliation is accomplished. Her sin is annulled; for she has received of the Lord's hand double for her sins. A voice of one crying in the wilderness, Prepare the ways of the Lord; make straight the paths of our God. Every valley shall be filled up, and every mountain and hill shall be brought low: and the crooked shall be made straight, and the rough way shall be plain ways; and the glory of the Lord thall be seen, and all flesh shall see the salvation of God: for the Lord hath spoken it. A voice of one saying, Cry; and I said, What shall I cry? All flesh is grass, and all the glory of man as the flower of grass. The grass has withered, and the flower of it has fallen away; but the word of the Lord endureth for ever. Thou that bringest good tidings to Zion, go up to the high mountain; thou that bringest good tidings to Jerusalem, lift up thy voice with strength. Lift ye up, be not afraid; tell the cities of Judah, Behold your God! Behold, the Lord comes with strength, and[His] arm comes with authority. Behold, His reward is with Him, and His work before Him. As a shepherd He will tend His flock, and will gather the lambs with[His] arm, and cheer on her that is with young. Who has measured the water with[his] hand, and the heaven with a span, and all the earth with[his] fist? Who has weighed the mountains, and[put] the valleys into a balance? Who has known the mind of the Lord? And who has been His counsellor, and who shall advise Him? Or with whom did He take counsel, and he instructed Him? Or who showed Him judgment? Or who made Him to know the way of understanding? All the nations are reckoned as a drop of a bucket, and as a turning of a balance, and shall be reckoned as spittle. But Lebanon is not sufficient to burn, nor the beasts sufficient for a burnt-offering; and all the nations are considered nothing, and for nothing.' "

CHAPTER LI -- IT IS PROVED THAT THIS PROPHECY HAS BEEN FULFILLED.

And when I ceased, Trypho said, "All the words of the prophecy you repeat, sir, are ambiguous, and have no force in proving what you wish to prove." Then I answered, "If the prophets had not ceased, so that there were no more in your nation, Trypho, after this John, it is evident that what I say in reference to Jesus Christ might be regarded perhaps as ambiguous. But if John came first calling on men to repent, and Christ, while[John] still sat by the river Jordan, having come, put an end to his prophesying and baptizing, and preached also Himself, saying that the kingdom of heaven is at hand, and that He must suffer many things from the Scribes and Pharisees, and be crucified, and on the third day rise again, and would appear again in Jerusalem, and would again eat and drink with His disciples; and foretold that in the interval between His[first and second] advent, as I previously said, priests and false prophets would arise in His name, which things do actually appear; then how can they be ambiguous, when you may be persuaded by the facts? Moreover, He referred to the fact that there would be no longer in your nation any prophet, and to the fact that men recognised how that the New Testament, which God formerly announced[His intention of] promulgating, was then present, i.e., Christ Himself; and in the following terms: 'The law and the prophets were until John the Baptist; from that time the kingdom of heaven suffereth violence, and the violent take it by force. And if you can receive it, he is Elijah, who was to come. He that hath ears to hear, let him hear.'

CHAPTER LII -- JACOB PREDICTED TWO ADVENTS OF CHRIST.

"And it was prophesied by Jacob the patriarch that there would be two advents of Christ, and that in the first He would suffer, and that after He came there would be neither prophet nor king in your nation(I proceeded), and that the nations who believed in the suffering Christ would look for His future appearance. And for this reason the Holy Spirit had uttered these truths in a parable, and obscurely: for," I added, "it is said, 'Judah, thy brethren have praised thee: thy hands[shall be] on the neck of thine enemies; the sons of thy father shall worship thee. Judah is a lion's whelp; from the germ, my son, thou art sprung up. Reclining, he lay down like a lion, and like [a lion's] whelp: who shall raise him up? A ruler shall not depart from Judah, or a leader from his

CHAPTER LVI -- GOD WHO APPEARED TO MOSES IS DISTINGUISHED FROM GOD THE FATHER.

"Moses, then, the blessed and faithful servant of God, declares that He who appeared to Abraham under the oak in Mamre is God, sent with the two angels in His company to judge Sodom by Another who remains ever in the supercelestial places, invisible to all men, holding personal intercourse with none, whom we believe to be Maker and Father of all things; for he speaks thus: 'God appeared to him under the oak in Mature, as he sat at his tent-door at noontide. And lifting up his eyes, he saw, and behold, three men stood before him; and when he saw them, he ran to meet them from the door of his tent; and he bowed himself toward the ground, and said;' "(and so on;) " 'Abraham gat up early in the morning to the place where he stood before the Lord: and he looked toward Sodom and Gomorrah, and toward the adjacent country, and beheld, and, lo, a flame went up from the earth, like the smoke of a furnace.'" And when I had made an end of quoting these words, I asked them if they had understood them.

And they said they had understood them, but that the passages adduced brought forward no proof that there is any other God or Lord, or that the Holy Spirit says so, besides the Maker of all things.

Then I replied, "I shall attempt to persuade you, since you have understood the Scriptures,[of the truth] of what I say, that there is, and that there is said to be, another God and Lord subject to the Maker of all things; who is also called an Angel, because He announces to men whatsoever the Maker of all things--above whom there is no other God--wishes to announce to them." And quoting once more the previous passage, I asked Trypho, "Do you think that God appeared to Abraham under the oak in Mature, as the Scripture asserts?"

He said, "Assuredly."

"Was He one of those three," I said, "whom Abraham saw, and whom the Holy Spirit of prophecy describes as men?"

He said, "No; but God appeared to him, before the vision of the three. Then those three whom the Scripture calls men, were angels; two of them sent to destroy Sodom, and one to announce the joyful tidings to Sarah, that she would bear a son; for which cause he was sent, and having accomplished his errand, went away."

"How then," said I, "does the one of the three, who was in the tent, and who said, 'I shall return to thee hereafter, and Sarah shall have a son,' appear to have returned when Sarah had begotten a son, and to be there declared, by the prophetic word, God? But that you may clearly discern what I say, listen to the words expressly employed by Moses; they are these: 'And Sarah saw the son of Hagar the Egyptian bond-woman, whom she bore to Abraham, sporting with Isaac her son, and said to Abraham, Cast out this bond-woman and her son; for the son of this bond-woman shall not share the inheritance of my son Isaac. And the matter seemed very grievous in Abraham's sight, because of his son. But God said to Abraham, Let it not be grievous in thy sight because of the son, and because of the bond-woman. In all that Sarah hath said unto thee, hearken to her voice; for in Isaac shall thy seed be called.' Have you perceived, then, that He who said under the oak that He would return, since He knew it would be necessary to advise Abraham to do what Sarah wished him, came back as it is written; and is God, as the words declare, when they so speak: 'God said to Abraham, Let it not be grievous in thy sight because of the son, and because of the bond-woman?' " I inquired. And Trypho said, "Certainly; but you have not proved from this that there is another God besides Him who appeared to Abraham, and who also appeared to the other patriarchs and prophets. You have proved, however, that we were wrong in believing that the three who were in the tent with Abraham were all angels."

I replied again, "If I could not have proved to you from the Scriptures that one of those three is God, and is called Angel, because, as I already said, He brings messages to those to whom God the Maker of all things wishes[messages to be brought], then in regard to Him who appeared to Abraham on earth in human form in like manner as the two angels who came with Him, and who was God even before the creation of the world, it were reasonable for you to entertain the same belief as is entertained by the whole of your nation."

"Assuredly," he said, "for up to this moment this has been our belief."

Then I replied, "Reverting to the Scriptures, I shall endeavour to persuade you, that He who is said to have appeared to Abraham, and to Jacob, and to Moses, and who is called God, is distinct from Him who made all things,--numerically, I mean, not[distinct] in will. For I affirm that He has never at any time done anything which He who made the world--above whom there is no other God--has not wished Him both to do and to engage Himself with."

And Trypho said, "Prove now that this is the case, that we also may agree with you. For we do not understand you to affirm that He has done or said anything contrary to the will of the Maker of all things."

Then I said, "The Scripture just quoted by me will make this plain to you. It is thus: 'The sun was risen on the earth, and Lot entered into Segor(Zoar); and the Lord rained on Sodom sulphur and fire from the Lord out of heaven, and overthrew these cities and all the neighbourhood.' "

Then the fourth of those who had remained with Trypho said, "It must therefore necessarily be said that one of the two angels who went to Sodom, and is named by Moses in the Scripture Lord, is different from Him who also is God and appeared to Abraham."

"It is not on this ground solely," I said, "that it must be admitted absolutely that some other one is called Lord by the Holy Spirit besides Him who is considered Maker of all things; not solely[for what is said] by Moses, but also[for what is said] by David. For there is written by him: 'The Lord says to my Lord, Sit on My right hand, until I make Thine enemies Thy footstool,' as I have already quoted. And again, in other words: 'Thy throne, O God, is for ever and ever. A sceptre of equity is the sceptre of Thy kingdom: Thou hast loved righteousness and hated iniquity: therefore God, even Thy God, hath anointed Thee with the oil of gladness above Thy fellows.' If, therefore, you assert that the Holy Spirit calls some other one God and Lord, besides the Father of all things and His Christ, answer me; for I undertake to prove to you from Scriptures themselves, that He whom the Scripture calls Lord is not one of the two angels that went to Sodom, but He who was with them, and is called God, that appeared to Abraham."

And Trypho said, "Prove this; for, as you see, the day advances, and we are not prepared for such perilous replies; since never yet have we heard any man investigating, or searching into, or proving these matters; nor would we have tolerated your conversation, had you not referred everything to the Scriptures: for you are very zealous in adducing proofs from them; and you are of opinion that there is no God above the Maker of all things."

Then I replied, "You are aware, then, that the Scripture says, 'And the Lord said to Abraham, Why did Sarah hugh, saying, Shall I truly conceive? for I am old. Is anything impossible with God? At the time appointed shall I return to thee according to the time of life, and Sarah shall have a son.' And after a little interval: 'And the men rose up from thence, and looked towards Sodom and Gomorrah; and Abraham went with them, to bring them on the way. And the Lord said, I will not conceal from Abraham, my servant, what I do.' And again, after a little, it thus says: 'The Lord said, The cry of Sodom and Gomorrah is great, and their sins are very grievous. I will go down now, and see whether they have done altogether according to their cry which has come unto me; and if not, that I may know. And the men turned away thence, and went to Sodom. But Abraham was standing before the Lord; and Abraham drew near, and said, Wilt Thou destroy the righteous with the wicked?' "(and so on, for I do not think fit to write over again the same words, having written them all before, but shall of necessity give those by which I established the proof to Trypho and his companions. Then I proceeded to what follows, in which these words are recorded:) " 'And the Lord went His way as soon as He had left communing with Abraham; and[Abraham] went to his place. And there came two angels to Sodom at even. And Lot sat in the gate of Sodom;' and what follows until, 'But the men put forth their hands, and pulled Lot into the house to them, and shut to the door of the house;' and what follows till, 'And the angels laid hold on his hand, and on the hand of his wife, and on the hands of his daughters, the Lord being merciful to him. And it came to pass, when they had brought them forth abroad, that they said, Save, save thy life. Look not behind thee, nor stay in all the neighbourhood; escape to the mountain, lest thou be taken along with[them]. And Lot said to them, I beseech[Thee], O Lord, since Thy servant bath found grace in Thy sight, and Thou hast magnified Thy righteousness, which Thou showest towards me in saving my life; but I cannot escape to the mountain, lest evil overtake me, and I die. Behold, this city is near to flee unto, and it is small: there I shall be safe, since it is small; and any soul shall live. And He said to him, Behold, I have accepted thee also in this matter, so as not to destroy the city for which thou hast spoken. Make haste to save thyself there; for I shall not do anything till thou be come thither. Therefore he called the name of the city Segor(Zoar). The sun was risen upon the earth; and Lot entered into Segor(Zoar). And the Lord rained on Sodom and Gomorrah sulphur and fire from the Lord out of heaven; and He overthrew these cities, and all the neighbourhood.'" And after another pause I added: "And now have you not perceived, my friends, that one of the three, who is both God and Lord, and ministers to Him who is in the heavens, is Lord of the two angels? For when[the angels] proceeded to Sodom, He remained behind, and communed with Abraham in the words recorded by Moses; and when He departed after the conversation, Abraham went back to his place. And when he came[to Sodom], the two angels no longer conversed with Lot, but Himself, as the Scripture makes evident; and He is the Lord who received commission from the Lord who[remains] in the heavens, i.e.,the Maker of all things, to inflict upon Sodom and Gomorrah the[judgments] which the Scripture describes in these terms:'The Lord rained down upon Sodom and Gomorrah sulphur and fire from the Lord out of heaven.' "

CHAPTER LVII -- THE JEW OBJECTS, WHY IS HE SAID TO HAVE EATEN, IF HE BE GOD? ANSWER OF JUSTIN.

Then Trypho said when I was silent, "That Scripture compels us to admit this, is manifest; but there is a matter about which we are deservedly at a loss--namely, about what was said to the effect that[the Lord] ate what was prepared and placed before him by Abraham; and you would admit this."

I answered, "It is written that they ate; and if we believe that it is said the three ate, and not the two alone--who were really angels, and are nourished in the heavens, as is evident to us, even though they are not nourished by food similar to that which mortals use--(for, concerning the sustenance of manna which supported your fathers in the desert, Scripture speaks thus, that they ate angels' food):[if we believe that three ate], then I would say that the Scripture which affirms they ate bears the same meaning as when we would say about fire that it has devoured all things; yet it is not certainly understood that they ate, masticating with teeth and jaws. So that not even here should we be at a loss about anything, if we are acquainted even slightly with figurative modes of expression, and able to rise above them."

And Trypho said, "It is possible that[the question] about the mode of eating may be thus explained:[the mode, that is to say,] in which it is written, they took and ate what had been prepared by Abraham: so that you may now proceed to explain to us how this God who appeared to Abraham, and is minister to God the Maker of all things, being born of the Virgin, became man, of like passions with all, as you said previously."

Then I replied, "Permit me first, Trypho, to collect some other proofs on this head, so that you, by the large number of them, may be persuaded of[the truth of] it, and thereafter I shall explain what you ask."

And he said, "Do as seems good to you; for I shall be thoroughly pleased."

CHAPTER LVIII -- THE SAME IS PROVED FROM THE VISIONS WHICH APPEARED TO JACOB.

Then I continued, "I purpose to quote to you Scriptures, not that I am anxious to make merely an artful display of words; for I possess no such faculty, but God's grace alone has been granted to me to the understanding of His Scriptures, of which grace I exhort all to become partakers freely and bounteously, in order that they may not, through want of it, incur condemnation in the judgment which God the Maker of all things shall hold through my Lord Jesus Christ."

And Trypho said, "What you do is worthy of the worship of God; but you appear to me to feign ignorance when you say that you do not possess a store of artful words."

I again replied, "Be it so, since you think so; yet I am persuaded that I speak the truth. But give me your attention, that I may now rather adduce the remaining proofs."

"Proceed," said he.

And I continued: "It is again written by Moses, my brethren, that He who is called God and appeared to the patriarchs is called both Angel and Lord, in order that from this you may understand Him to be minister to the Father of all things, as you have already admitted, and may remain firm, persuaded by additional arguments. The word of God, therefore,[recorded] by Moses, when referring to Jacob the grandson of Abraham, speaks thus: 'And it came to pass, when the sheep conceived, that I saw them with my eyes in the dream: And, behold, the he-goats and the rams which leaped upon the sheep and she-goats were spotted with white, and speckled and sprinkled with a dun colour. And the Angel of God said to me in the dream, Jacob, Jacob. And I said, What is it, Lord? And He said, Lift up thine eyes, and see that the he-goats and rams leaping on the sheep and she-goats are spotted with white, speckled, and sprinkled with a dun colour. For I have seen what Laban doeth unto thee. I am the God who appeared to thee in Bethel, where thou anointedst a pillar and vowedst a vow unto Me. Now therefore arise, and get thee out of this land, and depart to the land of thy birth, and I shall be with thee. And again, in other words, speaking of the same Jacob, it thus says: 'And having risen up that night, he took the two wives, and the two women-servants, and his eleven children, and passed over the ford Jabbok; and he took them and went over the brook, and sent over all his belongings. But Jacob was left behind alone, and an Angel wrestled with him until morning. And He saw that He is not prevailing against him, and He touched the broad part of his thigh; and the broad part of Jacob's thigh grew stiff while he wrestled with Him. And He said, Let Me go, for the day breaketh. But he said, I will not let Thee go, except Thou bless me. And He said to him, What is thy name? And he said, Jacob. And He said, Thy name shall be called no more Jacob, but Israel shall be thy name; for thou hast prevailed with God, and with men shalt be powerful. And Jacob asked Him, and said, Tell me Thy name. But he said, Why dost thou ask after My name? And He blessed him there. And Jacob called the name of that place Peniel, for I saw God face to face, and my soul rejoiced.' And again, in other terms, referring to the same Jacob, it says the following: 'And Jacob came to Luz, in the land of Canaan, which is Bethel, he and all the people that were with him. And there he built an altar, and called the name of that place Bethel; for there God appeared to him when he fled from the face of his brother Esau. And Deborah, Rebekah's nurse, died, and was buried beneath Bethel under an oak: and Jacob called the name of it The Oak of Sorrow. And God appeared again to Jacob in Luz, when he came out from Mesopotamia in Syria, and He blessed him. And God said to him, Thy name shall be no more called Jacob, but Israel shall he thy name.' He is called God, and He is and shall be God." And when all had agreed on these grounds, I continued: "Moreover, I consider it necessary to repeat to you the words which narrate how He who is both Angel and God and Lord, and who appeared as a man to Abraham, and who wrestled in human form with Jacob, was seen by him when he fled from his brother Esau. They are as follows: 'And Jacob went out from the well of the oath, and went toward Charran. And he lighted on a spot, and slept there, for the sun was set; and he gathered of the stones of the place, and put them under his head. And he slept in that place; and he dreamed, and, behold, a ladder was set up on the earth, whose top reached to heaven; and the angels of God ascended and descended upon it. And the Lord stood above it, and He said, I am the Lord, the God of Abraham thy father, and of Isaac; be not afraid: the land whereon thou liest, to thee will I give it, and to thy seed; and thy seed shall be as the dust of the earth, and shall be extended to the west, and south, and north, and east: and in thee, and in thy seed, shall all families of the earth be blessed. And, behold, I am with thee, keeping thee in every way wherein thou goest, and will bring thee again into this land; for I will not leave thee, until I have done all that I have spoken to thee of. And Jacob awaked out of his sleep, and said, Surely the Lord is in this place, and I knew it not. And he was afraid, and said, How dreadful is this place! this is none other than the house of God, and this is the gate of heaven. And Jacob rose up in the morning, and took the stone which he had placed under his head, and he set it up for a pillar, and poured oil upon the top of it; and Jacob called the name of the place The House of God, and the name of the city formerly was Ulammaus.'"

CHAPTER LIX -- GOD DISTINCT FROM THE FATHER CONVERSED WITH MOSES.

When I had spoken these words, I continued: "Permit me, further, to show you from the book of Exodus how this same One, who is both Angel, and God, and Lord, and man, and who appeared in human form to Abraham and Isaac, appeared in a flame of fire from the bush, and conversed with Moses." And after they said they would listen cheerfully, patiently, and eagerly, I went on: "These words are in the book which bears the title of Exodus: 'And after many days the king of Egypt died, and the children of Israel groaned by reason of the works;' and so on until,'Go and gather the elders of Israel, and thou shalt say unto them, The Lord God of your fathers, the God of Abraham, the God of Isaac, and the God of Jacob, hath appeared to me, saying, I am surely beholding you, and the things which have befallen you in Egypt.'" In addition to these words, I went on: "Have you perceived, sirs, that this very God whom Moses speaks of as an Angel that talked to him in the flame of fire, declares to Moses that He is the God of Abraham, of Isaac, and of Jacob?"

CHAPTER LX -- OPINIONS OF THE JEWS WITH REGARD TO HIM WHO APPEARED IN THE BUSH.

Then Trypho said, "We do not perceive this from the passage quoted by you, but[only this], that it was an angel who appeared in the flame of fire, but God who conversed with Moses; so that there were really two persons in company with each other, an angel and God, that appeared in that vision."

I again replied, "Even if this were so, my friends, that an angel and God were together in the vision seen by Moses, yet, as has already been proved to you by the passages previously quoted, it will not be the Creator of all things that is the God that said to Moses that He was the God of Abraham, and the God of Isaac, and the God of Jacob, but it will be He who has been proved to you to have appeared to Abraham, ministering to the will of the Maker of all things, and likewise carrying into execution His counsel in the judgment of Sodom; so that, even though it be as you say, that there were two--an angel and God--he who has but the smallest intelligence will not venture to assert that the Maker and Father of all things, having left all supercelestial matters, was visible on a little portion of the earth."

And Trypho said, "Since it has been previously proved that He who is called God and Lord, and appeared to Abraham, received from the Lord, who is in the heavens, that which He inflicted on the land of Sodom, even although an angel had accompanied the God who appeared to Moses, we shall perceive that the God who communed with Moses from the bush was not the Maker of all things, but He who has been shown to have manifested Himself to Abraham and to Isaac and to Jacob; who also is called and is perceived to be the Angel of God the Maker of all things, because He publishes to men the commands of the Father and Maker of all things."

And I replied, "Now assuredly, Trypho, I shall show that, in the vision of Moses, this same One alone who is called an Angel, and who is God, appeared to and communed with Moses. For the Scripture says thus:'The Angel of the Lord appeared to him in a flame of fire from the bush; and he sees that the bush bums with fire, but the bush was not consumed. And Moses said, I will turn aside and see this great sight, for the bush is not burnt. And when the Lord saw that he is turning aside to behold, the Lord called to him out of the bush.' In the same manner, therefore, in which the Scripture calls Him who appeared to Jacob in the dream an Angel, then[says] that the same Angel who appeared in the dream spoke to him, saying,'I am the God that appeared to thee when thou didst flee from the face of Esau thy brother;'and[again] says that, in the judgment which befell Sodom in the days of Abraham, the Lord had inflicted the punishment of the Lord who[dwells] in the heavens;--even so here, the Scripture, in announcing that the Angel of the Lord appeared to Moses, and in afterwards declaring him to be Lord and God, speaks of the same One, whom it declares by the many testimonies already quoted to be minister to God, who is above the world, above whom there is no other[God].

CHAPTER LXI--WISDOM IS BEGOTTEN OF THE FATHER, AS FIRE FROM FIRE.

"I shall give you another testimony, my friends," said I, "from the Scriptures, that God begat before all creatures a Beginning,[who was] a certain rational power[proceeding] from Himself, who is called by the Holy Spirit, now the Glory of the Lord, now the Son, again Wisdom, again an Angel, then God, and then Lord and Logos; and on another occasion He calls Himself Captain, when He appeared in human form to Joshua the son of Nave(Nun). For He can be called by all those names, since He ministers to the Father's will, and since He was begotten of the Father by an act of will; just as we see happening among ourselves: for when we give out some word, we beget the word; yet not by abscission, so as to lessen the word[which remains] in us, when we give it out: and just as we see also happening in the case of a fire, which is not lessened when it has kindled[another], but remains the same; and that which has been kindled by it likewise appears to exist by itself, not diminishing that from which it was kindled. The Word of Wisdom, who is Himself this God begotten of the Father of all things, and Word, and Wisdom, and Power, and the Glory of the Begetter, will bear evidence to me, when He speaks by Solomon the following: 'If I shall declare to you what happens daily, I shall call to mind events from everlasting, and review them. The Lord made me the beginning of His ways for His works. From everlasting He established me in the beginning, before He had made the earth, and before He had made the deeps, before the springs of the waters had issued forth, before the mountains had been established. Before all the hills He begets me. God made the country, and the desert, and the highest inhabited places under the sky. When He made ready the heavens, I was along with Him, and when He set up His throne on the winds: when He made the high clouds strong, and the springs of the deep safe, when He made the foundations of the earth,

I was with Him arranging. I was that in which He rejoiced; daily and at all times I delighted in His countenance, because He delighted in the finishing of the habitable world, and delighted in the sons of men. Now, therefore, O son, hear me. Blessed is the man who shall listen to me, and the mortal who shall keep my ways, watching daily at my doors, observing the posts of my ingoings. For my outgoings are the outgoings of life, and will has been prepared by the Lord. But they who sin against me, trespass against their own souls; and they who hate me love death.'

CHAPTER LXII -- THE WORDS "LET US MAKE MAN" AGREE WITH THE TESTIMONY OF PROVERBS.

"And the same sentiment was expressed, my friends, by the word of God[written] by Moses, when it indicated to us, with regard to Him whom it has pointed out, that God speaks in the creation of man with the very same design, in the following words:'Let Us make man after our image and likeness. And let them have dominion over the fish of the sea, and over the fowl of the heaven, and over the cattle, and over all the earth, and over all the creeping things that creep on the earth. And God created man: after the image of God did He create him; male and female created He them. And God blessed them, and said, Increase and multiply, and fill the earth, and have power over it. And that you may not change the[force of the] words just quoted, and repeat what your teachers assert,--either that God said to Himself,'Let Us make,'just as we, when about to do something, oftentimes say to ourselves,'Let us make;'or that God spoke to the elements, to wit, the earth and other similar substances of which we believe man was formed,'Let Us make,'--I shall quote again the words narrated by Moses himself, from which we can indisputably learn that[God] conversed with some one who was numerically distinct from Himself, and also a rational Being. These are the words:'And God said, Behold, Adam has become as one of us, to know good and evil.' In saying, therefore,'as one of us,'[Moses] has declared that[there is a certain] number of persons associated with one another, and that they are at least two. For I would not say that the dogma of that heresy which is said to be among you is true, or that the teachers of it can prove that[God] spoke to angels, or that the human frame was the workmanship of angels. But this Offspring, which was truly brought forth from the Father, was with the Father before all the creatures, and the Father communed with Him; even as the Scripture by Solomon has made clear, that He whom Solomon calls Wisdom, was begotten as a Beginning before all His creatures and as Offspring by God, who has also declared this same thing in the revelation made by Joshua the son of Nave(Nun). Listen, therefore, to the following from the book of Joshua, that what I say may become manifest to you; it is this: 'And it came to pass, when Joshua was near Jericho, he lifted up his eyes, and sees a man standing over against him. And Joshua approached to Him, and said, Art thou for us, or for our adversaries? And He said to him, I am Captain of the Lord's host: now have I come. And Joshua fell on his face on the ground, and said to Him, Lord, what commandest Thou Thy servant? And the Lord's Captain says to Joshua, Loose the shoes off thy feet; for the place whereon thou standest is holy ground. And Jericho was shut up and fortified, and no one went out of it. And the Lord said to Joshua, Behold, I give into thine hand Jericho, and its king,[and] its mighty men.'"

CHAPTER LXIII -- IT IS PROVED THAT THIS GOD WAS INCARNATE.

And Trypho said, "This point has been proved to me forcibly, and by many arguments, my friend. It remains, then, to prove that He submitted to become man by the Virgin, according to the will of His Father; and to be crucified, and to die. Prove also clearly, that after this He rose again and ascended to heaven." I answered, "This, too, has been already de- monstrated by me in the previously quoted words of the prophecies, my friends; which, by recalling and expounding for your sakes, I shall endover to lead you to agree with me also about this matter. The passage, then, which Isaiah records,'Who shall declare His generation? for His life is taken away from the earth,--does it not appear to you to refer to One who, not having descent from men, was said to be delivered over to death by God for the transgressions of the people?--of whose blood, Moses(as I mentioned before), when speaking in parable, said, that He would wash His garments in the blood of the grape; since His blood did not spring from the seed of man, but from the will of God. And then, what is said by David,'In the splendours of Thy holiness have I begotten Thee from the womb, before the morning star. The Lord hath sworn, and will not repent, Thou art a priest for ever, after the order of Melchizedek,'--does this not declare to you that[He was] from of old, and that the God and Father of all things intended Him to be begotten by a human womb? And speaking in other words, which also have been already quoted,[he says]:'Thy throne, O God, is for ever and ever: a sceptre of rectitude is the sceptre of Thy kingdom. Thou hast loved righteousness, and hast hated iniquity: therefore God, even thy God, hath anointed Thee with the oil of gladness above Thy fellows.[He hath anointed Thee] with myrrh, and oil, and cassia from Thy garments, from the ivory palaces, whereby they made Thee glad. Kings' daughters are in Thy honour. The queen stood at Thy right hand, clad in garments embroidered with gold. Hearken, O daughter, and behold, and incline thine ear, and forget thy people and the house of thy father; and the King shall desire thy beauty: because he is thy Lord, and thou shalt worship Him.' Therefore these words testify explicitly that He is witnessed to by Him who established these things, as deserving to be worshipped, as God and as Christ. Moreover, that the word of God speaks to those who believe in Him as being one soul, and one synagogue, and one church, as to a daughter; that it thus addresses the church which has sprung from His name and partakes of His name(for we are all called Christians), is distinctly proclaimed in like manner in the following words, which teach us also to forget[our] old ancestral customs, when they speak thus:'Hearken, O daughter, and behold, and incline thine ear; forget thy people and the house of thy father, and the King shall desire thy beauty: because He is thy Lord, and thou shalt worship Him.'"

CHAPTER LXIV -- JUSTIN ADDUCES OTHER PROOFS TO THE JEW, WHO DENIES THAT HE NEEDS THIS CHRIST.

Here Trypho said, "Let Him be recognised as Lord and Christ and God, as the Scriptures declare, by you of the Gentiles, who have from His name been all called Christians; but we who are servants of God that made this same[Christ], do not require to confess or worship Him."

To this I replied, "If I were to be quarrelsome and light-minded like you, Trypho,

I would no longer continue to converse with you, since you are prepared not to understand what has been said, but only to return some captious answer; but now, since I fear the judgment of God, I do not state an untimely opinion concerning any one of your nation, as to whether or not some of them may be saved by the grace of the Lord of Sabaoth. Therefore, although you act wrongfully, I shall continue to reply to any proposition you shall bring forward, and to any contradiction which you make; and, in fact, I do the very same to all men of every nation, who wish to examine along with me, or make inquiry at me, regarding this subject. Accordingly, if you had bestowed attention on the Scriptures previously quoted by me, you would already have understood, that those who are saved of your own nation are saved through this[man], and partake of His lot; and you would not certainly have asked me about this matter. I shall again repeat the words of David previously quoted by me, and beg of you to comprehend them, and not to act wrongfully, and stir each other up to give merely some contradiction. The words which David speaks, then, are these:'The Lord has reigned; let the nations be angry:[it is] He who sits upon the cherubim; let the earth be shaken. The Lord is great in Zion; and He is high above all the nations. Let them confess Thy great name, for it is fearful and holy; and the honour of the king loves judgment. Thou hast prepared equity; judgment and righteousness hast Thou performed in Jacob. Exalt the Lord our God, and worship the footstool of His feet; for He is holy. Moses and Aaron among His priests, and Samuel among them that call upon His name; they called on the Lord, and He heard them. In the pillar of the cloud He spake to them; for they kept His testimonies and His commandments which He gave them.' And from the other words of David, also previously quoted, which you foolishly affirm refer to Solomon,[because] inscribed for Solomon, it can be proved that they do not refer to Solomon, and that this[Christ] existed before the sun, and that those of your nation who are saved shall be saved through Him.[The words] are these:'O God, give Thy judgment to the king, and Thy righteousness unto the king's son. He shall judge Thy people with righteousness, and Thy poor with judgment. The mountains shall take up peace to the people, and the little hills righteousness. He shall judge the poor of the people, and shall save the children of the needy, and shall abase the slanderer: and He shall co-endure with the sun, and before the moon unto all generations;'and so on until, 'His name endureth before the sun, and all tribes of the earth shall be blessed in Him. All nations shall call Him blessed. Blessed be the Lord, the God of Israel, who only doeth wondrous things: and blessed be His glorious name for ever and ever: and the whole earth shall be filled with His glory. Amen, Amen.' And you remember from other words also spoken by David, and which I have mentioned before, how it is declared that He would come forth from the highest heavens, and again return to the same places, in order that you may recognise Him as God coming forth from above, and man living among men; and[how it is declared] that He will again appear, and they who pierced Him shall see Him, and shall bewail Him.[The words] are these: 'The heavens declare the glory of God, and the firmament showeth His handiwork. Day unto day uttereth speech, and night unto night showeth knowledge: They are not speeches or words whose voices are heard. Their sound has gone out through all the earth, and their words to the ends of the world. In the sun has he set his habitation; and he, like a bridegroom going forth from his chamber, will rejoice as a giant to run his race: from the highest heaven is his going forth, and he returns to the highest heaven, and there is not one who shall be hidden from his heat.' "

CHAPTER LXVI -- HE PROVES FROM ISAIAH THAT GOD WAS BORN FROM A VIRGIN.

And I, resuming the discourse where I had left off at a previous s when proving that He was born of a virgin, and that His birth of a virgin had been p cted by Isaiah, quoted again the same prophecy. It is as follows 'And the Lord spo ain to Ahaz, saying, Ask for thyself a sign from the Lord thy God, in the depth or in eight. And Ahaz said I will not ask, neither will I tempt the Lord. And Isaiah sai then, O house of David; Is it no small thing for you to contend with men? An do you contend with the Lord? Therefore the Lord Himself will give you a sign , the virgin shall conceive, and shall bear a son, and they shall call his name el. Butter and honey shall he eat; before he knows or prefers the evil he will c the good. For before the child knows ill or good, he rejects evil by choosin at good. For before the child knows how to call father or mother, he shall rec power of Damascus, and the spoil of Samaria, in presence of the king of Assyr the land shall be forsaken, which thou shalt with difficulty endure in consequen the presence of its two kings. But God shall bring on thee, and on thy people, an the house of thy father, days which have not yet come upon thee since the day in w Ephraim took away from Judah the king of Assyria.' " And I continued: "Now it evident to all, that in the race of Abraham according to the flesh no one has been bo of a virgin, or is said to have been born[of a virgin], save this our Christ."

CHAPTER LXVII -- TRYPHO COMPARES JESUS WITH PERSEUS; AND WOULD PREFER[TO SAY] THAT HE WAS ELECTED[TO BE CHRIST] ON ACCOUNT OF OBSERVANCE OF THE LAW. JUSTIN SPEAKS OF THE LAW AS FORMERLY.

And Trypho answered, "The Scripture has not, 'Behold, the virgin shall conceive, and bear a son,' but, 'Behold, the young woman shall conceive, and bear a son,' and so on, as you quoted. But the whole prophecy refers to Hezekiah, and it is proved that it was fulfilled in him, according to the terms of this prophecy. Moreover, in the fables of those who are called Greeks, it is written that Perseus was begotten of Danae, who was a virgin; he who was called among them Zeus having descended on her in the form of a golden shower. And you ought to feel ashamed when you make assertions similar to theirs, and rather[should] say that this Jesus was born man of men. And if you prove from the Scriptures that He is the Christ, and that on account of having led a life conformed to the law, and perfect, He deserved the honour of being elected to be Christ,[it is well]; but do not venture to tell monstrous phenomena, lest you be convicted of talking foolishly like the Greeks."

Then I said to this, "Trypho, I wish to persuade you, and all men in short, of this, that even though you talk worse things in ridicule and in jest, you will not move me from my fixed design; but I shall always adduce from the words which you think can be brought forward[by you] as proof[of your own views], the demonstration of what I have stated along with the testimony of the Scriptures. You are not, however, acting fairly or truthfully in attempting to undo those things in which there has been constantly agreement between us; namely, that certain commands were instituted by

Moses on account of the hardness of your people's hearts. For you said that, by reason of His living conformably to law, He was elected and became Christ, if indeed He were proved to be so."

And Trypho said, "You admitted to us that He was both circumcised, and observed the other legal ceremonies ordained by Moses."

And I replied, "I have admitted it, and do admit it: yet I have admitted that He endured all these not as if He were justified by them, but completing the dispensation which His Father, the Maker of all things, and Lord and God, wished Him[to complete]. For I admit that He endured crucifixion and death, and the incarnation, and the suffering of as many afflictions as your nation put upon Him. But since again you dissent from that to which you but lately assented, Trypho, answer me: Are those righteous patriarchs who lived before Moses, who observed none of those[ordinances] which, the Scripture shows, received the commencement of[their] institution from Moses, saved,[and have they attained to] the inheritance of the blessed?"

And Trypho said, "The Scriptures compel me to admit it."

"Likewise I again ask you," said I, "did God enjoin your fathers to present the offerings and sacrifices because He had need of them, or because of the hardness of their hearts and tendency to idolatry?"

"The latter," said he, "the Scriptures in like manner compel us to admit."

"Likewise," said I, "did not the Scriptures predict that God promised to dispense a new covenant besides that which[was dispensed] in the mountain Horeb?"

This, too, he replied, had been predicted.

Then I said again, "Was not the old covenant laid on your fathers with fear and trembling, so that they could not give ear to God?"

He admitted it.

"What then?" said I: "God promised that there would be another covenant, not like that old one, and said that it would be laid on them without fear, and trembling, and lightnings, and that it would be such as to show what kind of commands and deeds God knows to be eternal and suited to every nation, and what commandments He has given, suiting them to the hardness of your people's hearts, as He exclaims also by the prophets."

"To this also," said he, "those who are lovers of truth and not lovers of strife must assuredly assent."

Then I replied, "I know not how you speak of persons very fond of strife,[since] you yourself oftentimes were plainly acting in this very manner, frequently contradicting what you had agreed to."

CHAPTER LXVIII -- HE COMPLAINS OF THE OBSTINACY OF TRYPHO; HE ANSWERS HIS OBJECTION; HE CONVICTS THE JEWS OF BAD FAITH.

And Trypho said, "You endeavour to prove an incredible and well-nigh impossible thing;[namely], that God endured to be born and become man."

"If I undertook," said I, "to prove this by doctrines or arguments of man, you should not bear with me. But if I quote frequently Scriptures, and so many of them, referring to this point, and ask you to comprehend them, you are hard-hearted in the recognition of the mind and will of God. But if you wish to remain for ever so, I would not be injured at all; and for ever retaining the same[opinions] which I had before I met with you, I shall leave you."

And Trypho said," Look, my friend, you made yourself master of these[truths] with much labour and toil. And we accordingly must diligently scrutinize all that we meet with, in order to give our assent to those things which the Scriptures compel us[to believe]."

Then I said to this, "I do not ask you not to strive earnestly by all means, in making an investigation of the matters inquired into; but[I ask you], when you have nothing to say, not to contradict those things which you said you had admitted."

And Trypho said, "So we shall endeavour to do."

I continued again: "In addition to the questions I have just now put to you, I wish to put more: for by means of these questions I shall strive to bring the discourse to a speedy termination."

And Trypho said, "Ask the questions."

Then I said, "Do you think that any other one is said to be worthy of worship and called Lord and God in the Scriptures, except the Maker of all, and Christ, who by so many Scriptures was proved to you to have become man?"

And Trypho replied, "How can we admit this, when we have instituted so great an inquiry as to whether there is any other than the Father alone?"

Then I again said, "I must ask you this also, that I may know whether or not you are of a different opinion from that which you admitted some time ago."

He replied, "It is not, sir."

Then again I, "Since you certainly admit these things, and since Scripture says, 'Who shall declare His generation?' ought you not now to suppose that He is not the seed of a human race?"

And Trypho said, "How then does the Word say to David, that out of his loins God shall take to Himself a Son, and shall establish His kingdom, and shall set Him on the throne of His glory?"

And I said, "Trypho, if the prophecy which Isaiah uttered, "Behold, the virgin shall conceive,' is said not to the house of David, but to another house of the twelve tribes, perhaps the matter would have some difficulty; but since this prophecy refers to the house of David, Isaiah has explained how that which was spoken by God to David in mystery would take place. But perhaps you are not aware of this, my friends, that there were many sayings written obscurely, or parabolically, or mysteriously, and symbolical actions, which the prophets who lived after the persons who said or did them expounded." "Assuredly," said Trypho.

"If therefore, I shall show that this prophecy of Isaiah refers to our Christ, and not to Hezekiah, as you say, shall I not in this matter, too,

compel you not to believe your teachers, who venture to assert that the explanation which your seventy elders that were with Ptolemy the king of the Egyptians gave, is untrue in certain respects? For some statements in the Scriptures, which appear explicitly to convict them of a foolish and vain opinion, these they venture to assert have not been so written. But other statements, which they fancy they can distort and harmonize with human actions, these, they say, refer not to this Jesus Christ of ours, but to him of whom they are pleased to explain them. Thus, for instance, they have taught you that this Scripture which we are now discussing refers to Hezekiah, in which, as I promised, I shall show they are wrong. And since they are compelled, they agree that some Scriptures which we mention to them, and which expressly prove that Christ was to suffer, to be worshipped, and[to be called] God, and which I have already recited to you, do refer indeed to Christ, but they venture to assert that this man is not Christ. But they admit that He will come to suffer, and to reign, and to be worshipped, and to be God; and this opinion I shall in like manner show to be ridiculous and silly. But since I am pressed to answer first to what was said by you in jest, I shall make answer to it, and shall afterwards give replies to what follows.

CHAPTER LXIX -- THE DEVIL, SINCE HE EMULATES THE TRUTH, HAS INVENTED FABLES ABOUT BACCHUS, HERCULES, AND SCULAPIUS.

"Be well assured, then, Trypho," I continued, "that I am established in the knowledge of and faith in the Scriptures by those counterfeits which he who is called the devil is said to have performed among the Greeks; just as some were wrought by the Magi in Egypt, and others by the false prophets in Elijah's days. For when they tell that Bacchus, son of Jupiter, was begotten by[Jupiter's] intercourse with Semele, and that he was the discoverer of the vine; and when they relate, that being torn in pieces, and having died, he rose again, and ascended to heaven; and when they introduce wine into his mysteries, do I not perceive that[the devil] has imitated the prophecy announced by the patriarch Jacob, and recorded by Moses? And when they tell that Hercules was strong, and travelled over all the world, and was begotten by Jove of Alcmene, and ascended to heaven when he died, do I not perceive that the Scripture which speaks of Christ, 'strong as a giant to run his race,' has been in like manner imitated? And when he[the devil] brings forward sculapius as the raiser of the dead and healer of all diseases, may I not say that in this matter likewise he has imitated the prophecies about Christ? But since I have not quoted to you such Scripture as tells that Christ will do these things, I must necessarily remind you of one such: from which you can understand, how that to those destitute of a knowledge of God, I mean the Gentiles, who, 'having eyes, saw not, and having a heart, understood not,' worshipping the images of wood,[how even to them] Scripture prophesied that they would renounce these[vanities], and hope in this Christ. It is thus written: 'Rejoice, thirsty wilderness:

let the wilderness be glad, and blossom as the lily: the deserts of the Jordan shall both blossom and be glad: and the glory of Lebanon was given to it, and the honour of Carmel. And my people shall see the exaltation of the Lord, and the glory of God. Be strong, ye careless hands and enfeebled knees. Be comforted, ye faint in soul: be strong, fear not. Behold, our God gives, and will give, retributive judgment. He shall come and save us. Then the eyes of the blind shall be opened, and the ears of the deaf shall hear. Then the lame shall leap as an hart, and the tongue of the stammerers shall be distinct: for water has broken forth in the wilderness, and a valley in the thirsty land; and the parched ground shall become pools, and a spring of water shall[rise up] in the thirsty land.' The spring of living water which gushed forth from God in the land destitute of the knowledge of God, namely the land of the Gentiles, was this Christ, who also appeared in your nation, and healed those who were maimed, and deaf, and lame in body from their birth, causing them to leap, to hear, and to see, by His word. And having raised the dead, and causing them to live, by His deeds He compelled the men who lived at that time to recognise Him. But though they saw such works, they asserted it was magical art. For they dared to call Him a magician, and a deceiver of the people. Yet He wrought such works, and persuaded those who were[destined to] believe on Him; for even if any one be labouring under a defect of body, yet be an observer of the doctrines delivered by Him, He shall raise him up at His second advent perfectly sound, after He has made him immortal, and incorruptible, and free from grief.

CHAPTER LXX -- SO ALSO THE MYSTERIES OF MITHRAS ARE DISTORTED FROM THE PROPHECIES OF DANIEL AND ISAIAH.

"And when those who record the mysteries of Mithras say that he was begotten of a rock, and call the place where those who believe in him are initiated a cave, do I not perceive here that the utterance of Daniel, that a stone without hands was cut out of a great mountain, has been imitated by them, and that they have attempted likewise to imitate the whole of Isaiah's words? For they contrived that the words of righteousness be quoted also by them. But I must repeat to you the words of Isaiah referred to, in order that from them you may know that these things are so. They are these: 'Hear, ye that are far off, what I have done; those that are near shall know my might. The sinners in Zion are removed; trembling shall seize the impious. Who shall announce to you the everlasting place? The man who walks in righteousness, speaks in the right way, hates sin and unrighteousness, and keeps his hands pure from bribes, stops the ears from hearing the unjust judgment of blood closes the eyes from seeing unrighteousness: he shall dwell in the lofty cave of the strong rock. Bread shall be given to him, and his water[shall be] sure. Ye shall see the King with glory, and your eyes shall look far off. Your soul shall pursue diligently the fear of the Lord. Where is the scribe? where are the counsellors? where is he that numbers those who are nourished,--the small and great people? with whom they did not take counsel, nor knew the depth of the voices, so that they heard not. The people who are become depreciated, and there is no understanding in him who hears.' Now it is evident, that in this prophecy[allusion is made] to the bread which our Christ gave us to eat, in remembrance of His being made flesh for the sake of His believers, for whom also He suffered; and to the cup which He gave us to drink, in remembrance of His own blood, with giving of thanks.

CHAPTER LXXIV -- THE BEGINNING OF PS. XCVI. IS ATTRIBuTED TO THE FATHER[BY TRYPHO]. BUT[IT REFERS] TO CHRIST BY THESE WORDS: "TELL YE AMONG THE NATIONS THAT THE LORD," ETC.

Then Trypho said, "We know that you quoted these because we asked you. But it does not appear to me that this Psalm which you quoted last from the words of David refers to any other than the Father and Maker of the heavens and earth. You, however, asserted that it referred to Him who suffered, whom you also are eagerly endeavouring to prove to be Christ."

And I answered, "Attend to me, I beseech you, while I speak of the statement which the Holy Spirit gave utterance to in this Psalm; and you shall know that I speak not sinfully, and that we are not really bewitched; for so you shall be enabled of yourselves to understand many other statements made by the Holy Spirit. 'Sing unto the Lord a new song; sing unto the Lord, all the earth: sing unto the Lord, and bless His name; show forth His salvation from day to day, His wonderful works among all people.' He bids the inhabitants of all the earth, who have known the mystery of this salvation, i.e., the suffering of Christ, by which He saved them, sing and give praises to God the Father of all things, and recognise that He is to be praised and feared, and that He is the Maker of heaven and earth, who effected this salvation in behalf of the human race, who also was crucified and was dead, and who was deemed worthy by Him(God) to reign over all the earth. As[is clearly seen] also by the land into which[He said] He would bring[your fathers];[for He thus speaks]: 'This people[shall go a whoring after other gods], and shall forsake Me, and shall break my covenant which I made with them in that day; and I will forsake them, and will turn away My face from them; and they shall be devoured, and many evils and afflictions shall find them out; and they shall say in that day, Because the Lord my God is not amongst us, these misfortunes have found us out. And I shall certainly turn away My face from them in that day, on account of all the evils which they have committed, in that they have turned to other gods.'

CHAPTER LXXV -- IT IS PROVED THAT JESUS WAS THE NAME OF GOD IN THE BOOK OF EXODUS.

"Moreover, in the book of Exodus we have also perceived that the name of God Himself which, He says, was not revealed to Abraham or to Jacob, was Jesus, and was declared mysteriously through Moses. Thus it is written: 'And the Lord spake to Moses, Say to this people, Behold, I send My angel before thy face, to keep thee in the way, to bring thee into the land which I have prepared for thee. Give heed to Him, and obey Him; do not disobey Him. For He will not draw back from you; for My name is in Him.' Now understand that He who led your fathers into the land is called by this name Jesus, and first called Auses(Oshea). For if you shall understand this, you shall likewise perceive that the name of Him who said to Moses, 'for My name is in Him,' was Jesus. For, indeed, He was also called Israel, and Jacob's name was changed to this also. Now Isaiah shows that those prophets who are sent to publish tidings from God are called His angels and apostles. For Isaiah says in a certain place, 'Send me.'

And that the prophet whose name was changed, Jesus[Joshua], was strong and great, is manifest to all. If, then, we know that God revealed Himself in so many forms to Abraham, and to Jacob, and to Moses, how are we at a loss, and do not believe that, according to the will of the Father of all things, it was possible for Him to be born man of the Virgin, especially after we have such Scriptures, from which it can be plainly perceived that He became so according to the will of the Father?

CHAPTER LXXVI -- FROM OTHER PASSAGES THE SAME MAJESTY AND GOVERNMENT OF CHRIST ARE PROVED.

"For when Daniel speaks of 'one like unto the Son of man' who received the everlasting kingdom, does he not hint at this very thing? For he declares that, in saying 'like unto the Son of man,' He appeared, and was man, but not of human seed. And the same thing he proclaimed in mystery when he speaks of this stone which was cut out without hands. For the expression 'it was cut out without hands' signified that it is not a work of man, but[a work] of the will of the Father and God of all things, who brought Him forth. And when Isaiah says, 'Who shall declare His generation?' he meant that His descent could not be declared. Now no one who is a man of men has a descent that cannot be declared. And when Moses says that He will wash His garments in the blood of the grape, does not this signify what I have now often told you is an obscure prediction, namely, that He had blood, but not from men; just as not man, but God, has begotten the blood of the vine? And when Isaiah calls Him the Angel of mighty 1 counsel, did he not foretell Him to be the Teacher of those truths which He did teach when He came[to earth]? For He alone taught openly those mighty counsels which the Father designed both for all those who have been and shall be well-pleasing to Him, and also for those who have rebelled against His will, whether men or angels, when He said: 'They shall come from the east[and from the west], and shall sit down with Abraham, and Isaac, and Jacob, in the kingdom of heaven: but the children of the kingdom shall be cast out into outer darkness.' And, 'Many shall say to Me in that day, Lord, Lord, have we not eaten, and drunk, and prophesied, and cast out demons in Thy name? And I will say to them, Depart from Me.' Again, in other words, by which He shall condemn those who are unworthy of salvation, He said, Depart into outer darkness, which the Father has prepared for Satan and his, angels.' And again, in other words, He said, 'I give unto you power to tread on serpents, and on scorpions, and on scolopendras, and on all the might of the enemy.' And now we, who believe on our Lord Jesus, who was crucified under Pontius Pilate, when we exorcise all demons and evil spirits, have them subjected to us. For if the prophets declared obscurely that Christ would suffer, and thereafter be Lord of all, yet that[declaration] could not be understood by any man until He Himself persuaded the apostles that such statements were expressly related in the Scriptures. For He exclaimed before His crucifixion: 'The Son of man must suffer many things, and be rejected by the Scribes and Pharisees, and be crucified, and on the third day rise again.' And David predicted that He would be born from the womb before sun and moon, according to the Father's will, and made Him known, being Christ, as God strong and to be worshipped."

CHAPTER LXXVII -- HE RETURNS TO EXPLAIN THE PROPHECY OF ISAIAH.

Then Trypho said, "I admit that such and so great arguments are sufficient to persuade one; but I wish[you] to know that I ask you for the proof which you have frequently proposed to give me. Proceed then to make this plain to us, that we may see how you prove that that[passage] refers to this Christ of yours. For we assert that the prophecy relates to Hezekiah." And I replied, "I shall do as you wish. But show me yourselves first of all how it is said of Hezekiah, that before he knew how to call father or mother, he received the power of Damascus and the spoils of Samaria in the presence of the king of Assyria. For it will not be conceded to you, as you wish to explain it, that Hezekiah waged war with the inhabitants of Damascus and Samaria in presence of the king of Assyria. 'For before the child knows how to call father or mother,' the prophetic word said, 'He shall take the power of Damascus and spoils of Samaria in presence of the king of Assyria.' For if the Spirit of prophecy had not made the statement with an addition, 'Before the child knows how to call father or mother, he shall take the power of Damascus and spoils of Samaria,' but had only said, 'And shall bear a son, and he shall take the power of Damascus and spoils of Samaria,' then you might say that God foretold that he would take these things, since He fore-knew it. But now the prophecy has stated it with this addition: 'Before the child knows how to call father or mother, he shall take the power of Damascus and spoils of Samaria.' And you cannot prove that such a thing ever happened to any one among the Jews. But we are able to prove that it happened in the case of our Christ. For at the time of His birth, Magi who came from Arabia worshipped Him, coming first to Herod, who then was sovereign in your land, and whom the Scripture calls king of Assyria on account of his ungodly and sinful character. For you know," continued I, "that the Holy Spirit oftentimes announces such events by parables and similitudes; just as He did towards all the people in Jerusalem, frequently saying to them, 'Thy father is an Amorite, and thy mother a Hittite.

CHAPTER LXXVIII -- HE PROVES THAT THIS PROPHECY HARMONIZES WITH CHRIST ALONE, FROM WHAT IS AFTERWARDS WRITTEN.

"Now this king Herod, at the time when the Magi came to him from Arabia, and said they knew from a star which appeared in the heavens that a King had been born in your country, and that they had come to worship Him, learned from the elders of your people that it was thus written regarding Bethlehem in the prophet: 'And thou, Bethlehem, in the land of Judah, art by no means least among the princes of Judah; for out of thee shall go forth the leader who shall feed my people.' Accordingly the Magi from Arabia came to Bethlehem and worshipped the Child, and presented Him with gifts, gold and frankincense, and myrrh; but returned not to Herod, being warned in a revelation after worshipping the Child in Bethlehem. And Joseph, the spouse of Mary, who wished at first to put away his betrothed Mary, supposing her to be pregnant by intercourse with a man, i.e., from fornication, was commanded in a vision not to put away his wife; and the angel who appeared to him told him that what is in her womb is of the Holy Ghost. Then he was afraid, and did not put her away; but on the occasion of the first census which was taken in Jud a, under Cyrenius, he went up from Nazareth, where he lived, to Bethlehem, to which he belonged, to be enrolled; for his family was of the tribe of Judah, which then inhabited that region. Then along with Mary he is ordered to proceed into Egypt, and remain there with the Child until another revelation warn them to return into Jud a. But when the Child was born in Bethlehem, since Joseph could not find a lodging in that village, he took up his quarters in a certain cave near the village; and while they were there Mary brought forth the Christ and placed Him in a manger, and here the Magi who came from Arabia found Him. I have repeated to you," I continued, "what Isaiah foretold about the sign which foreshadowed the cave; but for the sake of those who have come with us to-day, I shall again remind you of the passage." Then I repeated the passage from Isaiah which I have already written, adding that, by means of those words, those who presided over the mysteries of Mithras were stirred up by the devil to say that in a place, called among them a cave, they were initiated by him. "So Herod, when the Magi from Arabia did not return to him, as he had asked them to do, but had departed by another way to their own country, according to the commands laid on them; and when Joseph, with Mary and the Child, had now gone into Egypt, as it was revealed to them to do; as he did not know the Child whom the Magi had gone to worship, ordered simply the whole of the children then in Bethlehem to be massacred. And Jeremiah prophesied that this would happen, speaking by the Holy Ghost thus: 'A voice was heard in Ramah, lamentation and much wailing, Rachel weeping for her children; and she would not be comforted, because they are not.' Therefore, on account of the voice which would be heard from Ramah, i.e., from Arabia(for there is in Arabia at this very time a place called Rama), wailing would come on the place where Rachel the wife of Jacob called lsrael, the holy patriarch, has been buried, i.e., on Bethlehem; while the women weep for their own slaughtered children, and have no consolation by reason of what has happened to them. For that expression of Isaiah 'He shall take the power of Damascus and spoils of Samaria,' foretold that the power of the evil demon that dwelt in Damascus should be overcome by Christ as soon as He was born; and this is proved to have happened. For the Magi, who were held in bondage for the commission of all evil deeds through the power of that demon, by coming to worship Christ, shows that they have revolted from that dominion which held them captive; and this[dominion] the Scripture has showed us to reside in Damascus. Moreover, that sinful and unjust power is termed well in parable, Samaria. And none of you can deny that Damascus was, and is, in the region of Arabia, although now it belongs to what is called Syrophoenicia. Hence it would be becoming for you, sirs, to learn what you have not perceived, from those who have received grace from God, namely, from us Christians; and not to strive in every way to maintain your own doctrines, dishonouring those of God. Therefore also this grace has been transferred to us, as Isaiah says, speaking to the following effect: 'This people draws near to Me, they honour Me with their lips, but their heart is far from Me; but in vain they worship Me, teaching the commands and doctrines of men. Therefore, behold, I will proceed to remove this people, and I shall remove them; and I shall take away the wisdom of their wise men, and bring to nothing the understanding of the prudent men.' "

CHAPTER LXXIX -- HE PROVES AGAINST TRYPHO THAT THE WICKED ANGELS HAVE REVOLTED FROM GOD.

On this, Trypho, who was somewhat angry, but respected the Scriptures, as was manifest from his countenance, said to me, "The utterances of God are holy, but your expositions are mere contrivances, as is plain from what has been explained by you; nay, even blasphemies, for you assert that angels sinned and revolted from God."

And I, wishing to get him to listen to me, answered in milder tones, thus: "I admire, sir, this piety of yours; and I pray that you may entertain the same disposition towards Him to whom angels are recorded to minister, as Daniel says; for[one] like the Son of man is led to the Ancient of days, and every kingdom is given to Him for ever and ever. But that you may know, sir," continued I, "that it is not our audacity which has induced us to adopt this exposition, which you reprehend, I shall give you evidence from Isaiah himself; for he affirms that evil angels have dwelt and do dwell in Tanis, in Egypt. These are[his] words: 'Woe to the rebellious children! Thus saith the Lord, You have taken counsel, but not through Me; and[made] agreements, but not through My Spirit, to add sins to sins; who have sinned in going down to Egypt(but they have not inquired at Me), that they may be assisted by Pharaoh, and be covered with the shadow of the Egyptians. For the shadow of Pharaoh shall be a disgrace to you, and a reproach to those who trust in the Egyptians; for the princes in Tanis are evil angels. In vain will they labour for a people which will not profit them by assistance, but[will be] for a disgrace and a reproach[to them].' And, further, Zechariah tells, as you yourself have related, that the devil stood on the right hand of Joshua the priest, to resist him; and[the Lord] said, 'The Lord, who has taken Jerusalem, rebuke thee.' And again, it is written in Job, as you said yourself, how that the angels came to stand before the Lord, and the devil came with them. And we have it recorded by Moses in the beginning of Genesis, that the serpent beguiled Eve, and was cursed. And we know that in Egypt there were magicians who emulated the mighty power displayed by God through the faithful servant Moses. And you are aware that David said, 'The gods of the nations are demons.'"

CHAPTER LXXX -- THE OPINION OF JUSTIN WITH REGARD TO THE REIGN OF A THOUSAND YEARS. SEVERAL CATHOLICS REJECT IT.

And Trypho to this replied, "I remarked to you sir, that you are very anxious to be safe in all respects, since you cling to the Scriptures. But tell me, do you really admit that this place, Jerusalem, shall be rebuilt; and do you expect your people to be gathered together, and made joyful with Christ and the patriarchs, and the prophets, both the men of our nation, and other proselytes who joined them before your Christ came? or have you given way, and admitted this in order to have the appearance of worsting us in the controversies?"

Then I answered, "I am not so miserable a fellow, Trypho, as to say one thing and think another. I admitted to you formerly, that I and many others are of this opinion, and[believe] that such will take place, as you assuredly are aware; but, on the other hand, I signified to you that many who belong to the pure and pious faith, and are true Christians, think otherwise. Moreover, I pointed out to you that some who are called Christians, but are godless, impious heretics, teach doctrines that are in every way blasphemous, atheistical, and foolish. But that you may know that I do not say this before you alone, I shall draw up a statement, so far as I can, of all the arguments which have passed between us; in which I shall record myself as admitting the very same things which I admit to you. For I choose to follow not men or men's doctrines, but God and the doctrines[delivered] by Him. For if you have fallen in with some who are called Christians, but who do not admit this[truth], and venture to blaspheme the God of Abraham, and the God of Isaac, and the God of Jacob; who say there is no resurrection of the dead, and that their souls, when they die, are taken to heaven; do not imagine that they are Christians, even as one, if he would rightly consider it, would not admit that the Sadducees, or similar sects of Genist , Meristae,Gelilaeans, Hellenists, Pharisees, Baptists, are Jews(do not hear me impatiently when I tell you what I think), but are[only] called Jews and children of Abraham, worshipping God with the lips, as God Himself declared, but the heart was far from Him. But I and others, who are right-minded Christians on all points, are assured that there will be a resurrection of the dead, and a thousand years in Jerusalem, which will then be built, adorned, and enlarged, the prophets Ezekiel and Isaiah and others declare.

CHAPTER LXXXI -- HE ENDEAVOURS TO PROVE THIS OPINION FROM ISAIAH AND THE APOCALYPSE.

"For Isaiah spake thus concerning this space of a thousand years: 'For there shall be the new heaven and the new earth, and the former shall not be remembered, or come into their heart; but they shall find joy and gladness in it, which things I create. For, Behold, I make Jerusalem a rejoicing, and My people a joy; and I shall rejoice over Jerusalem, and be glad over My I people. And the voice of weeping shall be no more heard in her, or the voice of crying. And there shall be no more there a person of immature years, or an old man who shall not fulfil his days. For the young man shall be an hundred years old; but the sinner who dies an hundred years old, he shall be accursed. And they shall build houses, and shall themselves inhabit them; and they shall plant vines, and shall themselves eat the produce of them, and drink the wine. They shall not build, and others inhabit; they shall not plant, and others eat. For according to the days of the tree of life shall be the days of my people; the works of their toil shall abound. Mine elect shall not toil fruitlessly, or beget children to be cursed; for they shall be a seed righteous and blessed by the Lord, and their offspring with them. And it shall come to pass, that before they call I will hear; while they are still speaking, I shall say, What is it? Then shall the wolves and the lambs feed together, and the lion shall eat straw like the ox; but the serpent[shall eat] earth as bread. They shall not hurt or maltreat each other on the holy mountain, i saith the Lord.' Now we have understood that the expression used among these words, 'According to the days of the tree[of life] shall be the days of my people; the works of their toil shall abound' obscurely predicts a thousand years. For as Adam was told that in the nay fie ate of the tree he would die, we know that he did not complete a thousand years. We have perceived, moreover, that the expression, 'The day of the Lord is as a thousand years,' is connected with this subject. And further, there was a certain man with us, whose name was John, one of the apostles of Christ, who prophesied, by a revelation that was made to him, that those who believed in our Christ would dwell a thousand years in Jerusalem; and that thereafter the general, and, in short, the eternal resurrection and judgment of all men would likewise take place. Just as our Lord also said, 'They shall neither marry nor be given in marriage, but shall be equal to the angels, the children of the God of the resurrection.'

CHAPTER LXXXII -- THE PROPHETICAL GIFTS OF THE JEWS WERE TRANSFERRED TO THE CHRISTIANS.

"For the prophetical gifts remain with us, even to the present time. And hence you ought to understand that[the gifts] formerly among your nation have been transferred to us. And just as there were false prophets contemporaneous with your holy prophets, so are there now many false teachers amongst us, of whom our Lord forewarned us to beware; so that in no respect are we deficient, since we know that He foreknew all that would happen to us after His resurrection from the dead and ascension to heaven. For He said we would be put to death, and hated for His name's sake; and that many false prophets and false Christs would appear in His name, and deceive many: and so has it come about. For many have taught godless, blasphemous, and unholy doctrines, forging them in His name; have taught, too, and even yet are teaching, those things which proceed from the unclean spirit of the devil, and which were put into their hearts. Therefore we are most anxious that you be persuaded not to be misled by such persons, since we know that every one who can speak the truth, and yet speaks it not, shall be judged by God, as God testified by Ezekiel, when He said, 'I have made thee a watchman to the house of Judah. If the sinner sin, and thou warn him not, he himself shall die in his sin; but his blood will I require at thine hand. But if thou warn him, thou shalt be innocent.' And on this account we are, through fear, very earnest in desiring to converse[with men] according to the Scriptures, but not from love of money, or of glory, or of pleasure. For no man can convict us of any of these[vices]. No more do we wish to live like the rulers of your people, whom God reproaches when He says, 'Your rulers are companions of thieves, lovers of bribes, followers of the rewards.' Now, if you know certain amongst us to be of this sort, do not for their sakes blaspheme the Scriptures and Christ, and do not assiduously strive to give falsified interpretations.

CHAPTER LXXXIII -- IT IS PROVED THAT THE PSALM, "THE LORD SAID TO MY LORD," ETC., DOES NOT SUIT HEZEKIAH.

"For your teachers have ventured to refer the passage, 'The Lord says to my Lord, Sit at my right hand, till I make Thine enemies Thy footstool,' to Hezekiah; as if he were requested to sit on the right side of the temple, when the king of Assyria sent to him and threatened him; and he was told by Isaiah not to be afraid. Now we know and admit that what Isaiah said took place; that the king of Assyria desisted from waging war against Jerusalem in Hezekiah's days, and the angel of the Lord slew about **185,000** of the host of the Assyrians. But it is manifest that the Psalm does not refer to him. For thus it is written, 'The Lord says to my Lord, Sit at My right hand, till I make Thine enemies Thy footstool. He shall send forth a rod of power over Jerusalem, and it shall rule in the midst of Thine enemies. In the splendour of the saints before the morning star have I begotten Thee. The Lord hath sworn, and will not repent, Thou art a priest for ever after the order of Melchizedek.' Who does not admit, then, that Hezekiah is no priest for ever after the order of Melchizedek? And who does not know that he is not the redeemer of Jerusalem? And who does not know that he neither sent a rod of power into Jerusalem, nor ruled in the midst of his enemies; but that it was God who averted from him the enemies, after he mourned and was afflicted? But our Jesus, who has not yet come in glory, has sent into Jerusalem a rod of power, namely, the word of calling and repentance[meant] for all nations over which demons held sway, as David says, 'The gods of the nations are demons.' And His strong word has prevailed on many to forsake the demons whom they used to serve, and by means of it to believe in the Almighty God because the gods of the nations are demons. And we mentioned formerly that the statement, 'In the splendour of the saints before the morning star have I begotten Thee from the womb,' is made to Christ.

CHAPTER LXXXIV -- THAT PROPHECY, "BEHOLD, A VIRGIN," ETC., SUITS CHRIST ALONE.

"Moreover, the prophecy, 'Behold, the virgin shall conceive, and bear a son,' was uttered respecting Him. For if He to whom Isaiah referred was not to be begotten of a virgin, of whom did the Holy Spirit declare, 'Behold, the Lord Himself shall give us a sign: behold, the virgin shall conceive, and bear a son?' For if He also were to be begotten of sexual intercourse, like all other first-born sons, why did God say that He would give a sign which is not common to all the first-born sons? But that which is truly a sign, and which was to be made trustworthy to mankind,--namely, that the first-begotten of all creation should become incarnate by the Virgin's womb, and be a child,--this he anticipated by the Spirit of prophecy, and predicted it, as I have repeated to you, in various ways; in order that, when the event should take place, it might be known as the operation of the power and will of the Maker of all things; just as Eve was made from one of Adam's ribs, and as all living beings were created in the beginning by the word of God. But you in these matters venture to pervert the expositions which your elders that were with Ptolemy king of Egypt gave forth, since you assert that the Scripture is not so as they have expounded it, but says, 'Behold, the young woman shall conceive,' as if great events were to be inferred if a woman should beget from sexual intercourse: which indeed all young women, with the exception of the barren, do; but even these, God, if He wills, is able to cause[to bear]. For Samuel's mother, who was barren, brought forth by 1 the will of God; and so also the wife of the holy patriarch Abraham; and Elisabeth, who bore John the Baptist, and other such. So that you must not suppose that it is impossible for God to do anything He wills. And especially when it was predicted that this would take place, do not venture to pervert or misinterpret the prophecies, since you will injure yourselves alone, and will not harm God.

CHAPTER LXXXV -- HE PROVES THAT CHRIST IS THE LORD OF HOSTS FROM PS. XXIV., AND FROM HIS AUTHORITY OVER DEMONS.

"Moreover, some of you venture to expound the prophecy which runs, 'Lift up your gates, ye rulers; and be ye lift up, ye everlasting doors, that the King of glory may enter,' as if it referred likewise to Hezekiah, and others of you[expound it] of Solomon; but neither to the latter nor to the former, nor, in short, to any of your kings, can it be proved to have reference, but to this our Christ alone, who appeared without comeliness, and inglorious, as Isaiah and David and all the Scriptures said; who is the Lord of hosts, by the will of the Father who conferred on Him[the dignity]; who also rose from the dead, and ascended to heaven, as the Psalm and the other Scriptures manifested when they announced Him to be Lord of hosts; and of this you may, if you will, easily be persuaded by the occurrences which take place before your eyes. For every demon, when exorcised in the name of this very Son of God--who is the First-born of every creature, who became man by the Virgin, who suffered, and was crucified under Pontius Pilate by your nation, who died, who rose from the dead, and ascended into heaven--is overcome and subdued. But though you exorcise any demon in the name of any of those who were amongst you--either kings, or righteous men, or prophets, or patriarchs--it will not be subject to you. But if any of you exorcise it in[the name of] the God of Abraham, and the God of Isaac, and the God of Jacob, it will perhaps be subject to you. Now assuredly your exorcists, I have said, make use of craft when they exorcise, even as the Gentiles do, and employ fumigations and incantations. But that they are angels and powers whom the word of prophecy by David[commands] to lift up the gates, that He who rose from the dead, Jesus Christ, the Lord of hosts, according to the will of the Father, might enter, the word of David has likewise showed; which I shall again recall to your attention for the sake of those who were not with us yesterday, for whose benefit, moreover, I sum up many things I said yesterday. And now, if I say this to you, although I have repeated it many times, I know that it is not absurd so to do. For it is a ridiculous thing to see the sun, and the moon, and the other stars, continually keeping the same course, and bringing round the different seasons; and to see the computer who may be asked how many are twice two, because he has frequently said that they are four, not ceasing to say again that they late four; and equally so other things, which are confidently admitted, to be continually mentioned and admitted in like manner; yet that he who founds his discourse on the prophetic Scriptures should leave them and abstain from constantly referring to the same Scriptures, because it is thought he can bring forth something better than Scripture. The passage, then, by which I proved that God reveals that there are both angels and hosts in heaven is this: 'Praise the Lord from the heavens: praise Him in the highest. Praise Him, all His angels: praise Him, all His hosts.' "

Then one of those who had come with them on the second day, whose name was Mnaseas, said, "We are greatly pleased that you undertake to repeat the same things on our account."

And I said, "Listen, my friends, to the Scripture which induces me to act thus. Jesus commanded to love even[our] enemies, as was predicted by Isaiah in many passages, in which also is contained the mystery of our own regeneration, as well, in fact, as the regeneration of all who expect that Christ will appear in Jerusalem, and by their works endeavour earnestly to please Him. These are the words spoken by Isaiah: 'Hear the word of the Lord, ye that tremble at His word. Say, our brethren, to them that hate you and detest you, that the name of the Lord has been glorified. He has appeared to your joy, and they shall be ashamed. A voice of noise from the city, a voice from the temple, a voice of the Lord who rendereth recompense to the proud. Before she that travailed brought forth, and before the pains of labour came, she brought forth a male child. Who hath heard such a thing? and who hath seen such a thing? has the earth brought forth in one day? and has she produced a nation at once? for Zion has travailed and borne her children. But I haye given such an expectation even to her that does not bring forth, said the Lord. Behold, I have made her that begetteth, and her that is barren, saith the Lord. Rejoice, O Jerusalem, and hold a joyous assembly, all ye that love her. Be glad, all ye that mourn for her, that ye may suck and be filled with the breast of her consolation, that having suck ye may be delighted with the entrance of His glory.' "

CHAPTER LXXXVI -- THERE ARE VARIOUS FIGURES IN THE OLD TESTAMENT OF THE WOOD OF THE CROSS BY WHICH CHRIST REIGNED.

And when I had quoted this, I added, "Hear, then, how this Man, of whom the Scriptures declare that He will come again in glory after His crucifixion, was symbolized both by the tree of life, which was said to have been planted in paradise, and by those events which should happen to all the just. Moses was sent with a rod to effect the redemption of the people; and with this in his hands at the head of the people, he divided the sea. By this he saw the water gushing out of the rock; and when he cast a tree into the waters of Marah, which were bitter, he made them sweet. Jacob, by putting rods into the water-troughs, caused the sheep of his uncle to conceive, so that he should obtain their young. With his rod the same Jacob boasts that he had crossed the river. He said he had seen a ladder, and the Scripture has declared that God stood above it. But that this was not the Father, we have proved from the Scriptures. And Jacob, having poured oil on a stone in the same place, is testified to by the very God who appeared to him, that he had anointed a pillar to the God who appeared to him. And that the stone symbolically proclaimed Christ, we have also proved by many Scriptures; and that the unguent, whether it was of oil, or of stacte, or of any other compounded sweet balsams, had reference to Him, we have also proved, inasmuch as the word says: 'Therefore God, even Thy God, hath anointed Thee with the oil of gladness above Thy fellows.' For indeed all kings and anointed persons obtained from Him their share in the names of kings and anointed: just as He Himself received from the Father the titles of King, and Christ, and Priest, and Angel, and such like other titles which He bears or did bear. Aaron's rod, which blossomed, declared him to be the high priest. Isaiah prophesied that a rod would come forth from the root of Jesse,[and this was] Christ. And David says that the righteous man is 'like the tree that is planted by the channels of waters, which should yield its fruit in its season, and whose leaf should not fade.' Again, the righteous is said to flourish like the palm-tree. God appeared from a tree to Abraham, as it is written, near the oak in Mature. The people found seventy willows and twelve springs after crossing the Jordan. David affirms that God comforted him with a rod and staff. Elisha, by casting a stick into the river Jordan, recovered the iron part of the axe with which the sons of the prophets had gone to cut down trees to build the house in which they wished to read and study the law and commandments of God; even as our Christ, by being crucified on the tree, and by purifying with water, has redeemed us, though plunged in the direst offences which we have committed, and has made a house of prayer and adoration. Moreover, it was a rod that pointed out Judah to be the father of Tamar's sons by a great mystery."

CHAPTER LXXXVII -- TRYPHO MAINTAINS IN OBJECTION THESE WORDS: "AND SHALL REST ON HIM," ETC. THEY ARE EXPLAINED BY JUSTIN.

Hereupon Trypho, after I had spoken these words, said, "Do not now suppose that I am endeavouring, by asking what I do ask, to overturn the statements you have made; but I wish to receive information respecting those very points about which I now inquire. Tell me, then, how, when the Scripture asserts by Isaiah, 'There shall come forth a rod from the root of Jesse; and a flower shall grow up from the root of Jesse; and the Spirit of God shall rest upon Him, the spirit of wisdom and understanding, the spirit of counsel and might, the spirit of knowledge and piety: and the spirit of the fear of the Lord shall fill Him:' (now you admitted to me," continued he, "that this referred to Christ, and you maintain Him to be pre-existent God, and having become incarnate by God's will, to be born man by the Virgin:) how He can be demonstrated to have been pre-existent, who is filled with the powers of the Holy Ghost, which the Scripture by Isaiah enumerates, as if He were in lack of them?"

Then I replied, "You have inquired most discreetly and most prudently, for truly there does seem to be a difficulty; but listen to what I say, that you may perceive the reason of this also. The Scripture says that these enumerated powers of the Spirit have come on Him, not because He stood in need of them, but because they would rest in Him, i.e., would find their accomplishment in Him, so that there would be no more prophets in your nation after the ancient custom: and this fact you plainly perceive. For after Him no prophet has arisen among you. Now, that [you may know that] your prophets, each receiving some one or two powers from God, did and spoke the things which we have learned from the Scriptures, attend to the following remarks of mine. Solomon possessed the spirit of wisdom, Daniel that of understanding and counsel, Moses that of might and piety, Elijah that of fear, and Isaiah that of knowledge; and so with the others: each possessed one power, or one joined alternately with another; also Jeremiah, and the twelve [prophets], and David, and, in short, the rest who existed amongst you. Accordingly He rested, i.e., ceased, when He came, after whom, in the times of this dispensation wrought out by Him amongst men, it was requisite that such gifts should cease from you; and having received their rest in Him, should again, as had been predicted, become gifts which, from the grace of His Spirit's power, He imparts to those who believe in Him, according as He deems each man worthy thereof. I have already said, and do again say, that it had been prophesied that this would be done by Him after His ascension to heaven. It is accordingly said, 'He ascended on high, He led captivity captive, He gave gifts unto the sons of men.' And again, in another prophecy it is said: 'And it shall come to pass after this, I will pour out My Spirit on all flesh, and on My servants, and on My handmaids, and they shall prophesy.'

CHAPTER LXXXVIII -- CHRIST HAS NOT RECEIVED THE HOLY SPIRIT ON ACCOUNT OF POVERTY.

"Now, it is possible to see amongst us women and men who possess gifts of the Spirit of God; so that it was prophesied that the powers enumerated by Isaiah would come upon Him, not because He needed power, but because these would not continue after Him. And let this be a proof to you, namely, what I told you was done by the Magi from Arabia, who as soon as the Child was born came to worship Him, for even at His birth He was in possession of His power; and as He grew up like all other men, by using the fitting means, He assigned its own [requirements] to each development, and was sustained by all kinds of nourishment, and waited for thirty years, more or less, until John appeared before Him as the herald of His approach, and preceded Him in the way of baptism, as I have already shown. And then, when Jesus had gone to the river Jordan, where John was baptizing, and when He had stepped into the water, a fire was kindled in the Jordan; and when He came out of the water, the Holy Ghost lighted on Him like a dove, the apostles of this very Christ of ours wrote. Now, we know that he did not go to the river because He stood in need of baptism, or of the descent of the Spirit like a dove; even as He submitted to be born and to be crucified, not because He needed such things, but because of the human race, which from Adam had fallen under the power of death and the guile of the serpent, and each one of which had committed personal transgression. For God, wishing both angels and men, who were endowed with freewill, and at their own disposal, to do whatever He had strengthened each to do, made them so, that if they chose the things acceptable to Himself, He would keep them free from death and from punishment; but that if they did evil, He would punish each as He sees fit. For it was not His entrance into Jerusalem sitting on an ass, which we have showed was prophesied, that empowered Him to be Christ, but it furnished men with a proof that He is the Christ; just as it was necessary in the time of John that men have proof, that they might know who is Christ. For when John remained by the Jordan, and preached the baptism of repentance, wearing only a leathern girdle and a vesture made of camels' hair, eating nothing but locusts and wild honey, men supposed him to be Christ; but he cried to them, 'I am not the Christ, but the voice of one crying; for He that is stronger than I shall come, whose shoes I am not worthy to bear.' And when Jesus came to the Jordan, He was considered to be the son of Joseph the carpenter; and He appeared without comeliness, as the Scriptures declared; and He was deemed a carpenter (for He was in the habit of working as a carpenter when among men, making ploughs and yokes; by which He taught the symbols of righteousness and an active life); but then the Holy Ghost, and for man's sake, as I formerly stated, lighted on Him in the form of a dove, and there came at the same instant from the heavens a voice, which was uttered also by David when he spoke, personating Christ, what the Father would say to Him: 'Thou art My Son: this day have I begotten Thee;' [the Father] saying that His generation would take place for men, at the time when they would become acquainted with Him: 'Thou art My Son; this day have I begotten thee.' "

CHAPTER LXXXIX -- THE CROSS ALONE IS OFFENSIVE TO TRYPHO ON ACCOUNT OF THE CURSE, YET IT PROVES THAT JESUS IS CHRIST.

Then Trypho remarked, "Be assured that all our nation waits for Christ; and we admit that all the Scriptures which you have quoted refer to Him. Moreover, I do also admit that the name of Jesus, by which the the son of Nave (Nun) was called, has inclined me very strongly to adopt this view. But whether Christ should be so shamefully crucified, this we are in doubt about. For whosoever is crucified is said in the law to be accursed, so that I am exceedingly incredulous on this point. It is quite clear, indeed, that the Scriptures announce that Christ had to suffer; but we wish to learn if you can prove it to us whether it was by the suffering cursed in the law."

I replied to him, "If Christ was not to suffer, and the prophets had not foretold that He would be led to death on account of the sins of the people, and be dishonoured and scourged, and reckoned among the transgressors, and as a sheep be led to the slaughter, whose generation, the prophet says, no man can declare, then you would have good cause to wonder. But if these are to be characteristic of Him and mark Him out to all, how is it possible for us to do anything else than believe in Him most confidently? And will not as many as have understood the writings of the prophets, whenever they hear merely that He was crucified, say that this is He and no other?"

CHAPTER XC -- THE STRETCHED-OUT HANDS OF MOSES SIGNIFIED BEFOREHAND THE CROSS.

"Bring us on, then," said [Trypho], "by the Scriptures, that we may also be persuaded by you; for we know that He should suffer and be led as a sheep. But prove to us whether He must be crucified and die so disgracefully and so dishonourably by the death cursed in the law. For we cannot bring ourselves even to think of this."

"You know," said I, "that what the prophets said and did they veiled by parables and types, as you admitted to us; so that it was not easy for all to understand the most [of what they said], since they concealed the truth by these means, that those who are eager to find out and learn it might do so with much labour."

They answered, "We admitted this."

"Listen, therefore," say I, "to what follows; for Moses first exhibited this seeming curse of Christ's by the signs which he made."

"Of what [signs] do you speak?" said he.

"When the people," replied I, "waged war with Amalek, and the son of Nave (Nun) by name Jesus (Joshua), led the fight, Moses himself prayed to God, stretching out both hands, and Hur with Aaron supported them during the whole day, so that they might not hang down when he got wearied. For if he gave up any part of this sign, which was an imitation of the cross, the people were beaten, as is recorded in the writings of Moses; but if he remained in this form, Amalek was proportionally defeated, and he who prevailed prevailed by the cross. For it was not because Moses so prayed that the people were stronger, but because, while one who bore the name of Jesus (Joshua) was in the forefront of the battle, he himself made the sign of the cross. For who of you knows not that the prayer of one who accompanies it with lamentation and tears, with the body prostrate, or with bended knees, propitiates God most of all? But in such a manner neither he nor any other one, while sitting on a stone, prayed. Nor even the stone symbolized Christ, as I have shown.

CHAPTER XCI -- THE CROSS WAS FORETOLD IN THE BLESSINGS OF JOSEPH, AND IN THE SERPENT THAT WAS LIFTED UP..

"And God by Moses shows in another way the force of the mystery of the cross, when He said in the blessing wherewith Joseph was blessed, 'From the blessing of the Lord is his land; for the seasons of heaven, and for the dews, and for the deep springs from beneath, and for the seasonable fruits of the sun, and for the coming together of the months, and for the heights of the everlasting mountains, and for the heights of the hills, and for the ever-flowing rivers, and for the fruits of the fatness of the earth; and let the things accepted by Him who appeared in the bush come on the head and crown of Joseph. Let him be glorified among his brethren; his beauty is [like] the firstling of a bullock; his horns the horns of an unicorn: with these shall he push the nations from one end of the earth to another.' Now, no one could say or prove that the horns of an unicorn represent any other fact or figure than the type which portrays the cross. For the one beam is placed upright, from which the highest extremity is raised up into a horn, when the other beam is fitted on to it, and the ends appear on both sides as horns joined on to the one horn. And the part which is fixed in the centre, on which are suspended those who are crucified, also stands out like a horn; and it also looks like a horn conjoined and fixed with the other horns. And the expression, 'With these shall he push as with horns the nations from one end of the earth to another,' is indicative of what is now the fact among all the nations. For some out of all the nations, through the power of this mystery, having been so pushed, that is, pricked in their hearts, have turned from vain idols and demons to serve God. But the same figure is revealed for the destruction and condemnation of the unbelievers; even as Amalek was defeated and Israel victorious when the people came out of Egypt, by means of the type of the stretching out of Moses' hands, and the name of Jesus (Joshua), by which the son of Nave (Nun) was called. And it seems that the type and sign, which was erected to counteract the serpents which bit Israel, was intended for the salvation of those who believe that death was declared to come thereafter on the serpent through Him that would be crucified, but salvation to those who had been bitten by him and had betaken themselves to Him that sent His Son into the world to be crucified. For the Spirit of prophecy by Moses did not teach us to believe in the serpent, since it shows us that he was cursed by God from the beginning; and in Isaiah tells us that he shall be put to death as an enemy by the mighty sword, which is Christ.

CHAPTER XCII -- UNLESS THE SCRIPTURES BE UNDERSTOOD THROUGH GOD'S GREAT GRACE, GOD WILL NOT APPEAR TO HAVE TAUGHT ALWAYS THE SAME RIGHTEOUSNESS..

"Unless, therefore, a man by God's great grace receives the power to understand what has been said and done by the prophets, the appearance of being able to repeat the words or the deeds will not profit him, if he cannot explain the argument of them. And will they not assuredly appear contemptible to many, since they are related by those who understood them not? For if one should wish to ask you why, since Enoch, Noah with his sons, and all others in similar circumstances, who neither were circumcised nor kept the Sabbath, pleased God, God demanded by other leaders, and by the giving of the law after the lapse of so many generations, that those who lived between the times of Abraham and of Moses be justified by circumcision, and that those who lived after Moses be justified by circumcision and the other ordinances--to wit, the Sabbath, and sacrifices, and libations, and offerings; [God will be slandered] unless you show, as I have already said, that God who foreknew was aware that your nation would deserve expulsion from Jerusalem, and that none would be permitted to enter into it.(For you are not distinguished in any other way than by the fleshly circumcision, as I remarked previously. For Abraham was declared by God to be righteous, not on account of circumcision, but on account of faith. For before he was circumcised the following statement was made regarding him: 'Abraham believed God, and it was accounted unto him for righteousness.' And we, therefore, in the uncircumcision of our flesh, believing God through Christ, and having that circumcision which is of advantage to us who have acquired it--namely, that of the heart--we hope to appear righteous before and well-pleasing to God: since already we have received His testimony through the words of the prophets.) [And, further, God will be slandered unless you show] that you were commanded to observe the Sabbath, and to present offerings, and that the Lord submitted to have a place called by the name of God, in order that, as has been said, you might not become impious and godless by worshipping idols and forgetting God, as indeed you do always appear to have been. (Now, that God enjoined the ordinances of Sabbaths and offerings for these reasons, I have proved in what I previously remarked; but for the sake of those who came to-day, I wish to repeat nearly the whole.) For if this is not the case, God will be slandered, as having no foreknowledge, and as not teaching all men to know and to do the same acts of righteousness (for many. generations of men appear to have existed before Moses); and the Scripture is not true which affirms that 'God is true and righteous, and all His ways are judgments, and there is no unrighteousness in him.' But since the Scripture is true, God is always willing that such even as you be neither foolish nor lovers of yourselves, in order that you may obtain the salvation of Christ, who pleased God, and received testimony from Him, as I have already said, by alleging proof from the holy words of prophecy.

CHAPTER XCIII -- THE SAME KIND OF RIGHTEOUSNESS IS BESTOWED ON ALL. CHRIST COMPREHENDS IT IN TWO PRECEPTS.

"For [God] sets before every race of mankind that which is always and universally just, as well as all righteousness; and every race knows that adultery, and fornication, and homicide, and such like, are sinful; and though they all commit such practices, yet they do not escape from the knowledge that they act unrighteously whenever they so do, with the exception of those who are possessed with an unclean spirit, and who have been debased by education, by wicked customs, and by sinful institutions, and who have lost, or rather quenched and put under, their natural ideas. For we may see that such persons are unwilling to submit to the same things which they inflict upon others, and reproach each other with hostile consciences for the acts which they perpetrate. And hence I think that our Lord and Saviour Jesus Christ spoke well when He summed up all righteousness and piety in two commandments. They are these: 'Thou shalt love the Lord thy God with all thy heart, and with all thy strength, and thy neighbour as thyself.' For the man who loves God with all the heart, and with all the strength, being filled with a God-fearing mind, will reverence no other god; and since God wishes it, he would reverence that angel who is beloved by the same Lord and God. And the man who loves his neighbour as himself will wish for him the same good things that he wishes for himself, and no man will wish evil things for himself. Accordingly, he who loves his neighbour would pray and labour that his neighbour may be possessed of the same benefits as himself. Now nothing else is neighbour to man than that similarly-affectioned and reasonable being--man. Therefore, since all righteousness is divided into two branches, namely, in so far as it regards God and men, whoever, says the Scripture, loves the Lord God with all the heart, and all the strength, and his neighbour as himself, would be truly a righteous man. But you were never shown to be possessed of friendship or love either towards God, or towards the prophets, or towards yourselves, but, as is evident, you are ever found to be idolaters and murderers of righteous men, so that you laid hands even on Christ Himself; and to this very day you abide in your wickedness, execrating those who prove that this man who was crucified by you is the Christ. Nay, more than this, you suppose that He was crucified as hostile to and cursed by God, which supposition is the product of your most irrational mind. For though you have the means of understanding that this man is Christ from the signs given by Moses, yet you will not; but, in addition, fancying that we can have no arguments, you put whatever question comes into your minds, while you yourselves are at a loss for arguments whenever you meet with some firmly established Christian.

CHAPTER XCIV -- IN WHAT SENSE HE WHO HANGS ON A TREE IS CURSED.

"For tell me, was it not God who commanded by Moses that no image or likeness of anything which was in heaven above or which was on the earth should be made, and yet who caused the brazen serpent to be made by Moses in the wilderness, and set it up for a sign by which those bitten by serpents were saved? Yet is He free from unrighteousness. For by this, as I previously remarked, He proclaimed the mystery, by which He declared that He would break the power of the serpent which occasioned the transgression of Adam, and [would bring] to them that believe on Him [who was foreshadowed] by this sign, i.e., Him who was to be crucified, salvation from the fangs of the serpent, which are wicked deeds, idolatries, and other unrighteous acts. Unless the matter be so understood, give me a reason why Moses set up the brazen serpent for a sign, and bade those that were bitten gaze at it, and the wounded were healed; and this, too, when he had himself commanded that no likeness of anything whatsoever should be made."

On this, another of those who came on the second day said, "You have spoken truly: we cannot give a reason. For I have frequently interrogated the teachers about this matter, and none of them gave me a reason: therefore continue what you are speaking; for we are paying attention while you unfold the mystery, on account of which the doctrines of the prophets are falsely slandered."

Then I replied, "Just as God commanded the sign to be made by the brazen serpent, and yet He is blameless; even so, though a curse lies in the law against persons who are crucified, yet no curse lies on the Christ of God, by whom all that have committed things worthy of a curse are saved.

CHAPTER XCV -- CHRIST TOOK UPON HIMSELF THE CURSE DUE TO US.

"For the whole human race will be found to be under a curse. For it is written in the law of Moses, 'Cursed is every one that continueth not in all things that are written in the book of the law to do them.' And no one has accurately done all, nor will you venture to deny this; but some more and some less than others have observed the ordinances enjoined. But if those who are under this law appear to be under a curse for not having observed all the requirements, how much more shall all the nations appear to be under a curse who practise idolatry, who seduce youths, and commit other crimes? If, then, the Father of all wished His Christ for the whole human family to take upon Him the curses of all, knowing that, after He had been crucified and was dead, He would raise Him up, why do you argue about Him, who submitted to suffer these things according to the Father's will, as if He were accursed, and do not rather bewail yourselves? For although His Father caused Him to suffer these things in behalf of the human family, yet you did not commit the deed as in obedience to the will of God. For you did not practise piety when you slew the prophets. And let none of you say: If His Father wished Him to suffer this, in order that by His stripes the human race might be healed, we have done no wrong. If, indeed, you repent of your sins, and recognise Him to be Christ, and observe His commandments, then you may assert this; for, as I have said before, remission of sins shall be yours. But if you curse Him and them that believe on Him, and, when you have the power, put them to death, how is it possible that requisition shall not be made of you, as of unrighteous and sinful men, altogether hard-hearted and without understanding, because you laid your hands on Him?

CHAPTER XCVI -- THAT CURSE WAS A PREDICTION OF THE THINGS WHICH THE JEWS WOULD DO.

"For the statement in the law, 'Cursed is every one that hangeth on a tree,' confirms our hope which depends on the crucified Christ, not because He who has been crucified is cursed by God, but because God foretold that which would be done by you all, and by those like to your, who do not know that this is He who existed before all, who is the eternal Priest of God, and King, and Christ. And you clearly see that this has come to pass. For you curse in your synagogues all those who are called from Him Christians; and other nations effectively carry out the curse, putting to death those who simply confess themselves to be Christians; to all of whom we say, You are our brethren; rather recognise the truth of God. And while neither they nor you are persuaded by us, but strive earnestly to cause us to deny the name of Christ, we choose rather and submit to death, in the full assurance that all the good which God has promised through Christ He will reward us with. And in addition to all this we pray for you, that Christ may have mercy upon you. For He taught us to pray for our enemies also, saying, 'Love your enemies; be kind and merciful, as your heavenly Father is.' For we see that the Almighty God is kind and merciful, causing His sun to rise on the un-thankful and on the righteous, and sending rain on the holy and on the wicked; all of whom He has taught us He will judge.

CHAPTER XCVII -- OTHER PREDICTIONS OF THE CROSS OF CHRIST.

"For it was not without design that the prophet Moses, when Hur and Aaron upheld his hands, remained in this form until evening. For indeed the Lord remained upon the tree almost until evening, and they buried Him at eventide; then on the third day He rose again. This was declared by David thus: 'With my voice I cried to the Lord, and He heard me out of His holy hill. I laid me down, and slept; I awaked, for the Lord sustained me.' And Isaiah likewise mentions concerning Him the manner in which He would die, thus: 'I have spread out My hands unto a people disobedient, and gainsaying, that walk in a way which is not good.' And that He would rise again, Isaiah himself said: 'His burial has been taken away from the midst, and I will give the rich for His death.' And again, in other words, David in the twenty-first Psalm thus refers to the suffering and to the cross in a parable of mystery: 'They pierced my hands and my feet; they counted all my bones. They considered and gazed on me; they parted my garments among themselves, and cast lots upon my vesture.' For when they crucified Him, driving in the nails, they pierced His hands and feet; and those who crucified Him parted His garments among themselves, each casting lots for what he chose to have, and receiving according to the decision of the lot. And this very Psalm you maintain does not refer to Christ; for you are in all respects blind, and do not understand that no one in your nation who has been called King or Christ has ever had his hands or feet pierced while alive, or has died in this mysterious fashion--to wit, by the cross--save this Jesus alone.

CHAPTER XCVIII -- PREDICTIONS OF CHRIST IN PS. XXII.

"I shall repeat the whole Psalm, in order that you may hear His reverence to the Father, and how He refers all things to Him, and prays to be delivered by Him from this death; at the same time declaring in the Psalm who they are that rise up against Him, and showing that He has truly become man capable of suffering. It is as follows: 'O God, my God, attend to me why hast Thou forsaken me? The words of my transgressions are far from my salvation. O my God, I will cry to Thee in the day-time, and Thou wilt not hear; and in the night-season, and it is not for want of understanding in me. But Thou, the Praise of Israel, inhabitest the holy place. Our fathers trusted in Thee; they trusted, and Thou didst deliver them. They cried unto Thee, and were delivered: they trusted in Thee, and were not confounded. But I am a worm, and no man; a reproach of men, and despised of the people. All they that see me laughed me to scorn; they spake with the lips, they shook the head: He trusted on the Lord: let Him deliver him, let Him save him, since he desires Him. For Thou art He that took me out of the womb; my hope from the breasts of my mother I was cast upon Thee from the womb. Thou art my God from my mother's belly: be not far from me, for trouble is near; for there is none to help. Many calves have compassed me; fat bulls have beset me round. They opened their mouth upon me, as a ravening and roaring lion. All my bones are poured out and dispersed like water. My heart has become like wax melting in the midst of my belly. My strength is dried up like a potsherd; and my tongue has cleaved to my throat; and Thou hast brought me into the dust of death. For many dogs have surrounded me; the assembly of the wicked have beset me round. They pierced my hands and my feet, they did tell all my bones. They did look and stare upon me; they parted my garments among them, and cast lots upon my vesture. But do not Thou remove Thine assist-ante from me, O Lord: give heed to help me; deliver my soul from the sword, and my only-begotten from the hand of the dog. Save me from the lion's mouth, and my humility from the horns of the unicorns. I will declare Thy name to my brethren; in the midst of the Church will I praise Thee. Ye that fear the Lord, praise Him: all ye the seed of Jacob, glorify Him. Let all the seed of Israel fear Him.' "

CHAPTER XCIX -- IN THE COMMENCEMENT OF THE PSALM ARE CHRIST'S DYING WORDS.

And when I had said these words, I continued: "Now I will demonstrate to you that the whole Psalm refers thus to Christ, by the words which I shall again explain. What is said at first--'O God, my God, attend to me: why hast Thou forsaken me?'--announced from the beginning that which was to be said in the time of Christ. For when crucified, He spake: 'O God, my God, why hast Thou forsaken me?' And what follows: 'The words of my transgressions are far from my salvation. O my God, I will cry to Thee in the day-time, and Thou wilt not hear; and in the night-season, and it is not for want of understanding in me.' These, as well as the things which He was to do, were spoken. For on the day on which He was to be crucified, having taken three of His disciples to the hill called Olivet, situated opposite to the temple in Jerusalem, He prayed in these words: 'Father, if it be possible, let this cup pass from me.' And again He prayed: "Not as I will, but as Thou wilt;' showing by this that He had become truly a suffering man. But lest any one should say, He did not know then that He had to suffer, He adds immediately in the Psalm: 'And it is not for want of under standing in me.' Even as there was no ignorance on God's part when He asked Adam where he was, or asked Cain where Abel was; but [it was done] to convince each what kind of man he was, and in order that through the record [of Scripture] we might have a knowledge of all: so likewise Christ declared that ignorance was not on His side, but on theirs, who thought that He was not the Christ, but fancied they would put Him to death, and that He, like some common mortal, would remain in Hades.

CHAPTER C -- IN WHAT SENSE CHRIST IS [CALLED] JACOB, AND ISRAEL, AND SON OF MAN.

"Then what follows--'But Thou, the praise of Israel, inhabitest the holy place'-- declared that He is to do something worthy of praise and wonderment, being about to rise again from the dead on the third day after the crucifixion; and this He has obtained from the Father. For I have showed already that Christ is called both Jacob and Israel; and I have proved that it is not in the blessing of Joseph and Judah alone that what relates to Him was proclaimed mysteriously, but also in the Gospel it is written that He said: 'All things are delivered unto me by My Father;' and, 'No man knoweth the Father but the Son; nor the Son but the Father, and they to whom the Son will reveal Him.' Accordingly He revealed to us all that we have perceived by His grace out of the Scriptures, so that we know Him to be the first-begotten of God, and to be before all creatures; likewise to be the Son of the patriarchs, since He assumed flesh by the Virgin of their family, and submitted to become a man without comeliness, dishonoured, and subject to suffering. Hence, also, among His words He said, when He was discoursing about His future sufferings: "The Son of man must suffer many things, and be rejected by the Pharisees and Scribes, and be crucified, and on the third day rise again.' He said then that He was the Son of man, either because of His birth by the Virgin, who was, as I said, of the family of David and Jacob, and Isaac, and Abraham; or because Adam was the father both of Himself and of those who have been first enumerated from whom Mary derives her descent. For we know that the fathers of women are the fathers likewise of those children whom their daughters bear. For [Christ] called one of His disciples--previously known by the name of Simon--Peter; since he recognised Him to be Christ the Son. of God, by the revelation of His Father: and since we find it recorded in the memoirs of His apostles that He is the Son of God, and since we call Him the Son, we have understood that He proceeded before all creatures from the Father by His power and will (for He is addressed in the writings of the prophets in one way or another as Wisdom, and the Day, and the East, and a Sword, and a Stone, and a Rod, and Jacob, and Israel); and that He became man by the Virgin, in order that the disobedience which proceeded from the serpent might receive its destruction in the same manner in which it derived its origin. For Eve, who was a virgin and undefiled, having conceived the word of the serpent, brought forth disobedience and death. But the Virgin Mary received faith and joy, when the angel Gabriel announced the good tidings to her that the Spirit of the Lord would come upon her, and the power of the Highest would overshadow her: wherefore also the Holy Thing begotten of her is the Son of God; and she replied, 'Be it unto me according to thy word.' And by her has He been born, to whom we have proved so many Scriptures refer, and by whom God destroys both the serpent and those angels and men who are like him; but works deliverance from death to those who repent of their wickedness and believe upon Him.

CHAPTER CI -- CHRIST REFERS ALL THINGS TO THE FATHER

"Then what follows of the Psalm is this, in which He says: 'Our fathers trusted in Thee; they trusted, and Thou didst deliver them. They cried unto Thee, and were not confounded. But I am a worm, and no man; a reproach of men, and despised of the people;' which show that He admits them to be His fathers, who trusted in God and were saved by Him, who also were the fathers of the Virgin, by whom He was born and became man; and He foretells that He shall be saved by the same God, but boasts not in accomplishing anything through His own will or might. For when on earth He acted in the very same manner, and answered to one who addressed Him as' Good Master:' Why callest thou me good? One is good, my Father who is in heaven.' But when He says, I am a worm, and no man; a reproach of men, and despised of the people,' He prophesied the things which do exist, and which happen to Him. For we who believe on Him are everywhere a reproach, 'despised of the people;' for, rejected and dishonoured by your nation, He suffered those indignities which you planned against Him. And the following: 'All they that see me laughed me to scorn; they spake with the lips, they shook the head: He trusted in the Lord; let Him deliver him, since he desires Him;' this likewise He foretold should happen to Him. For they that saw Him crucified shook their heads each one of them, and distorted their lips, and twisting their noses to each other, they spake in mockery the words which are recorded in the memoirs of His apostles: 'He said he was the Son of God: let him come down; let God save him.'

CHAPTER CII -- THE PREDICTION OF THE EVENTS WHICH HAPPENED TO CHRIST WHEN HE WAS BORN. WHY GOD PERMITTED IT.

"And what follows--'My hope from the breasts of my mother. On Thee have I been cast from the womb; from my mother's belly Thou art my God: for there is no helper. Many calves have compassed me; fat bulls have beset me round. They opened their mouth upon me, as a ravening and a roaring lion. All my bones are poured out and dispersed like water. My heart has become likes wax melting in the midst of my belly. My strength is become dry like a potsherd; and my tongue has cleaved to my throat'--foretold what would come to pass; for the statement, 'My hope from the breasts of my mother,' [is thus explained]. As soon as He was born in Bethlehem, as I previously remarked, king Herod, having learned from the Arabian Magi about Him, made a plot to put Him to death and by God's command Joseph took Him with Mary and departed into Egypt. For the Father had decreed that He whom He had begotten should be put to death, but not before He had grown to manhood, and proclaimed the word which proceeded from Him. But if any of you say to us, Could not God rather have put Herod to death? I return answer by anticipation: Could not God have cut off in the beginning the serpent, so that he exist not, rather than have said, 'And I will put enmity between him and the woman, and between his seed and her seed?' Could He not have at once created a multitude of men? But yet, since He knew that it would be good, He created both angels and men free to do that which is righteous, and He appointed periods of time during which He knew it would be good for them to have the exercise of free-will; and because He likewise knew it would be good, He made general and particular judgments; each one's freedom of will, however, being guarded. Hence Scripture says the following, at the destruction of the tower, and division and alteration of tongues: 'And the Lord said, Behold, the people is one, and they have all one language; and this they have begun to do: and now nothing will be restrained from them of all which they have attempted to do.' And the statement, 'My strength is become dry like a potsherd, and my tongue has cleaved to my throat,' was also a prophecy of what would be done by Him according to the Father's will. For the power of His strong word, by which He always confuted the Pharisees and Scribes, and, in short, all your nation's teachers that questioned Him, had a cessation like a plentiful and strong spring, the waters of which have been turned off, when He kept silence, and chose to return no answer to any one in the presence of Pilate; as has been declared in the memoirs of His apostles, in order that what is recorded by Isaiah might have efficacious fruit, where it is written, 'The Lord gives me a tongue, that I may know when I ought to speak.' Again, when He said, 'Thou art my God; be not far from me,' He taught that all men ought to hope in God who created all things, and seek salvation and help from Him alone; and not suppose, as the rest of men do, that salvation can be obtained by birth, or wealth, or strength, or wisdom. And such have ever been your practices: at one time you made a calf, and always you have shown yourselves ungrateful, murderers of the righteous, and proud of your descent. For if the Son of God evidently states that He can be saved, [neither] because He is a son, nor because He is strong or wise, but that without God He cannot be saved, even though He be sinless, as Isaiah declares in words to the effect that even in regard to His very language He committed no sin (for He committed no iniquity or guile with His mouth), how do you or others who expect to be saved without this hope, suppose that you are not deceiving yourselves?

CHAPTER CIII -- THE PHARISEES ARE THE BULLS: THE ROARING LION IS HEROD OR THE DEVIL.

"Then what is next said in the Psalm--'For trouble is near, for there is none to help me. Many calves have compassed me; fat bulls have beset me round. They opened their mouth upon me as a ravening and roaring lion. All my bones are poured out and dispersed like water,'--was likewise a prediction of the events which happened to Him. For on that night when some of your nation, who had been sent by the Pharisees and Scribes, and teachers, came upon Him from the Mount of Olives, those whom Scripture called butting and prematurely destructive calves surrounded Him. And the expression, 'Fat bulls have beset me round,' He spoke beforehand of those who acted similarly to the calves, when He was led before your teachers. And the Scripture described them as bulls, since we know that bulls are authors of calves' existence. As therefore the bulls are the begetters of the calves, so your teachers were the cause why their children went out to the Mount of Olives to take Him and bring Him to them. And the expression, 'For there is none to help,' is also indicative of what took place. For there was not even a single man to assist Him as an innocent person. And the expression, 'They opened their mouth upon me like a roaring lion,' designates him who was then king of the Jews, and was called Herod, a successor of the Herod who, when Christ was born, slew all the infants in Bethlehem born about the same time, because he imagined that amongst them He would assuredly be of whom the Magi from Arabia had spoken; for he was ignorant of the will of Him that is stronger than all, how He had commanded Joseph and Mary to take the Child and depart into Egypt, and there to remain until a revelation should again be made to them to return into their own country. And there they did remain until Herod, who slew the infants in Bethlehem, was dead, and Archelaus had succeeded him. And he died before Christ came to the dispensation on the cross which was given Him by His Father. And when Herod succeeded Archelaus, having received the authority which had been allotted to him, Pilate sent to him by way of compliment Jesus bound; and God foreknowing that this would happen, had thus spoken: 'And they brought Him to the Assyrian, a present to the king.' Or He meant the devil by the lion roaring against Him: whom Moses calls the serpent, but in Job and Zechariah he is called the devil, and by Jesus is addressed as Satan, showing that a compounded name was acquired by him from the deeds which he performed. For 'Sata' in the Jewish and Syrian tongue means apostate; and 'Nas' is the word from which he is called by interpretation the serpent, i.e., according to the interpretation of the Hebrew term, from both of which there arises the single word Satanas. For this devil, when [Jesus] went up from the river Jordan, at the time when the voice spake to Him, 'Thou art my Son: this day have I begotten Thee,' is recorded in the memoirs of the apostles to have come to Him and tempted Him, even so far as to say to Him, 'Worship me;' and Christ answered him, 'Get thee behind me, Satan: thou shalt worship the Lord thy God, and Him only shalt thou serve.' For as he had deceived Adam, so he hoped that he might contrive some mischief against Christ also. Moreover, the statement, 'All my bones are poured out and dispersed like water; my heart has become like wax, melting in the midst of my belly,' was a prediction of that which happened to Him on that night when men came out against Him to the Mount of Olives to seize Him. For in the memoirs which I say were drawn up by His apostles and those who followed them, [it is recorded] that His sweat fell down like drops of blood while He was praying, and saying, 'If it be possible, let this cup pass:' His heart and also His bones trembling; His heart being like wax melting in His belly: in order that we may perceive that the Father wished His Son really to undergo such sufferings for our sakes, and may not say that He, being the Son of God, did not feel what was happening to Him and inflicted on Him. Further, the expression, 'My strength is dried up like a potsherd, and my tongue has cleaved to my throat,' was a prediction, as I previously remarked, of that silence, when He who convicted all your teachers of being unwise returned no answer at all.

CHAPTER CIV -- CIRCUMSTANCES OF CHRIST'S DEATH ARE PREDICTED IN THIS BALM.

"And the statement, 'Thou hast brought me into the dust of death; for many dogs have surrounded me: the assembly of the wicked have beset me round. They pierced my hands and my feet. They did tell all my bones. They did look and stare upon me. They parted my garments among them, and cast lots upon my vesture,'--was a prediction, as I said before, of the death to which the synagogue of the wicked would condemn Him, whom He calls both dogs and hunters, declaring that those who hunted Him were both gathered together and assiduously striving to condemn Him. And this is recorded to have happened in the memoirs of His apostles. And I have shown that, after His crucifixion, they who crucified Him parted His garments among them.

CHAPTER CV -- THE PSALM ALSO PREDICTS THE CRUCIFIXION AND THE SUBJECT OF THE LAST PRAYERS OF CHRIST ON EARTH.

"And what follows of the Psalm,--'But Thou, Lord, do not remove Thine assistance from me; give heed to help me. Deliver my soul from the sword, and my only-begotten from the hand of the dog; save me from the lion's mouth, and my humility from the horns of the unicorns,'--was also information and prediction of the events which should befall Him. For I have already proved that He was the only-begotten of the Father of all things, being begotten in a peculiar manner Word and Power by Him, and having afterwards become man through the Virgin, as we have learned from the memoirs. Moreover, it is similarly foretold that He would die by crucifixion. For the passage, 'Deliver my soul from the sword, and my only-begotten from the hand of the dog; save me from the lion's mouth, and my humility from the horns of the unicorns,' is indicative of the suffering by which He should die, i.e., by crucifixion. For the 'horns of the, unicorns,' I have already explained to you, are the figure of the cross only. And the prayer that His soul should be saved from the sword, and lion's mouth, and hand of the dog, was a prayer that no one should take possession of His soul: so that, when we arrive at the end of life, we may ask the same petition from God, who is able to turn away every shameless evil angel from taking our souls. And that the souls survive, I have shown to you from the fact that the soul of Samuel was called up by the witch, as Saul demanded. And it appears also, that all the souls of similiar righteous men and prophets fell under the dominion of such powers, as is indeed to be inferred from the very facts in the case of that witch. Hence also God by His Son teaches us for whose sake these things seem to have been done, always to strive earnestly, and at death to pray that our souls may not fall into the hands of any such power. For when Christ was giving up His spirit on the cross, He said, 'Father, into Thy hands I commend my spirit,' as I have learned also from the memoirs. For He exhorted His disciples to surpass the pharisaic way of living, with the warning, that if they did not, they might be sure they could not be saved; and these words are recorded in the memoirs: 'Unless your righteousness exceed that of the Scribes and Pharisees, ye shall not enter into the kingdom of heaven.'

CHAPTER CVI -- CHRIST'S RESURRECTION IS FORETOLD IN THE CONCLUSION OF THE PSALM.

"The remainder of the Psalm makes it manifest that He knew His Father would grant to Him all things which He asked, and would raise Him from the dead; and that He urged all who fear God to praise Him because He had compassion on all races of believing men, through the mystery of Him who was crucified; and that He stood in the midst of His brethren the apostles (who repented of their flight from Him when He was crucified, after He rose from the dead, and after they were persuaded by Himself that, before His passion He had mentioned to them that He must suffer these things, and that they were announced beforehand by the prophets), and when living with them sang praises to God, as is made evident in the memoirs of the apostles. The words are the following: 'I will declare Thy name to my brethren; in the midst of the Church will I praise Thee. Ye that fear the Lord, praise Him; all ye, the seed of Jacob, glorify Him. Let all the seed of Israel fear Him.' And when it is said that He changed the name of one of the apostles to Peter; and when it is written in the memoirs of Him that this so happened, as well as that He changed the names of other two brothers, the sons of Zebedee, to Boanerges, which means sons of thunder; this was an announcement of the fact that it was He by whom Jacob was called Israel, and Oshea called Jesus (Joshua), under whose name the people who survived of those that came from Egypt were conducted into the land promised to the patriarchs. And that He should arise like a star from the seed of Abraham, Moses showed before hand when he thus said, 'A star shall arise from Jacob, and a leader from Israel;' and another Scripture says, 'Behold a man; the East is His name.' Accordingly, when a star rose in heaven at the time of His birth, as is recorded in the memoirs of His apostles, the Magi from Arabia, recognising the sign by this, came and worshipped Him.

CHAPTER CVII -- THE SAME IS TAUGHT FROM THE HISTORY OF JONAH.

"And that He would rise again on the third day after the crucifixion, it is written in the memoirs that some of your nation, questioning Him, said, 'Show us a sign;' and He replied to them, 'An evil and adulterous generation seeketh after a sign; and no sign shall be given them, save the sign of Jonah.' And since He spoke this obscurely, it was to be understood by the audience that after His crucifixion He should rise again on the third day. And He showed that your generation was more wicked and more adulterous than the city of Nineveh; for the latter, when Jonah preached to them, after he had been cast up on the third day from the belly of the great fish, that after three (in other versions, forty) days they should all perish, proclaimed a fast of all creatures, men and beasts, with sackcloth, and with earnest lamentation, with true repentance from the heart, and turning away from unrighteousness, in the belief that God is merciful and kind to all who turn from wickedness; so that the king of that city himself, with his nobles also, put on sackcloth and remained fasting and praying, and obtained their request that the city should not be overthrown. But when Jonah was grieved that on the (fortieth) third day, as he proclaimed, the city was not overthrown, by the dispensation of a gourd springing up from the earth for him, under which he sat and was shaded from the heat (now the gourd had sprung up suddenly, and Jonah had neither planted nor watered it, but it had come up all at once to afford him shade), and by the other dispensation of its withering away, for which Jonah grieved, [God] convicted him of being unjustly displeased because the city of Nineveh had not been overthrown, and said, 'Thou hast had pity on the gourd, for the which thou hast not laboured, neither madest it grow; which came up in a night, and perished in a night. And shall I not spare Nineveh, the great city, wherein dwell more than six score thousand persons that cannot discern between their right hand and their left hand; and also much cattle?'

CHAPTER CVII -- THE RESURRECTION OF CHRIST DID NOT CONVERT THE JEWS. BUT THROUGH THE WHOLE WORLD THEY HAVE SENT MEN TO ACCUSE CHRIST.

"And though all the men of your nation knew the incidents in the life of Jonah, and though Christ said amongst you that He would give the sign of Jonah, exhorting you to repent of your wicked deeds at least after He rose again from the dead, and to mourn before God as did the Ninevites, in order that your nation and city might not be taken and destroyed, as they have been destroyed; yet you not only have not repented, after you learned that He rose from the dead, but, as I said before you have sent chosen and ordained men throughout all the world to proclaim that a godless and lawless heresy had sprung from one Jesus, a Galilaean deceiver, whom we crucified, but his disciples stole him by night from the tomb, where he was laid when unfastened from the cross, and now deceive men by asserting that he has risen from the dead and ascended to heaven. Moreover, you accuse Him of having taught those godless, lawless, and unholy doctrines which you mention to the condemnation of those who confess Him to be Christ, and a Teacher from and Son of God. Besides this, even when your city is captured, and your land ravaged, you do not repent, but dare to utter imprecations on Him and all who believe in Him. Yet we do not hate you or those who, by your means, have conceived such prejudices against us; but we pray that even now all of you may repent and obtain mercy from God, the compassionate and long-suffering Father of all.

CHAPTER CIX -- THE CONVERSION OF THE GENTILES HAS BEEN PREDICTED BY MICAH.

"But that the Gentiles would repent of the evil in which they led erring lives, when they heard the doctrine preached by His apostles from Jerusalem, and which they learned through them, suffer me to show you by quoting a short statement from the prophecy of Micah, one of the twelve [minor prophets]. This is as follows: 'And in the last days the mountain of the Lord shall be manifest, established on the top of the mountains; it shall be exalted above the hills, arid people shall flow unto it. And many nations shall go, and say, Come, let us go up to the mountain of the Lord, and to the house of the God of Jacob; and they shall enlighten us in His way, and we shall walk in His paths: for out of Zion shall go forth the law, and the word of the Lord from Jerusalem. And He shall judge among many peoples, and shall rebuke strong nations afar off; and they shall beat their swords into ploughshares, and their spears into sickles: nation shall not lift up a sword against nation, neither shall they learn war any more. And each man shall sit under his vine and under his fig tree; and there shall be none to terrify: for the mouth of the Lord of hosts hath spoken it. For all people will walk in the name of their gods; but we will walk in the name of the Lord our God for ever. And it shall come to pass in that day, that I will assemble her that is afflicted, and gather her that is driven out, and whom I had plagued; and I shall make her that is afflicted a remnant, and her that is oppressed a strong nation. And the Lord shall reign over them in Mount Zion from henceforth, and even for ever.' "

CHAPTER CX -- A PORTION OF THE PROPHECY ALREADY FULFILLED IN THE CHRISTIANS: THE REST SHALL BE FULFILLED AT THE SECOND ADVENT.

And when I had finished these words, I continued: "Now I am aware that your teachers, sirs, admit the whole of the words of this passage to refer to Christ; and I am likewise aware that they maintain He has not yet come; or if they say that He has come, they assert that it is not known who He is; but when He shall become manifest and glorious, then it shall be known who He is. And then, they say, the events mentioned in this passage shall happen, just as if there was no fruit as yet from the words of the prophecy. O unreasoning men! understanding not what has been proved by all these passages, that two advents of Christ have been announced: the one, in which He is set forth as suffering, inglorious, dishonoured, and crucified; but the other, in which He shall come from heaven with glory, when the man of apostasy, who speaks strange things against the Most High, shall venture to do unlawful deeds on the earth against us the Christians, who, having learned the true worship of God from the law, and the word which went forth from Jerusalem by means of the apostles of Jesus, have fled for safety to the God of Jacob and God of Israel; and we who were filled with war, and mutual slaughter, and every wickedness, have each through the whole earth changed our warlike weapons,--our swords into ploughshares, and our spears into implements of tillage,--and we cultivate piety, righteousness, philanthropy, faith, and hope, which we have from the Father Himself through Him who was crucified; and sitting each under his vine, i.e., each man possessing his own married wife. For you are aware that the prophetic word says, 'And his wife shall be like a fruitful vine.' Now it is evident that no one can terrify or subdue us who have believed in Jesus over all the world. For it is plain that, though beheaded, and crucified, and thrown to wild beasts, and chains, and fire, and all other kinds of torture, we do not give up our confession; but the more such things happen, the more do others and in larger numbers become faithful, and worshippers of God through the name of Jesus. For Just as if one should cut away the fruit-bearing parts of a vine, it grows up again, and yields other branches flourishing and fruitful; even so the same thing happens with us. For the vine planted by God and Christ the Saviour is His people. But the rest of the prophecy shall be fulfilled at His second coming. For the expression, 'He that is afflicted [and driven out],' i.e., from the world, [implies] that, so far as you and all other men have it in your power, each Christian has been driven out not only from his own property, but even from the whole world; for you permit no Christian to live. But you say that the same fate has befallen your own nation. Now, if you have been cast out after defeat in battle, you have suffered such treatment justly indeed, as all the Scriptures bear witness; but we, though we have done no such [evil acts] after we knew the truth of God, are testified to by God, that, together with the most righteous, and only spotless and sinless Christ, we are taken away out of the earth. For Isaiah cries, 'Behold how the righteous perishes, and no man lays it to heart; and righteous men are taken away, and no man considers it.'

CHAPTER CXI -- THE TWO ADVENTS WERE SIGNIFIED BY THE TWO GOATS. OTHER FIGURES OF THE FIRST ADVENT, IN WHICH THE GENTILES ARE FREED BY THE BLOOD OF CHRIST.

"And that it was declared by symbol, even in the time of Moses, that there would be two advents of this Christ, as I have mentioned previously, [is manifest] from the symbol of the goats presented for sacrifice during the fast. And again, by what Moses and Joshua did, the same thing was symbolically announced and told beforehand. For the one of them, stretching out his hands, remained till evening on the hill, his hands being supported; and this reveals a type of no other thing than of the cross: and the other, whose name was altered to Jesus (Joshua), led the fight, and Israel conquered. Now this took place in the case of both those holy men and prophets of God, that you may perceive how one of them could not bear up both the mysteries: I mean, the type of the cross and the type of the name. For this is, was, and shall be the strength of Him alone, whose name every power dreads, being very much tormented because they shall be destroyed by Him. Therefore our suffering and crucified Christ was not cursed by the law, but made it manifest that He alone would save those who do not depart from His faith. And the blood of the passover, sprinkled on each man's door-posts and lintel, delivered those who were saved in Egypt, when the first-born of the Egyptians were destroyed. For the passover was Christ, who was afterwards sacrificed, as also Isaiah said, 'He was led as a sheep to the slaughter.' And it is written, that on the day of the passover you seized Him, and that also during the passover you crucified Him. And as the blood of the passover saved those who were in Egypt, so also the blood of Christ will deliver from death those who have believed. Would God, then, have been deceived if this sign had not been above the doors? I do not say that; but I affirm that He announced beforehand the future salvation for the human race through the blood of Christ. For the sign of the scarlet thread, which the spies, sent to Jericho by Joshua, son of Nave (Nun), gave to Rahab the harlot, telling her to bind it to the window through which she let them down to escape from their enemies, also manifested the symbol of the blood of Christ, by which those who were at one time harlots and unrighteous persons out of all nations are saved, receiving remission of sins, and continuing no longer in sin.

CHAPTER CXII -- THE JEWS EXPOUND THESE SIGNS JEJUNELY AND FEEBLY, AND TAKE UP THEIR ATTENTION ONLY WITH INSIGNIFICANT MATTERS.

"But you, expounding these things in a low [and earthly] manner, impute much weakness to God, if you thus listen to them merely, and do not investigate the force of the words spoken. Since even Moses would in this way be considered a transgressor: for he enjoined that no likeness of anything in heaven, or on earth, or in the sea, be made; and then he himself made a brazen serpent and set it on a standard, and bade those who were bitten look at it: and they were saved when they looked at it. Will the serpent, then, which (I have already said) God had in the beginning cursed and cut off by the great sword, as Isaiah says, be understood as having preserved at that time the people? and shall we receive these things in the foolish acceptation of your teachers, and [regard] them not as signs? And shall we not rather refer the standard to the resemblance of the crucified Jesus, since also Moses by his outstretched hands, together with him who was named Jesus (Joshua), achieved a victory for your people? For in this way we shall cease to be at a loss about the things which the lawgiver did, when he, without forsaking God, persuaded the people to hope in a beast through which transgression and disobedience had their origin. And this was done and said by the blessed prophet with much intelligence and mystery; and there is nothing said or done by any one of the prophets, without exception, which one can justly reprehend, if he possess the knowledge which is in them. But if your teachers only expound to you why female cancels are spoken of in this passage, and are not in that; or why so many measures of fine flour and so many measures of oil [are used] in the offerings; and do so in a low and sordid manner, while they never venture either to speak of or to expound the points which are great and worthy of investigation, or command you to give no audience to us while we expound them, and to come not into conversation with us; will they not deserve to hear what our Lord Jesus Christ said to them: 'Whited sepulchres, which appear beautiful outward, and within are full of dead men's bones; which pay tithe of mint, and swallow a camel: ye blind guides!' If, then, you will not despise the doctrines of those who exalt themselves and wish to be called Rabbi, Rabbi, and come with such earnestness and intelligence to the words of prophecy as to suffer the same inflictions from your own people which the prophets themselves did, you cannot receive any advantage whatsoever from the prophetic writings.

CHAPTER CXIII. --JOSHUA WAS A FIGURE OF CHRIST.

"What I mean is this. Jesus (Joshua), as I have now frequently remarked, who was called Oshea, when he was sent to spy out the land of Canaan, was named by Moses Jesus (Joshua). Why he did this you neither ask, nor are at a loss about it, nor make strict inquiries. Therefore Christ has escaped your notice; and though you read, you understand not; and even now, though you hear that Jesus is our Christ, you consider not that the name was bestowed on Him not purposelessly nor by chance. But you make a theological discussion as to why one rho was added to Abraham's first name; and as to why one 'p' was added to Sarah's name, you use similar high-sounding disputations. But why do you not similarly investigate the reason why the name of Oshea the son of Nave (Nun), which his father gave him, was changed to Jesus (Joshua)? But since not only was his name altered, but he was also appointed successor to Moses, being the only one of his contemporaries who came out from Egypt, he led the surviving people into the Holy Land; and as he, not Moses, led the people into the Holy Land, and as he distributed it by lot to those who entered along with him, so also Jesus the Christ will turn again the dispersion of the people, and will distribute the good land to each one, though not in the same manner. For the former gave them a temporary inheritance, seeing he was neither Christ who is God, nor the Son of God; but the latter, after the holy resurrection, shall give us the eternal possession. The former, after he had been named Jesus (Joshua), and after he had received strength from. His Spirit, caused the sun to stand still. For I have proved that it was Jesus who appeared to and conversed with Moses, and Abraham, and all the other patriarchs without exception, ministering to the will of the Father; who also, I say, came to be born man by the Virgin Mary, and I lives for ever. For the latter is He after whom and by whom the Father will renew both the heaven and the earth; this is He who shall shine an eternal light in Jerusalem; this is he who is the king of Salem after the order of Melchizedek, and the eternal Priest of the Most High. The former is said to have circumcised the people a second time with knives of stone (which was a sign of this circumcision with which Jesus Christ Himself has circumcised us from the idols made of stone and of other materials), and to have collected together those who were circumcised from the uncircumcision, i.e., from the error of the world, in every place by the knives of stone, to wit, the words of our Lord Jesus. For I have shown that Christ was proclaimed by the prophets in parables a Stone and a Rock. Accordingly the knives of stone we shall take to mean His words, by means of which so many who were in error have been circumcised from uncircumcision with the circumcision of the heart, with which God by Jesus commanded those from that time to be circumcised who derived their circumcision from Abraham, saying that Jesus (Joshua) would circumcise a second time with knives of stone those who entered into that holy land.

CHAPTER CXIV -- SOME RULES FOR DISCERNING WHAT IS SAID ABOUT CHRIST. THE CIRCUMCISION OF THE JEWS IS VERY DIFFERENT FROM THAT WHICH CHRISTIANS RECEIVE.

"For the Holy Spirit sometimes brought about that something, which was the type of the future, should be done clearly; sometimes He uttered words about what was to take place, as if it was then taking place, or had taken place. And unless those who read perceive this art, they will not be able to follow the words of the prophets as they ought. For example's sake, I shall repeat some prophetic passages, that you may understand what I say. When He speaks by Isaiah, 'He was led as a sheep to the slaughter, and like a lamb before the shearer,' He speaks as if the suffering had already taken place. And when He says again, 'I have stretched out my hands to a disobedient and gainsaying people;' and when He says, 'Lord, who hath believed our report?'--the words are spoken as if announcing events which had already come to pass. For I have shown that Christ is oftentimes called a Stone in parable, and in figurative speech Jacob and Israel. And again, when He says, 'I shall behold the heavens, the works of Thy fingers,' unless I understand His method of using words, I shall not understand intelligently, but just as your teachers suppose, fancying that the Father of all, the unbegotten God, has hands and feet, and fingers, and a soul, like a composite being; and they for this reason teach that it was the Father Himself who appeared to Abraham and to Jacob. Blessed therefore are we who have been circumcised the second time with knives of stone. For your first circumcision was and is performed by iron instruments, for you remain hard-hearted; but our circumcision, which is the second, having been instituted after yours, circumcises us from idolatry and from absolutely every kind of wickedness by sharp stones, i.e., by the words [preached] by the apostles of the corner-stone cut out without hands. And our hearts are thus circumcised from evil, so that we are happy to die for the name of the good Rock, which causes living water to burst forth for the hearts of those who by Him have loved the Father of all, and which gives those who are willing to drink of the water of life. But you do not comprehend me when I speak these things; for you have not understood what it has been prophesied that Christ would do, and you do not believe us who draw your attention to what has been written. For Jeremiah thus cries: 'Woe unto you! because you have forsaken the living fountain, and have digged for yourselves broken cisterns that can hold no water. Shall there be a wilderness where Mount Zion is, because I gave Jerusalem a bill of divorce in your sight?'

CHAPTER CXV -- PREDICTION ABOUT THE CHRISTIANS IN ZECHARIAH. THE MALIGNANT WAY WHICH THE JEWS HAVE IN DISPUTATIONS.

"But you ought to believe Zechariah when he shows in parable the mystery of Christ, and announces it obscurely. The following are his words: 'Rejoice, and be glad, O daughter of Zion: for, lo, I come, and I shall dwell in the midst of thee, saith the Lord. And many nations shall be added to the Lord in that day. And they shall be my people, and I will dwell in the midst of thee; and they shall know that the Lord of hosts hath sent me unto thee. And the Lord shall inherit Judah his portion in the holy land, and He shall choose Jerusalem again. Let all flesh fear before the Lord, for He is raised up out of His holy clouds. And He showed me Jesus (Joshua) the high priest standing before the angel [of the Lord]; and the devil stood at his right hand to resist him. And the Lord said to the devil, The Lord who hath chosen Jerusalem rebuke thee. Behold, is not this a brand plucked out of the fire?' "

As Trypho was about to reply and contradict me, I said, "Wait and hear what I say first: for I am not to give the explanation which you suppose, as if there had been no priest of the name of Joshua (Jesus) in the land of Babylon, where your nation were prisoners. But even if I did, I have shown that if there was a priest named Joshua (Jesus) in your nation, yet the prophet had not seen him in his revelation, just as he had not seen either the devil or the angel of the Lord by eyesight, and in his waking condition, but in a trance, at the time when the revelation was made to him. But I now say, that as [Scripture] said that the Son of Nave (Nun) by the name Jesus (Joshua) wrought powerful works and exploits which proclaimed beforehand what would be performed by our Lord; so I proceed now to show that the revelation made among your people in Babylon in the days of Jesus (Joshua) the priest, was an announcement of the things to be accomplished by our Priest, who is God, and Christ the Son of God the Father of all.

"Indeed, I wondered," continued I, "why a little ago you kept silence while I was speaking, and why you did not interrupt me when I said that the son of Nave (Nun) was the only one of contemporaries who came out of Egypt that entered the Holy Land along with the men described as younger than that generation. For you swarm and light on sores like flies. For though one should speak ten thousand words well, if there happen to be one little word displeasing to you, because not sufficiently intelligible or accurate, you make no account of the many good words, but lay hold of the little word, and are very zealous in setting it up as something impious and guilty; in order that, when you are judged with the very same judgment by God, you may have a much heavier account to render for your great audacities, whether evil actions, or bad interpretations which you obtain by falsifying the truth. For with what judgment you judge, it is righteous that you be judged withal.

CHAPTER CXVI -- IT IS SHOWN HOW THIS PROPHECY SUITS THE CHRISTIANS.

"But to give you the account of the revelation of the holy Jesus Christ, I take up again my discourse, and I assert that even that revelation was made for us who believe on Christ the High Priest, namely this crucified One; and though we lived in fornication and all kinds of filthy conversation, we have by the grace of our Jesus, according to His Father's will, stripped ourselves of all those filthy wickednesses with which we were imbued. And though the devil is ever at hand to resist us, and anxious to seduce all to himself, yet the Angel of God, i.e., the Power of God sent to us through Jesus Christ, rebukes him, and he departs from us. And we are just as if drawn out from the fire, when purified from our former sins, and [rescued] from the affliction and the fiery trial by which the devil and all his coadjutors try us; out of which Jesus the Son of God has promised again to deliver us, and invest us with prepared garments, if we do His commandments; and has undertaken to provide an eternal kingdom [for us]. For just as that Jesus (Joshua), called by the prophet a priest, evidently had on filthy garments because he is said to have taken a harlot for a wife, and is called a brand plucked out of the fire, because he had received remission of sins when the devil that resisted him was rebuked; even so we, who through the name of Jesus have believed as one man in God the Maker of all, have been stripped, through the name of His first-begotten Son, of the filthy garments, i.e., of our sins; and being vehemently inflamed by the word of His calling, we are the true high priestly race of God, as even God Himself bears witness, saying that in every place among the Gentiles sacrifices are presented to Him well-pleasing and pure. Now God receives sacrifices from no one, except through His priests.

CHAPTER CXVII -- MALACHI'S PROPHECY CONCERNING THE SACRIFICES OF THE CHRISTIANS. IT CANNOT BE TAKEN AS REFERRING TO THE PRAYERS OF JEWS OF THE DISPERSION.

"Accordingly, God, anticipating all the sacrifices which we offer through this name, and which Jesus the Christ enjoined us to offer, i.e., in the Eucharist of the bread and the cup, and which are presented by Christians in all places throughout the world, bears witness that they are well-pleasing to Him. But He utterly rejects those presented by you and by those priests of yours, saying, 'And I will not accept your sacrifices at your hands; for from the rising of the sun to its setting my name is glorified among the Gentiles (He says); but ye profane it.' Yet even now, in your love of contention, you assert that God does not accept the sacrifices of those who dwelt then in Jerusalem, and were called Israelites; but says that He is pleased with the prayers of the individuals of that nation then dispersed, and calls their prayers sacrifices. Now, that prayers and giving of thanks, when offered by worthy men, are the only perfect and well-pleasing sacrifices to God, I also admit. For such alone Christians have undertaken to offer, and in the remembrance effected by their solid and liquid food, whereby the suffering of the Son of God which He endured is brought to mind, whose name the high priests of your nation and your teachers have caused to be profaned and blasphemed over all the earth. But these filthy garments, which have been put by you on all who have become Christians by the name of Jesus, God shows shall be taken away from us, when He shall raise all men from the dead, and appoint some to be incorruptible, immortal, and free from sorrow in the everlasting and imperishable kingdom; but shall send others away to the everlasting punishment of fire. But as to you and your teachers deceiving yourselves when you interpret what the Scripture says as referring to those of your nation then in dispersion, and maintain that their prayers and sacrifices offered in every place are pure and well-pleasing, learn that you are speaking falsely, and trying by all means to cheat yourselves: for, first of all, not even now does your nation extend from the rising to the setting of the sun, but there are nations among which none of your race ever dwelt. For there is not one single race of men, whether barbarians, or Greeks, or whatever they may be called, nomads, or vagrants, or herdsmen living in tents, among whom prayers and giving of thanks are not offered through the name of the crucified Jesus. And then, as the Scriptures show, at the time when Malachi wrote this, your dispersion over all the earth, which now exists, had not taken place.

CHAPTER CXVIII -- -HE EXHORTS TO REPENTANCE BEFORE CHRIST COMES; IN WHOM CHRISTIANS, SINCE THEY BELIEVE, ARE FAR MORE RELIGIOUS THAN JEWS.

"So that you ought rather to desist from the love of strife, and repent before the great day of judgment come, wherein all those of your tribes who have pierced this Christ shall mourn as I have shown has been declared by the Scriptures. And I have explained that the Lord swore, 'after the order of Melchizedek,' and what this prediction means; and the prophecy of Isaiah which says, 'His burial is taken away from the midst,' I have already said, referred to the future burying and rising again of Christ; and I have frequently remarked that this very Christ is the Judge of all the living and the dead. And Nathan likewise, speaking to David about Him, thus continued: 'I will be His Father, and He shall be my Son; and my mercy shall I not take away from Him, as I did from them that went before Him; and I will establish Him in my house, and in His kingdom for ever.' And Ezekiel says, 'There shall be no other prince in the house but He.' For He is the chosen Priest and eternal King, the Christ, inasmuch as He is the Son of God; and do not suppose that Isaiah or the other prophets speak of sacrifices of blood or libations being presented at the altar on His second advent, but of true and spiritual praises and giving of thanks. And we have not in vain believed in Him, and have not been led astray by those who taught us such doctrines; but this has come to pass through the wonderful foreknowledge of God, in order that we, through the calling of the new and eternal covenant, that is, of Christ, might be found more intelligent and God-fearing than yourselves, who are considered to be lovers of God and men of understanding, but are not. Isaiah, filled with admiration of this, said: 'And kings shall shut their mouths: for those to whom no announcement has been made in regard to Him shall see; and those who heard not shall understand. Lord, who hath believed our report? and to whom is the arm of the Lord revealed?'

"And in repeating this, Trypho," I continued, "as far as is allowable, I endeavour to do so for the sake of those who came with you to-day, yet briefly and concisely."

Then he replied, "You do well; and though you repeat the same things at considerable length, be assured that I and my companions listen with I pleasure ."

CHAPTER CXIX -- CHRISTIANS ARE THE HOLY PEOPLE PROMISED TO ABRAHAM. THEY HAVE BEEN CALLED LIKE ABRAHAM.

Then I said again, "Would you suppose, sirs, that we could ever have understood these matters in the Scriptures, if we had not received grace to discern by the will of Him whose pleasure it was? in order that the saying of Moses might come to pass, 'They provoked me with strange [gods], they provoked me to anger with their abominations. They sacrificed to demons whom they knew not; new gods that came newly up, whom their fathers knew not. Thou hast forsaken God that begat thee, and forgotten God that brought thee up. And the Lord saw, and was jealous, and was provoked to anger by reason of the rage of His sons and daughters: and He said, I will turn My face away from them, and I will show what shall come on them at the last; for it is a very froward generation, children in whom is no faith. They have moved Me to jealousy with that which is not God, they have provoked Me to anger with their idols; and I will move them to jealousy with that which is not a nation, I will provoke them to anger with a foolish people. For a fire is kindled from Mine anger, and it shall burn to Hades. It shall consume the earth and her increase, and set on fire the foundations of the mountains; I will heap mischief on them.' And after that Righteous One was put to death, we flourished as another people, and shot forth as new and prosperous corn; as the prophets said, 'And many nations shall betake themselves to the Lord in that day for a people: and they shall dwell in the midst of all the earth.' But we are not only a people, but also a holy people, as we have shown already. 'And they shall call them the holy people, redeemed by the Lord.' Therefore we are not a people to be despised, nor a barbarous race, nor such as the Carian and Phrygian nations; but God has even chosen us and He has become manifest to those who asked not after Him. 'Behold, I am God,' He says, 'to the nation which called not on My name.' For this is that nation which God of old promised to Abraham, when He declared that He would make him a father of many nations; not meaning, however, the Arabians, or Egyptians, or Idumaeans, since Ishmael became the father of a mighty nation, and so did Esau; and there is now a great multitude of Ammonites. Noah, moreover, was the father of Abraham, and in fact of all men; and others were the progenitors of others. What larger measure of grace, then, did Christ bestow on Abraham? This, namely, that He called him with His voice by the like calling, telling him to quit the land wherein he dwelt. And He has called all of us by that voice, and we have left already the way of living in which we used to spend our days, passing our time in evil after the fashions of the other inhabitants of the earth; and along with Abraham we shall inherit the holy land, when we shall receive the inheritance for an endless eternity, being children of Abraham through the like faith. For as he believed the voice of God, and it was imputed to him for righteousness, in like manner we having believed God's voice spoken by the apostles of Christ, and promulgated to us by the prophets, have renounced even to death all the things of the world. Accordingly, He promises to him a nation of similar faith, God-fearing, righteous, and delighting the Father; but it is not you, 'in whom is no faith.'

CHAPTER CXX. -- CHRISTIANS WERE PROMISED TO ISAAC, JACOB, AND JUDAH.

"Observe, too, how the same promises are made to Isaac and to Jacob. For thus He speaks to Isaac: 'And in thy seed shall all the nations of the earth be blessed.' And to Jacob: 'And in thee and in thy seed shall all families of the earth be blessed.' He says that neither to Esau nor to Reuben, nor to any other; only to those of whom the Christ should arise, according to the dispensation, through the Virgin Mary. But if you would consider the blessing of Judah, you would perceive what I say. For the seed is divided from Jacob, and comes down through Judah, and Phares, and Jesse, and David. And this was a symbol of the fact that some of your nation would be found children of Abraham, and found, too, in the lot of Christ; but that others, who are indeed children of Abraham, would be like the sand on the sea-shore, barren and fruitless, much in quantity, and without number indeed, but bearing no fruit whatever, and only drinking the water of the sea. And a vast multitude in your nation are convicted of being of this kind, imbibing doctrines of bitterness and godlessness, but spurning the word of God. He speaks therefore in the passage relating to Judah: 'A prince shall not fail from Judah, nor a ruler from his thighs, till that which is laid up for him come; and He shall be the expectation of the nations.' And it is plain that this was spoken not of Judah, but of Christ. For all we out of all nations do expect not Judah, but Jesus, who led your fathers out of Egypt. For the prophecy referred even to the advent of Christ: 'Till He come for whom this is laid up, and He shall be the expectation of nations.' Jesus came, therefore, as we have shown at length, and is expected again to appear above the clouds; whose name you profane, and labour hard to get it profaned over all the earth. It were possible for me, sirs," I continued, "to contend against you about the reading which you so interpret, saying it is written, 'Till the things laid up for Him come;' though the Seventy have not so explained it, but thus, 'Till He comes for whom this is laid up.' But since what follows indicates that the reference is to Christ (for it is, 'and He shall be the expectation of nations'), I do not proceed to have a mere verbal controversy with you, as I have not attempted to establish proof about Christ from the passages of Scripture which are not admitted by you? which I quoted from the words of Jeremiah the prophet, and Esdras, and David; but from those which are even now admitted by you, which had your teachers comprehended, be well assured they would have deleted them, as they did those about the death of Isaiah, whom you sawed asunder with a wooden saw. And this was a mysterious type of Christ being about to cut your nation in two, and to raise those worthy of the honour to the everlasting kingdom along with the holy patriarchs and prophets; but He has said that He will send others to the condemnation of the unquenchable fire along with similar disobedient and impenitent men from all the nations. 'For they shall come,' He said, 'from the west and from the east, and shall sit down with Abraham, and Isaac, and Jacob in the kingdom of heaven; but the children of the kingdom shall be cast out into outer darkness.' And I have mentioned these things, taking nothing whatever into consideration, except the speaking of the truth, and refusing to be coerced by any one, even though I should be forthwith torn in pieces by you. For I gave no thought to any of my people, that is, the Samaritans, when I had a communication in writing with Caesar, but stated that they were wrong in trusting to the magician Simon of their own nation, who, they say, is God above all power, and authority, and might."

CHAPTER CXXI -- FROM THE FACT THAT THE GENTILES BELIEVE LN JESUS, IT IS EVIDENT THAT HE IS CHRIST.

And as they kept silence, I went on: "[The Scripture], speaking by David about this Christ, my friends, said no longer that 'in His seed' the nations should be blessed, but 'in Him.' So it is here: 'His name shall rise up for ever above the sun; and in Him shall all nations be blessed.' But if all nations are blessed in Christ, and we of all nations believe in Him, then He is indeed the Christ, and we are those blessed by Him. God formerly gave the sun as an object of worship, as it is written, but no one ever was seen to endure death on account of his faith in the sun; but for the name of Jesus you may see men of every nation who have endured and do endure all sufferings, rather than deny Him. For the word of His truth and wisdom is more ardent and more light-giving than the rays of the sun, and sinks down into the depths of heart and mind. Hence also the Scripture said, 'His name shall rise up above the sun.' And again, Zechariah says, 'His name is the East.' And speaking of the same, he says that 'each tribe shall mourn.' But if He so shone forth and was so mighty in His first advent (which was without honour and comeliness, and very contemptible), that in no nation He is unknown, and everywhere men have repented of the old wickedness in each nation's way of living, so that even demons were subject to His name, and all powers and kingdoms feared His name more than they feared all the dead, shall He not on His glorious advent destroy by all means all those who hated Him, and who unrighteously departed from Him, but give rest to His own, rewarding them with all they have looked for? To us, therefore, it has been granted to hear, and to understand, and to be saved by this Christ, and to recognise all the [truths revealed] by the Father. Wherefore He said to Him: 'It is a great thing for Thee to be called my servant, to raise up the tribes of Jacob, and turn again the dispersed of Israel. I have appointed Thee for a light to the Gentiles, that Thou mayest be their salvation unto the end of the earth.'

CHAPTER CXXII -- THE JEWS UNDERSTAND THIS OF THE PROSELYTES WITHOUT REASON.

"You think that these words refer to the stranger and the proselytes, but in fact they refer to us who have been illumined by Jesus. For Christ would have borne witness even to them; but now you are become twofold more the children of hell, as He said Himself. Therefore what was written by the prophets was spoken not of those persons, but of us, concerning whom the Scripture speaks: 'I will lead the blind by a way which they knew not; and they shall walk in paths which they have not known. And I am witness, saith the Lord God, and my servant whom I have chosen.' To whom, then, does Christ bear witness? Manifestly to those who have believed. But the proselytes not only do not believe, but twofold more than yourselves blaspheme His name, and wish to torture and put to death us who believe in Him; for in all points they strive to be like you. And again in other words He cries: 'I the Lord have called Thee in righteousness, and will hold Thine hand, and will strengthen Thee, and will give Thee for a covenant of the people, for a light of the Gentiles, to open the eyes of the blind, to bring out the prisoners from their bonds.' These words, indeed, sirs, refer also to Christ, and concern the enlightened nations; or will you say again, He speaks to them of the law and the proselytes?"

Then some of those who had come on the second day cried out as if they had been in a theatre, "But what? does He not refer to the law, and to those illumined by it? Now these are proselytes."

"No," I said, looking towards Trypho, "since, if the law were able to enlighten the nations and those who possess it, what need is there of a new covenant? But since God announced beforehand that He would send a new covenant, and an everlasting law and commandment, we will not understand this of the old law and its proselytes, but of Christ and His proselytes, namely us Gentiles, whom He has illumined, as He says somewhere: 'Thus saith the Lord, In an acceptable time have I heard Thee, and in a day of salvation have I helped Thee, and I have given Thee for a covenant of the people, to establish the earth, and to inherit the deserted.' What, then, is Christ's inheritance? Is it not the nations? What is the covenant of God? Is it not Christ? As He says in another place: 'Thou art my Son; this day have I begotten Thee. Ask of Me, and I shall give Thee the nations for Thine inheritance, and the uttermost parts of the earth for Thy possession.'

CHAPTER CXXIII -- RIDICULOUS INTERPRETATIONS OF THE JEWS. CHRISTIANS ARE THE TRUE ISRAEL.

"As, therefore, all these latter prophecies refer to Christ and the nations, you should believe that the former refer to Him and them in like manner. For the proselytes have no need of a covenant, if, since there is one and the same law imposed on all that are circumcised, the Scripture speaks about them thus: 'And the stranger shall also be joined with them, and shall be joined to the house of Jacob;' and because the proselyte, who is circumcised that he may have access to the people, becomes like one of themselves, while we who have been deemed worthy to be called a people are yet Gentiles, because we have not been circumcised. Besides, it is ridiculous for you to imagine that the eyes of the proselytes are to be opened while your own are not, and that you be understood as blind and deaf while they are enlightened. And it will be still more ridiculous for you, if you say that the law has been given to the nations, but you have not known it. For you would have stood in awe of God's wrath, and would not have been lawless, wandering sons; being much afraid of hearing God always say, 'Children in whom is no faith. And who are blind, but my servants? and deaf, but they that rule over them? And the servants of God have been made blind. You see often, but have not observed; your ears have been opened, and you have not heard.' Is God's commendation of you honourable? and is God's testimony seemly for His servants? You are not ashamed though you often hear these words. You do not tremble at God's threats, for you are a people foolish and hard-hearted. 'Therefore, behold, I will proceed to remove this people,' saith the Lord;' and I will remove them, and destroy the wisdom of the wise, and hide the understanding of the prudent.' Deservedly too: for you are neither wise nor prudent, but crafty and unscrupulous; wise only to do evil, but utterly incompetent to know the hidden counsel of God, or the faithful covenant of the Lord, or to find out the everlasting paths. 'Therefore, saith the Lord, I will raise up to Israel and to Judah the seed of men and the seed of beasts.' And by Isaiah He speaks thus concerning another Israel: 'In that day shall there be a third Israel among the Assyrians and the Egyptians, blessed in the land which the Lord of Sabaoth hath blessed, saying, blessed shall my people in Egypt and in Assyria be, and Israel mine inheritance.' Since then God blesses this people, and calls them Israel, and declares them to be His inheritance, how is it that you repent not of the deception you practise on yourselves, as if you alone were the Israel, and of execrating the people whom God has blessed? For when He speaks to Jerusalem and its environs, He thus added: 'And I will beget men upon you, even my people Israel; and they shall inherit you, and you shall be a possession for them; and you shall be no longer bereaved of them.'"

"What, then?" says Trypho; "are you Israel? and speaks He such things of you?"

"If, indeed," I replied to him, "we had not entered into a lengthy discussion on these topics, I might have doubted whether you ask this question in ignorance; but since we have brought the matter to a conclusion by demonstration and with your assent, I do not believe that you are ignorant of what I have just said, or desire again mere contention, but that you are urging me to exhibit the same proof to these men." And in compliance with the assent expressed in his eyes, I continued: "Again in Isaiah, if you have ears to hear it, God, speaking of Christ in parable, calls Him Jacob and Israel. He speaks thus: 'Jacob is my servant, I will uphold Him; Israel is mine elect, I will put my Spirit upon Him, and He shall bring forth judgment to the Gentiles. He shall not strive, nor cry, neither shall any one hear His voice in the street: a bruised reed He shall not break, and smoking flax He shall not quench; but He shall bring forth judgment to truth: He shall shine, and shall not be broken till He have set judgment on the earth. And in His name shall the Gentiles trust.' As therefore from the one man Jacob, who was surnamed Israel, all your nation has been called Jacob and Israel; so we from Christ, who begat us unto God, like Jacob, and Israel, and Judah, and Joseph, and David, are called and are the true sons of God, and keep the commandments of Christ."

CHAPTER CXXIV -- CHRISTIANS ARE THE SONS OF GOD.

And when I saw that they were perturbed because I said that we are the sons of God, I anticipated their questioning, and said, "Listen, sirs, how the Holy Ghost speaks of this people, saying that they are all sons of the Highest; and how this very Christ will be present in their assembly, rendering judgment to all men. The words are spoken by David, and are, according to your version of them, thus: 'God standeth in the congregation of gods; He judgeth among the gods. How long do ye judge unjustly, and accept the persons of the wicked? Judge for the orphan and the poor, and do justice to the humble and needy. Deliver the needy, and save the poor out of the hand of the wicked. They know not, neither have they understood; they walk on in darkness: all the foundations of the earth shall be shaken. I said, Ye are gods, and are all children of the Most High. But ye die like men, and fall like one of the princes. Arise, O God! judge the earth, for Thou shalt inherit all nations.' But in the version of the Seventy it is written, 'Behold, ye die like men, and fall like one of the princes, in order to manifest the disobedience of men,--I mean of Adam and Eve,--and the fall of one of the princes, i.e., of him who was called the serpent, who fell with a great overthrow, because he deceived Eve. But as my discourse is not intended to touch on this point, but to prove to you that the Holy Ghost reproaches men because they were made like God, free from suffering and death, provided that they kept His commandments, and were deemed deserving of the name of His sons, and yet they, becoming like Adam and Eve, work out death for themselves; let the interpretation of the Psalm be held just as you wish, yet thereby it is demonstrated that all men are deemed worthy of becoming "gods," and of having power to become sons of the Highest; and shall be each by himself judged and condemned like Adam and Eve. Now I have proved at length that Christ is called God.

CHAPTER CXXV -- HE EXPLAINS WHAT FORCE THE WORD ISRAEL HAS, AND HOW IT SUITS CHRIST.

"I wish, sirs," I said, "to learn from you what is the force of the name Israel." And as they were silent, I continued: "I shall tell you what I know: for I do not think it fight, when I know, not to speak; or, suspecting that you do know, and yet from envy or from voluntary ignorance deceive yourselves, to be continually solicitous; but I speak all things simply and candidly, as my Lord said: 'A sower went forth to sow the seed; and some fell by the wayside; and some among thorns, and some on stony ground, and some on good ground.' I must speak, then, in the hope of finding good ground somewhere; since that Lord of mine, as One strong and powerful, comes to demand back His own from all, land will not condemn His steward if He recognises that he, by the knowledge that the Lord is powerful and has come to demand His own, has given it to every bank, and has not digged for any cause whatsoever. Accordingly the name Israel signifies this, A man who overcomes power; for Isra is a man overcoming, and El is power. And that Christ would act so when He became man was foretold by the mystery of Jacob's wrestling with Him who appeared to him, in that He ministered to the will of the Father, yet nevertheless is God, in that He is the first-begotten of all creatures. For when He became man, as I previously remarked, the devil came to Him--i.e., that power which is called the serpent and Sa-tan--tempting Him, and striving to effect His downfall by asking Him to worship him. But He destroyed and overthrew the devil, having proved him to be wicked, in that he asked to be worshipper as God, contrary to the Scripture; who is an apostate from the will of God. For He answers him, 'It is written, Thou shalt worship the Lord thy God, and Him only shall thou serve.' Then, overcome and convicted, the devil departed at that time. But since our Christ was to be numbed, i.e., by pain and experience of suffering, He made a previous intimation of this by touching Jacob's thigh, and causing it to shrink. But Israel was His name from the beginning, to which He altered the name of the blessed Jacob when He blessed him with His own name, proclaiming thereby that all who through Him have fled for refuge to the Father, constitute the blessed Israel. But you, having understood none of this, and not being prepared to understand, since you are the children of Jacob after the fleshly seed, expect that you shall be assuredly saved. But that you deceive yourselves in such matters, I have proved by many words.

CHAPTER CXXVI -- THE VARIOUS NAMES OF CHRIST ACCORDING TO BOTH NATURES. IT IS SHOWN THAT HE IS GOD, AND APPEARED TO THE PATRIARCHS.

"But if you knew, Trypho," continued I, "who He is that is called at one time the Angel of great counsel, and a Man by Ezekiel, and like the Son of man by Daniel, and a Child by Isaiah, and Christ and God to be worshipped by David, and Christ and a Stone by many, and Wisdom by Solomon, and Joseph and Judah and a Star by Moses, and the East by Zechariah, and the Suffering One and Jacob and Israel by Isaiah again, and a Rod, and Flower, and Corner-Stone, and Son of God, you would not have blasphemer Him who has now come, and been born, and suffered, and ascended to heaven; who shall also come again, and then your twelve tribes shall mourn. For if you had understood what has been written by the prophets, you would not have denied that He was God, Son of the only, unbegotten, unutterable God. For Moses says somewhere in Exodus the following: 'The Lord spoke to Moses, and said to him, I am the Lord, and I appeared to Abraham, to Isaac, and to Jacob, being their God; and my name I revealed not to them, and I established my covenant with them.' And thus again he says, 'A man wrestled with Jacob,' and asserts it was God; narrating that Jacob said, 'I have seen God face to face, and my life is preserved.' And it is recorded that he called the place where He wrestled with him, appeared to and blessed him, the Face of God (Peniel). And Moses says that God appeared also to Abraham near the oak in Mature, when he was sitting at the door of his tent at mid-day. Then he goes on to say: 'And he lifted up his eyes and looked, and, behold, three men stood before him; and when he saw them, he ran to meet them.' a After a little, one of them promises a son to Abraham: 'Wherefore did Sarah laugh, saying, Shall. I of a surety bear a child, and I am old? Is anything impossible with God? At the time appointed I will return, according to the time of life, and Sarah shall have a son. And they went away from Abraham.' Again he speaks of them thus: 'And the men rose up from thence, and looked toward Sodom.' Then to Abraham He who was and is again speaks: 'I will not hide from Abraham, my servant, what I intend to do.'" And what follows in the writings of Moses I quoted and explained; "from which I have demonstrated," I said, "that He who is described as God appeared to Abraham, to Isaac, and to Jacob, and the other patriarchs, was appointed under the authority of the Father and Lord, and ministers to His will." Then I went on to say what I had not said before: "And so, when the people desired to eat flesh, and Moses had lost faith in Him, who also there is called the Angel, and who promised that God would give them to satiety, He who is both God and the Angel, sent by the Father, is described as saying and doing these things. For thus the Scripture says: 'And the Lord said to Moses Will the Lord's hand not be sufficient? thou shall know now whether my word shall conceal thee or not.' And again, in other words, it thus says: 'But the Lord spoke unto me, Thou shalt not go over this Jordan: the Lord thy God, who goeth before thy face, He shall cut off the nations.'

CHAPTER CXXVII -- THESE PASSAGES OF SCRIPTURE DO NOT APPLY TO THE FATHER, BUT TO THE WORD.

"These and other such sayings are recorded by the lawgiver and by the prophets; and I suppose that I have stated sufficiently, that wherever God says, 'God went up from Abraham,' or, 'The Lord spake to Moses,' and 'The Lord came down to behold the tower which the sons of men had built,' or when 'God shut Noah into the ark,' you must not imagine that the unbegotten God Himself came down or went up from any place. For the ineffable Father and Lord of all neither has come to any place, nor walks, nor sleeps, nor rises up, but remains in His own place, wherever that is, quick to behold and quick to hear, having neither eyes nor ears, but being of indescribable might; and He sees all things, and knows all things, and none of us escapes His observation; and He is not moved or confined to a spot in the whole world, for He existed before the world was made. How, then, could He talk with any one, or be seen by any one, or appear on the smallest portion of the earth, when the people at Sinai were not able to look even on the glory of Him who was sent from Him; and Moses himself could not enter into the tabernacle which he had erected, when it was filled with the glory of God; and the priest could not endure to stand before the temple when Solomon conveyed the ark into the house in Jerusalem which he had built for it? Therefore neither Abraham, nor Isaac, nor Jacob, nor any other man, saw the Father and ineffable Lord of all, and also of Christ, but [saw] Him who was according to His will His Son, being God, and the Angel because He ministered to His will; whom also it pleased Him to be born man by the Virgin; who also was fire when He conversed with Moses from the bush. Since, unless we thus comprehend the Scriptures, it must follow that the Father and Lord of all had not been in heaven when what Moses wrote took place: 'And the Lord rained upon Sodom fire and brimstone from the Lord out of heaven;' and again, when it is thus said by David: 'Lift up your gates, ye rulers; and be ye lift up, ye everlasting gates; and the King of glory shall enter;' and again, when He says: 'The Lord says to my Lord, Sit at My right hand, till I make Thine enemies Thy footstool.'

CHAPTER CXXVIII -- THE WORD IS SENT NOT AS AN INANIMATE POWER, BUT AS A PERSON BEGOTTEN OF THE FATHER'S SUBSTANCE.

"And that Christ being Lord, and God the Son of God, and appearing formerly in power as Man, and Angel, and in the glory of fire as at the bush, so also was manifested at the judgment executed on Sodom, has been demonstrated fully by what has been said." Then I repeated once more all that I had previously quoted from Exodus, about the vision in the bush, and the naming of Joshua (Jesus), and continued: "And do not suppose, sirs, that I am speaking superfluously when I repeat these words frequently: but it is because I know that some wish to anticipate these remarks, and to say that the power sent from the Father of all which appeared to Moses, or to Abraham, or to Jacob, is called an Angel because He came to men (for by Him the commands of the Father have been proclaimed to men); is called Glory, because He appears in a vision sometimes that cannot be borne; is called a Man, and a human being, because He appears strayed in such forms as the Father pleases; and they call Him the Word, because He carries tidings from the Father to men: but maintain that this power is indivisible and inseparable from the Father, just as they say that the light of the sun on earth is indivisible and inseparable from the sun in the heavens; as when it sinks, the light sinks along with it; so the Father, when He chooses, say they, causes His power to spring forth, and when He chooses, He makes it return to Himself. In this way, they teach, He made the angels. But it is proved that there are angels who always exist, and are never reduced to that form out of which they sprang. And that this power which the prophetic word calls God, as has been also amply demonstrated, and Angel, is not numbered [as different] in name only like the light of the sun but is indeed something numerically distinct, I have discussed briefly in what has gone before; when I asserted that this power was begotten from the Father, by His power and will, but not by abscission, as if the essence of the Father were divided; as all other things partitioned and divided are not the same after as before they were divided: and, for the sake of example, I took the case of fires kindled from a fire, which we see to be distinct from it, and yet that from which many can be kindled is by no means made less, but remains the same.

CHAPTER CXXIX -- THAT IS CONFIRMED FROM OTHER PASSAGES OF SCRIPTURE.

"And now I shall again recite the words which I have spoken in proof of this point. When Scripture says,' The Lord rained fire from the Lord out of heaven,' the prophetic word indicates that there were two in number: One upon the earth, who, it says, descended to behold the cry of Sodom; Another in heaven, who also is Lord of the Lord on earth, as He is Father and God; the cause of His power and of His being Lord and God. Again, when the Scripture records that God said in the beginning, 'Behold, Adam has become like one of Us,' this phrase, 'like one of Us,' is also indicative of number; and the words do not admit of a figurative meaning, as the sophists endeavour to affix on them, who are able neither to tell nor to understand the truth. And it is written in the book of Wisdom: 'If I should tell you daily events, I would be mindful to enumerate them from the beginning. The Lord created me the beginning of His ways for His works. From everlasting He established me in the beginning, before He formed the earth, and before He made the depths, and before the springs of waters came forth, before the mountains were settled; He begets me before all the hills.'" When I repeated these words, I added: "You perceive, my hearers, if you bestow attention, that the Scripture has declared that this Offspring was begotten by the Father before all things created; and that which is begotten is numerically distinct from that which begets, any one will admit."

CHAPTER CXXX -- HE RETURNS TO THE CONVERSION OF THE GENTILES, AND SHOWS THAT IT WAS FORETOLD.

And when all had given assent, I said: "I would now adduce some passages which I had not recounted before. They are recorded by the faithful servant Moses in parable, and are as follows: 'Rejoice, O ye heavens, with Him, and let all the angels of God worship Him;'" and I added what follows of the passage: "'Rejoice, O ye nations, with His people, and let all the angels of God be strengthened in Him: for the blood of His sons He avenges, and will avenge, and will recompense His enemies with vengeance, and will recompense those that hate Him; and the Lord will purify the land of His people.' And by these words He declares that we, the nations, rejoice with His people,--to wit, Abraham, and Isaac, and Jacob, and the prophets, and, in short, all of that people who are well-pleasing to God, according to what has been already agreed on between us. But we will not receive it of all your nation; since we know from Isaiah that the members of those who have transgressed shall be consumed by the worm and unquenchable fire, remaining immortal; so that they become a spectacle to all flesh. But in addition to these, I wish, sin," said I, "to add some other passages from the very words of Moses, from which you may understand that God has from of old dispersed all men according to their kindreds and tongues; and out of all kindreds has taken to Himself your kindred, a useless, disobedient, and faithless generation; and has shown that those who were selected out of every nation have obeyed His will through Christ,--whom He calls also Jacob, and names Israel,--and these, then, as I mentioned fully previously, must be Jacob and Israel. For when He says, 'Rejoice, O ye nations, with His people,' He allots the same inheritance to them, and does not call them by the same name; but when He says that they as Gentiles rejoice with His people, He calls them Gentiles to reproach you. For even as you provoked Him to anger by your idolatry, so also He has deemed those who were idolaters worthy of knowing His will, and of inheriting His inheritance.

CHAPTER CXXXI -- HOW MUCH MORE FAITHFUL TO GOD THE GENTILES ARE WHO ARE CONVERTED TO CHRIST THAN THE JEWS.

"But I shall quote the passage by which it is made known that God divided all the nations. It is as follows: 'Ask thy father, and he will show thee; thine eiders, and they will tell thee; when the Most High divided the nations, as He dispersed the sons of Adam. He set the bounds of the nations according to the numbers of the children of Israel; and the Lord's portion became His people Jacob, and Israel was the lot of His inheritance.'" And having said this, I added: "The Seventy have translated it, 'He set the bounds of the nations according to the number of the angels of God.' But because my argument is again in nowise weakened by this, I have adopted your exposition. And you yourselves, if you will confess the truth, must acknowledge that we, who have been called by God through the despised and shameful mystery of the cross (for the confession of which, and obedience to which, and for our piety, punishments even to death have been inflicted on us by demons, and by the host of the devil, through the aid ministered to them by you), and endure all torments rather than deny Christ even by word, through whom we are called to the salvation prepared beforehand by the Father, are more faithful to God than you, who were redeemed from Egypt with a high hand and a visitation of great glory, when the sea was parted for you, and a passage left dry, in which [God] slew those @ho pursued you with a very great equipment, and splendid chariots, bringing back upon them the sea which had been made a way for your sakes; on whom also a pillar of light shone, in order that you, more than any other nation in the world, might possess a peculiar light, never-failing and never-setting; for whom He rained manna as nourishment, fit for the heavenly angels, in order that you might have no need to prepare your food; and the water at Marah was made sweet; and a sign of Him that was to be crucified was made, both in the matter of the serpents which bit you, as I already mentioned (God anticipating before the proper times these mysteries, in order to confer grace upon you, to whom you are always convicted of being thankless), as well as in the type of the extending of the hands of Moses, and of Oshea being named Jesus (Joshua); when you fought against Amalek: concerning which God enjoined that the incident be recorded, and the name of Jesus laid up in your understandings; saying that this is He who would blot out the memorial of Amalek from under heaven. Now it is clear that the memorial of Amalek remained after the son of Nave (Nun): but He makes it manifest through Jesus, who was crucified, of whom also those symbols were fore-announcements of all that would happen to Him, the demons would be destroyed, and would dread His name, and that all principalities and kingdoms would fear Him; and that they who believe in Him out of all nations would be shown as God-fearing and peaceful men; and the facts already quoted by me, Trypho, indicate this. Again, when you desired flesh, so vast a quantity of quails was given you, that they could not be told; for whom also water gushed from the rock; and a cloud followed you for a shade from heat, and covering from cold, declaring the manner and signification of another and new heaven; the latchets of your shoes did not break, and your shoes waxed not old, and your garments wore not away, but even those of the children grew along with them.

CHAPTER CXXXII -- HOW GREAT THE POWER WAS OF THE NAME OF JESUS IN THE OLD TESTAMENT.

"Yet after this you made a calf, and were very zealous in committing fornication with the daughters of strangers, and in serving idols. And again, when the land was given up to you with so great a display of power, that you witnessed the sun stand still in the heavens by the order of that man whose name was Jesus (Joshua), and not go down for thirty-six hours, as well as all the other miracles which were wrought for you as time served; and of these it seems good to me now to speak of another, for it conduces to your hereby knowing Jesus, whom we also know to have been Christ the Son of God, who was crucified, and rose again, and ascended to heaven, and will come again to judge all men, even up to Adam himself. You are aware, then," I continued, "that when the ark of the testimony was seized by the enemies of Ashdod, and a terrible and incurable malady had broken out among them, they resolved to place it on a cart to which they yoked cows that had recently calved, for the purpose of ascertaining by trial whether or not they had been plagued by God's power on account of the ark, and if God wished it to be taken back to the place from which it had been carried away. And when they had done this, the cows, led by no man, went not to the place whence the ark had been taken, but to the fields of a certain man whose name was Oshea, the same as his whose name was altered to Jesus (Joshua), as has been previously mentioned, who also led the people into the land and meted it out to them: and when the cows had come into these fields they remained there, showing to you thereby that they were guided by the name of power; just as formerly the people who survived of those that came out of Egypt, were guided into the land by him who had received the name Jesus (Joshua), who before was called Oshea.

CHAPTER CXXXIII -- THE HARD-HEARTEDNESS OF THE JEWS, FOR WHOM THE CHRISTIANS PRAY.

"Now, although these and all other such unexpected and marvellous works were wrought amongst and seen by you at different times, yet you are convicted by the prophets of having gone to such a length as offering your own children to demons; and besides all this, of having dared to do such things against Christ; and you still dare to do them: for all which may it be granted to you to obtain mercy and salvation from God and His Christ. For God, knowing before that you would do such things, pronounced this curse upon you by the prophet Isaiah: 'Woe unto their soul! they have devised evil counsel against themselves, saying, Let us bind the righteous man, for he is distasteful to us. Therefore they shall eat the fruit of their own doings. Woe to the wicked! evil, according to the works of his hands, shall befall him. O my people, your exactors glean you, and those who extort from you shall rule over you. O my people, they who call you blessed cause you to err, and disorder the way of your paths. But now the Lord shall sist His people to judgment, and He shall enter into judgment with the elders of the people and the princes thereof. But why have you burnt up my vineyard? and why is the spoil of the poor found in your houses? Why do you wrong my people, and put to shame the countenance of the humble?' Again, in other words, the same prophet spake to the same effect: 'Woe unto them that draw their iniquity as with a long cord, and their transgressions as with the harness of an heifer's yoke: who say, Let His speed come near, and let the counsel of the Holy One of Israel come, that we may know it. Woe unto them that call evil good, and good evil! that put light for darkness, and darkness for light! that put bitter for sweet, and sweet for bitter! Woe unto them that are wise in their own eyes, and prudent in their own sight! Woe unto those that are mighty among you, who drink wine, who are men of strength, who mingle strong drink! who justify the wicked for a reward, and take away justice from the righteous! Therefore, as the stubble shall be burnt by the coal of fire, and utterly consumed by the burning flame, their root shall be as wool, and their flower shall go up like dust. For they would not have the law of the Lord of Sabaoth, but despised the word of the Lord, the Holy One of Israel. And the Lord of Sabaoth was very angry, and laid His hands upon them, and smote them; and He was provoked against the mountains, and their carcases were in the midst like dung on the road. And for all this they have not repented, but their hand is still high.' For verily your hand is high to commit evil, because ye slew the Christ, and do not repent of it; but so far from that, ye hate and murder us who have believed through Him in the God and Father of all, as often as ye can; and ye curse Him without ceasing, as well as those who side with Him; while all of us pray for you, and for all men, as our Christ and Lord taught us to do, when He enjoined us to pray even for our enemies, and to love them that hate us, and to bless them that curse us.

CHAPTER CXXXIV -- THE MARRIAGES OF JACOB ARE A FIGURE OF THE CHURCH.

"If, then, the teaching of the prophets and of Himself moves you, it is better for you to follow God than your imprudent and blind masters, who even till this time permit each man to have four or five wives; and if any one see a beautiful woman and desire to have her, they quote the doings of Jacob [called] Israel, and of the other patriarchs, and maintain that it is not wrong to do such things; for they are miserably ignorant in this matter. For, as I before said, certain dispensations of weighty mysteries were accomplished in each act of this sort. For in the marriages of Jacob I shall mention what dispensation and prophecy were accomplished, in order that you may thereby know that your teachers never looked at the divine motive which prompted each act, but only at the grovelling and corrupting passions. Attend therefore to what I say. The marriages of Jacob were types of that which Christ was about to accomplish. For it was not lawful for Jacob to marry two sisters at once. And he serves Laban for [one of] the daughters; and being deceived in [the obtaining of] the younger, he again served seven years. Now Leah is your people and synagogue; but Rachel is our Church. And for these, and for the servants in both, Christ even now serves. For while Noah gave to the two sons the seed of the third as servants, now on the other hand Christ has come to restore both the free sons and the servants amongst them, conferring the same honour on all of them who keep His commandments; even as the children of the free women and the children of the bond women born to Jacob were all sons, and equal in dignity. And it was foretold what each should be according to rank and according to fore-knowledge. Jacob served Laban for speckled and many-spotted sheep; and Christ served, even to the slavery of the cross, for the various and many-formed races of mankind, acquiring them by the blood and mystery of the cross. Leah was weak-eyed; for the eyes of your souls are excessively weak. Rachel stole the gods of Laban, and has hid them to this day; and we have lost our paternal and material gods. Jacob was hated for all time by his brother; and we now, and our Lord Himself, are hated by you and by all men, though we are brothers by nature. Jacob was called Israel; and Israel has been demonstrated to be the Christ, who is, and is called, Jesus.

CHAPTER CXXXV -- CHRIST IS KING OF ISRAEL, AND CHRISTIANS ARE THE ISRAELITIC RACE.

"And when Scripture says, 'I am the Lord God, the Holy One of Israel, who have made known Israel your King,' will you not understand that truly Christ is the everlasting King? For you are aware that Jacob the son of Isaac was never a king. And therefore Scripture again, explaining to us, says what king is meant by Jacob and Israel: 'Jacob is my Servant, I will uphold Him; and Israel is mine Elect, my soul shall receive Him. I have given Him my Spirit; and He shall bring forth judgment to the Gentiles. He shall not cry, and His voice shall not be heard without. The bruised reed He shall not break, and the smoking flax He shall not quench, until He shall bring forth judgment to victory. He shall shine, and shall not be broken, until He set judgment on the earth. And in His name shall the Gentiles trust.' Then is it Jacob the patriarch in whom the Gentiles and yourselves shall trust? or is it not Christ? As, therefore, Christ is the Israel and the Jacob, even so we, who have been quarried out from the bowels of Christ, are the true Israelitic race. But let us attend rather to the very word: 'And I will bring forth,' He says, 'the seed out of Jacob, and out of Judah: and it shall inherit My holy mountain; and Mine Elect and My servants shall possess the inheritance, and shall dwell there; and there shall be folds of flocks in the thicket, and the valley of Achor shall be a resting-place of cattle for the people who have sought Me. But as for you, who forsake Me, and forget My holy mountain, and prepare a table for demons, and fill out drink for the demon, I shall give you to the sword. You shall all fall with a slaughter; for I called you, and you hearkened not, and did evil before me, and did choose that wherein I delighted not.' Such are the words of Scripture; understand, therefore, that the seed of Jacob now referred to is something else, and not, as may be supposed, spoken of your people. For it is not possible for the seed of Jacob to leave an entrance for the descendants of Jacob, or for [God] to have accepted the very same persons whom He had reproached with unfitness for the inheritance, and promise it to them again; but as there the prophet says, 'And now, O house of Jacob, come and let us walk in the light of the Lord; for He has sent away His people, the house of Jacob, because their land was full, as at the first, of soothsayers and divinations;' even so it is necessary for us here to observe that there are two seeds of Judah, and two races, as there are two houses of Jacob: the one begotten by blood and flesh, the other by faith and the Spirit.

CHAPTER CXXXVI -- THE JEWS, IN REJECTING CHRIST, REJECTED GOD WHO SENT HIM.

"For you see how He now addresses the people, saying a little before: 'As the gape shah be found in the cluster, and they will say, Destroy it not, for a blessing is in it; so will I do for My servant's sake: for His sake I will not destroy them all.' And thereafter He adds: 'And I shall bring forth the seed out of Jacob, and out of Judah.' It is plain then that if He thus be angry with them, and threaten to leave very few of them, He promises to bring forth certain others, who shall dwell in His mountain. But these are the persons whom He said He would sow and beget. For you neither suffer Him when He calls you, nor hear Him when He speaks to you, but have done evil in the presence of the Lord. But the highest pitch of your wickedness lies in this, that you hate the Righteous One, and slew Him; and so treat those who have received from Him all that they are and have, and who are pious, righteous, and humane. Therefore 'woe unto their soul,' says' the Lord, 'for they have devised an evil counsel against themselves, saying, Let us take away the righteous, for he is distasteful to us.' For indeed you are not in the habit of sacrificing to Baal, as were your fathers, or of placing cakes in groves and on high places for the host of heaven: but you have not accepted God's Christ. For he who knows not Him, knows not the will of God; and he who insults and hates Him, insults and hates Him that sent Him. And whoever believes not in Him, believes not the declarations of the prophets, who preached and proclaimed Him to all.

CHAPTER CXXXVII -- HE EXHORTS THE JEWS TO BE CONVERTED.

"Say no evil thing, my brothers, against Him that was crucified, and treat not scornfully the stripes wherewith all may be healed, even as we are healed. For it will be well if, persuaded by the Scriptures, you are circumcised from hard-heartedness: not that circumcision which you have from the tenets that are put into you; for that was given for a sign, and not for a work of righteousness, as the Scriptures compel you [to admit]. Assent, therefore, and pour no ridicule on the Son of God; obey not the Pharisaic teachers, and scoff not at the King of Israel, as the rulers of your synagogues teach you to do after your prayers: for if he that touches those who are not pleasing to God, is as one that touches the apple of God's eye, how much more so is he that touches His beloved! And that this is He, has been sufficiently demonstrated."

And as they kept silence, I continued: "My friends, I now refer to the Scriptures as the Seventy have interpreted them; for when I quoted them formerly as you possess them, I made proof of you [to ascertain] how you were disposed. For, mentioning the Scripture which says, 'Woe unto them! for they have devised evil counsel against themselves, saying (as the Seventy have translated, I continued): 'Let us take away the righteous, for he is distasteful to us;' whereas at the commencement of the discussion I added what your version has: 'Let us bind the righteous, for he is distaste fill to us.' But you had been busy about some other matter, and seem to have listened to the words without attending to them. But now, since the day is drawing to a close, for the sun is about to set, I shall add one remark to what I have said, and conclude. I have indeed made the very same remark already, but I think it would be right to bestow some consideration on it again.

CHAPTER CXXXVIII -- NOAH IS A FIGURE OF CHRIST, WHO HAS REGENERATED US BY WATER, AND FAITH, AND WOOD: [i.e., the Cross.]

"You know, then, sirs," I said, "that God has said in Isaiah to Jerusalem: 'I saved thee in the deluge of Noah.' By this which God said was meant that the mystery of saved men appeared in the deluge. For righteous Noah, along with the other mortals at the deluge, i.e., with his own wife, his three sons and their wives, being eight in number, were a symbol of the eighth day, wherein Christ appeared when He rose from the dead, for ever the first in power. For Christ, being the first-born of every creature, became again the chief of another race regenerated by Himself through water, and faith, and wood, containing the mystery of the cross; even as Noah was saved by wood when he rode over the waters with his household. Accordingly, when the prophet says, 'I saved thee in the times of Noah,' as I have already remarked, he addresses the people who are equally faithful to God, and possess the same signs. For when Moses had the rod in his hands, he led your nation through the sea. And you believe that this was spoken to your nation only, or to the land. But the whole earth, as the Scripture says, was inundated, and the water rose in height fifteen cubits above all the mountains: so that it is evident this was not spoken to the land, but to the people who obeyed Him: for whom also He had before prepared a resting-place in Jerusalem, as was previously demonstrated by all the symbols of the deluge; I mean, that by water, faith, and wood, those who are afore-prepared, and who repent of the sins which they have committed, shall escape from the impending judgment of God.

CHAPTER CXXXIX -- THE BLESSINGS, AND ALSO THE CURSE, PRONOUNCED BY NOAH WERE PROPHECIES OF THE FUTURE.

"For another mystery was accomplished and predicted in the days of Noah, of which you are not aware. It is this: in the blessings wherewith Noah blessed his two sons, and in the curse pronounced on his son's son. For the Spirit of prophecy would not curse the son that had been by God blessed along with [his brothers]. But since the punishment of the sin would cleave to the whole descent of the son that mocked at his father's nakedness, he made the curse originate with his son. Now, in what he said, he foretold that the descendants of Shem would keep in retention the property and dwellings of Canaan: and again that the descendants of Japheth would take possession of the property of which Shem's descendants had dispossessed Canaan's descendants; and spoil the descendants of Shem, even as they plundered the sons of Canaan. And listen to the way in which it has so come to pass. For you, who have derived your lineage from Shem, invaded the territory of the sons of Canaan by the will of God; and you possessed it. And it is manifest that the sons of Japheth, having invaded you in turn by the judgment of God, have taken your land from you, and have possessed it. Thus it is written: 'And Noah awoke from the wine, and knew what his younger son had done unto him; and he said, Cursed be Canaan, the servant; a servant shall he be unto his brethren. And he said, Blessed be the Lord God of Shem; and Canaan shall be his servant. May the Lord enlarge Japheth, and let him dwell in the houses of Shem; and let Canaan be his servant.' Accordingly, as two peoples were blessed,--those from Shem, and those from Japheth,--and as the offspring of Shem were decreed first to possess the dwellings of Canaan, and the offspring of Japheth were predicted as in turn receiving the same possessions, and to the two peoples there was the one people of Canaan handed over for servants; so Christ has come according to the power given Him from the Almighty Father, and summoning men to friendship, and blessing, and repentance, and dwelling together, has promised, as has already been proved, that there shall be a future possession for all the saints in this same land. And hence all men everywhere, whether bond or free, who believe in Christ, and recognise the truth in His own words and those of His prophets, know that they shall be with Him in that land, and inherit everlasting and incorruptible good.

CHAPTER CXL -- IN CHRIST ALL ARE FREE. THE JEWS HOPE FOR SALVATION IN VAIN BECAUSE THEY ARE SONS OF ABRAHAM.

"Hence also Jacob, as I remarked before, being himself a type of Christ, had married the two handmaids of his two free wives, and of them begat sons, for the purpose of indicating beforehand that Christ would receive even all those who amongst Japheth's race are descendants of Canaan, equally with the free, and would have the children fellow-heirs. And we are such; but you cannot comprehend this, because you cannot drink of the living fountain of God, but of broken cisterns which can hold no water, as the Scripture says. But they are cisterns broken, and holding no water, which your own teachers have digged, as the Scripture also expressly asserts, 'teaching for doctrines the commandments of men.' And besides, they beguile themselves and you, supposing that the everlasting kingdom will be assuredly given to those of the dispersion who are of Abraham after the flesh, although they be sinners, and faithless, and disobedient towards God, which the Scriptures have proved is not the case. For if so, Isaiah would never have said this: 'And unless the Lord of Sabaoth had left us a seed, we would have been like Sodom and Gomorrah.' And Ezekiel: 'Even if Noah, and Jacob, and Daniel were to pray for sons or daughters, their request should not be granted.' But neither shall the father perish for the son, nor the son for the father; but every one for his own sin, and each shall be saved for his own righteousness. And again Isaiah says:

‘They shall look on the car; cases of them that have transgressed: their worm shall not cease, and their fire shall not be quenched; and they shall be a spectacle to all flesh.’ And our Lord, according to the will of Him that sent Him, who is the Father and Lord of all, would not have said, ‘They shall come from the east, and from the west, and shall sit down with Abraham, and Isaac, and Jacob in the kingdom of heaven. But the children of the kingdom shall be cast out into outer darkness.’ Furthermore, I have proved in what has preceded,” that those who were foreknown to be unrighteous, whether men or angels, are not made wicked by God’s fault, but each man by his own fault is what he will appear to be.

CHAPTER CXLI -- FREE-WILL IN MEN AND ANGELS.

“But that you may not have a pretext for saying that Christ must have been crucified, and that those who transgressed must have been among your nation, and that the matter could not have been otherwise, I said briefly by anticipation, that God, wishing men and angels to follow His will, resolved to create them free to do righteousness; possessing reason, that they may know by whom they are created, and through whom they, not existing formerly, do now exist; and with a law that they should be judged by Him, if they do anything contrary to right reason: and of ourselves we, men and angels, shall be convicted of having acted sinfully, unless we repent beforehand. But if the word of God foretells that some angels and men shall be certainly punished, it did so because it foreknew that they would be unchangeably [wicked], but not because God had created them so. So that if they repent, all who wish for it can obtain mercy from God: and the Scripture foretells that they shall be blessed, saying, ‘Blessed is the man to whom the Lord imputeth not sin;’ that is, having repented of his sins, that he may receive remission of them from God; and not as you deceive yourselves, and some others who resemble you in this, who say, that even though they be sinners, but know God, the Lord will not impute sin to them. We have as proof of this the one fall of David, which happened through his boasting, which was forgiven then when he so mourned and wept, as it is written. But if even to such a man no remission was granted before repentance, and only when this great king, and anointed one, and prophet, mourned and conducted himself so, how can the impure and utterly abandoned, if they weep not, and mourn not, and repent not, entertain the hope that the Lord will not impute to them sin? And this one fall of David, in the matter of Uriah’s wife, proves, sirs,” I said, “that the patriarchs had many wives, not to commit fornication, but that a certain dispensation and all mysteries might be accomplished by them; since, if it were allowable to take any wife, or as many wives as one chooses, and how he chooses, which the men of your nation do over all the earth, wherever they sojourn, or wherever they have been sent, taking women under the name of marriage, much more would David have been permitted to do this.”

When I had said this, dearest Marcus Pompeius, I came to an end.

CHAPTER CXLII -- THE JEWS RETURN THANKS, AND LEAVE JUSTIN.

Then Trypho, after a little delay, said, "You see that it was not intentionally that we came to discuss these points. And I confess that I have been particularly pleased with the conference; and I think that these are of quite the same opinion as myself. For we have found more than we expected, and more than it was possible to have expected. And if we could do this more frequently, we should be much helped in the searching of the Scriptures themselves. But since," he said, "you are on the eve of departure, and expect daily to set sail, do not hesitate to remember us as friends when you are gone."

"For my part," I replied, "if I had remained, I would have wished to do the same thing daily. But now, since I expect, with God's will and aid, to set sail, I exhort you to give all diligence in this very great struggle for your own salvation, and to be earnest in setting a higher value on the Christ of the Almighty God than on your own teachers."

After this they left me, wishing me safety in my voyage, and from every misfortune. And I, praying for them, said, "I can wish no better thing for you, sirs, than this, that, recognising in this way that intelligence is given to every man, you may be of the same opinion as ourselves, and believe that Jesus is the Christ of God."